The

The Fangirl Diaries

Finding Community in Anime Fandom of the '90s and '00s

ERICA VICTORIA ESPEJO

McFarland & Company, Inc., Publishers

Jefferson, North Carolina

All photographs are from the author's collection

LIBRARY OF CONGRESS CATALOGING-IN-PUBLICATION DATA

Names: Espejo, Erica Victoria, author.
Title: The fangirl diaries : finding community in anime fandom
of the '90s and '00s / Erica Victoria Espejo.
Description: Jefferson, North Carolina : McFarland & Company, Inc.,
Publishers, 2025. | Includes index.
Identifiers: LCCN 2024051311 | ISBN 9781476696508 (paperback : acid free paper) ∞
ISBN 9781476654904 (ebook)
Subjects: LCSH: Espejo, Erica Victoria. | Fans (Persons)—United States—Biography. |
Anime (Television programs)—Social aspects—United States. | Popular
culture—Social aspects—United States. | LCGFT: Autobiographies.
Classification: LCC P94.5.F362 U647 2025 | DDC 791.45/34092 [B]—dc23/eng/20241107
LC record available at https://lccn.loc.gov/2024051311

ISBN (print) 978-1-4766-9650-8
ISBN (ebook) 978-1-4766-5490-4

Front cover: The author, Erica Espejo (in the mirror), as a cosplay character
at SiliCon 2005 (author's collection); anime illustration from Adobe Firefly

Printed in the United States of America

*McFarland & Company, Inc., Publishers
Box 611, Jefferson, North Carolina 28640
www.mcfarlandpub.com*

To Kevin Lillard,
a pioneer of fandom who showed us
a fan's view of conventions.
You will always be my inspiration.
I will never forget you.
And to anyone who has found themselves
and a sense of community in fandom—this is also your story.

Acknowledgments

Thank you to my fandom studies mentors, Rob Miles, Gilles Poitras, and Helen McCarthy, for encouraging me to take the next step in my blogging hustle. Thank you for being shining examples and for encouraging the millennial generation to keep on writing and documenting fandom history. I wouldn't have been able to get to this publishing stage without fandom's most intellectual minds and contributors. Thank you for believing in what I have called "The Fangirl Project."

Thank you to my friends and family for believing in this project. So many of you have shown your support and excitement for "The Fangirl Project." This is for all of you who have found a safe place in online fandom spaces and at fandom conventions to be who you truly are. Thank you for all of the support from shared hotel rooms, rides to conventions, cosplay advice, and your friendship. If it wasn't for our love of anime and Japanese pop culture in fandom, we would not be here today.

And, of course, to the dearest friends whom I reconnected with again from the good old days: This written lived experience would not be where it is without us reminiscing about our memories when we were young and cringe but free at Anime Expo and Anime Central. I hope we can still continue to live it up as the years go by.

And last but not least, to Miko, the Holstein cat, thank you for keeping me company while I was writing this book in my cabin retreat in the woods. I will miss our teatime and conversations at the August cottage. Thank you for being this book's "mews."

Table of Contents

Table of Contents

Preface

I've never been a TikTok person. I've always felt that I was too old. Too jaded. I'm already on too many social media apps to keep up. I tried the clock app during the legendary and dreary 2020 lockdown to cope with the ennui. "I could lip sync some classic '90s *Sailor Moon* DIC dub lines while cosplaying as Sailor Mars," I thought to myself. I got my cosplay out from storage and put it on. The last time I wore her was Anime Expo 2019 for a nearly complete *Sailor Moon* cosplay group. I recorded a few videos and saw that my clips were not getting much love. No traction. Not much in the likes department. Maybe I wasn't using the right hashtags? Maybe it's all about the timing, when during the day I was posting? I was too old, too jaded to figure out this new app. This TikTok trend was not for me. Instead, I decided to support my friends who were getting a thousand more views and followers. I was a serial liker—mostly of internet cats doing silly things and friends lip syncing to trending sounds while in cosplay. I was supporting their content from the sidelines.

And "Y2KCore" happened to be a social media trend among Generation Z. I thought: Wait ... you mean things from my high school days are totally cool again? Okay, I'll add a little something to the Y2KCore social media rabbit hole! What if I could post my old cosplay photos? Would that get any traction? It was worth a shot. I happened to be at my parents' house. My photo albums were still in my childhood bedroom. I decided to see what I could find. I found the pink album that I got at a Borders bookstore a while back. In the album, there were about 100 or so photos from the best summer of my life, Anime Expo 2002. I was not sure how the Y2KCore aesthetic crowd would respond to fandom of the early 2000s.

On a Saturday in April 2023, I compiled all of my Anime Expo 2002 photos into a video collage set to the trending city pop tune of Mariya Takeuchi's "Plastic Love." The 50-second video was uploaded. I immediately ignored my phone. I had plans that Saturday afternoon. I was staffing a local one-day fandom convention, TouhouFest. While I was familiar with the video game franchise, I was not what you would call a hard-core fan. A friend had asked if I could staff the convention centered on super kawaii magical girls and their franchise that spawns a universe of bullet hell games and giant plushes. It was local. It was in Torrance. It was 10 minutes away from my parents' house. I had nothing else better to do on a Saturday. Why not?

At three o'clock in the afternoon I took a break from taking photos and documenting the convention. I figured I'd take a seat in one of the panel rooms. I cannot remember what the panel was about. I had been on my feet for a few hours. I was exhausted. I felt like I needed a nap. I remembered when I could still have energy at a fandom convention in the mid-afternoon. I could have used another trip to Starbucks for an additional caffeine boost. I went back into my phone. A red dot was hovering over my TikTok app. I immediately opened the app. My notifications were going haywire. What I saw next surprised me.

The Anime Expo 2002 video already had five thousand views?! This had to be a glitch. I'd never gotten this much traction on social media! I shrugged it off. I continued my staffing duties, greeting guests and taking photos of masculine folks in super cute floofy dresses from the beloved video game series. "I love your Marisa cosplay!" I said to the TouhouFest convention chair. He was wearing a frilly and whimsical witch outfit. Think *Alice in Wonderland* meets *Kiki's Delivery Service*. I may have taken 50 or so photos at the small one-day event. I wanted to make time to play the video game the convention was centered on, but the room was too crowded and noisy. Maybe next time.

At five o'clock I had just finished documenting TouhouFest. I was just about ready for the short drive back to my parents' house to sort and make a post for my blog. An outsider's view looking into the *Touhou* scene. But first, I needed to lie down. I'd been on my feet all day, socializing with *Touhou* fans, making sure their photos were taken and that guests were having a good time. I rested my head on my memory foam pillow. I had my phone beside me. I went back into my phone to check the clock app.

Fifteen thousand views?! HOW?!

I'm an elder millennial who's jaded with most social media. I don't even know how to create and edit content for TikTok. How am I getting this many views? I was lucky to get 300 on any given cosplay lip sync I posted.

Numbers by the thousands were going higher and higher. By the end of the day, I had reached 30,000 views for a simple TikTok video of my old Anime Expo 2002 photos.

I wasn't a well-known cosplayer in 2002. My friends and I cosplayed for fun. Anime Expo 2002 was our celebration before moving away to university. We were cringe, but we were free to be ourselves without judgment of "normal people." We didn't have the best materials or access to high-quality wigs back in 2002. We used shiny costume satin because it was cheap, and we were cheap. We either used our real hair or whatever neon party wig we could find to look like our favorite anime characters.

I looked at the comments—and I'm not one to look at comments. I was afraid of being trolled. I apprehensively started scrolling down to read each comment posted. What I read was unexpected.

"They walked so we could run."

"True pioneers, ahead of their time."

"Our ancestors."

"THE ancestors."

I was in shock. So many of these comments came from people who were born around the time of Anime Expo 2002. For them, it was looking through the pages of a history book. For me, it was my high school summer memories set to the city pop tune of fleeting romance. Much like fleeting romance, the summer before going off to university is a short-lived time.

A whopping 107,000 views later, I decided to give story and life to these old anime convention photos from my high school years. I bring you *The Fangirl Diaries*. Seeing that this TikTok video had garnered so many views and positive comments, and after 20 years of blogging about anime conventions and fandom, I knew it was time to put all the history down chapter by chapter. I had to recall memories of the early days of the internet, finding information about anime and how to get anime, even if it was trusting a stranger to send me VHS tapes of the *Evangelion* movies and *Gundam Wing*. These were the days before streaming.

My lived experience as a fangirl speaks to whom anime was targeting at the turn of the millennium. What was it like to be in your youth and catch up with *Sailor Moon*, stay up all night to catch the latest episode of *Cowboy Bebop*, and how was I, a high school student with no part-time job focused on extracurriculars and then a broke university student, going to afford this hobby? The joke back then was "Anime: Drugs Would Be Cheaper" because the anime hobby entails owning home video equipment, buying merchandise, attending conventions, dressing up like your favorite characters, and more.

The Fangirl Diaries is a story 20 years in the making of what it was like for a teen otaku finding herself within the anime fandom. These were more than just pictures set to trending tunes on TikTok. They were curated memories of friends spending one last summer together before going their separate ways to university.

Let me take you back to a time before you could snap cosplay selfies on your iPhone, order cosplays directly from China, read manga on your phone, create anime Spotify playlists, or stream your favorite anime on Crunchyroll. To a time before TikTok. From the pages of my *Cardcaptor Sakura* diary and the old blog posts I saved on LiveJournal and on my website, I present *The Fangirl Diaries*.

"Thank you for letting us live your memory with you!!!"—a TikTok user

Prologue
Fall 2019: An Auditorium
in South Orange County

The auditorium lights dimmed. The show was about to begin. I never thought in 20 years that I would watch a high school production of anime convention life. "Welcome to Fire-Con!" Two teens navigate an anime convention and run into their own series of unfortunate events that could only happen at a con. Actors in capes, Party City masks, Halloween costumes, and cat ears cavorted on the stage as these intrepid teens were on their quest at Fire-Con to ... well, that's a spoiler. Go watch *Geek!* to find out what happens next.

A coworker at my liberal arts university day job had asked me to check out his kid's play. He had let the teacher know that there would be a ... gasp ... cosplayer in the audience! I was curious, and I wanted to support the local high school theater. After all, I too was very much involved in performing arts when I was in high school.

I sat in my seat viewing the show, thinking to myself that it was strange and therapeutic to see my college days onstage. I had been to many Fire-Cons and seen many similar stories play out—good, bad, and cringe.

And then we went into intermission.

This was the final dress rehearsal for this production. One of the parents who worked at a local Mexican food place catered the late-night dinner for the kiddos and the guest. "Great day to wear white," I murmured sarcastically, realizing that my dinner was going to involve tacos, enchiladas, and salsa; this was going to get messy. I was wearing my *Sailor Moon*–inspired cardigan and a white circle skirt. I almost looked like I was dressed as a retro 1940s pinup version of the Stay-Puft Marshmallow Man from *Ghostbusters*.

"We have a guest with us!" the drama teacher announced. "We have a guest from Soka University who has cosplayed and attended conventions for over 20 years." I had originally thought I was just going to watch a play about anime convention goers getting into some kind of trouble, the trouble that you would privately share with your friends on LiveJournal. Okay, I love giving speeches. I've done shotgun presentations on NCAA requirements for high school students at the last second. Let's go!

"Hi. My name is Erica, and thank you for having me as a guest," I paused now, realizing that I had the full attention of the high school thespians on me. Wow, so well-behaved and quiet. No one was on their phones! "I was invited to speak to your drama class this evening. I work as a counselor at Soka University in Aliso Viejo. I really enjoyed seeing the first part of your play this evening. I think all of you did an amazing job! So much of what I've seen onstage reminds me of when I started going to anime conventions. In fact, I've been cosplaying and going to conventions for 20 years." But what was 20 years to these high school students? It's not like I had not worked with high school students before. I got my master's degree in high school counseling, and I worked at a university with young people from all over the world every day.

"I started going to conventions when I was your age. Anime conventions were where my people were." I paused again. Don't overshare. Don't talk about the time your friend nearly got into a fistfight with some famous YouTuber at Anime Expo. You've got this, Eri.

"My people," I emphasized. "In high school, anime was my go-to for entertainment. We didn't have Crunchyroll, Netflix, or streaming. I had to order VHS tapes online and hope they arrived at my doorstep. How many of you know what a VHS tape is?" A laugh came from the adults in the room.

"I went to a Catholic high school. I wore my school uniform—cardigan, skirt, white button-up, saddle shoes, knee-high socks, and sometimes cat ears. I was a wannabe cat girl in a school uniform. Sometimes, I brought a cat plush with me to school." Embrace your cringe culture, but don't talk about the boys love and yaoi *Gundam Wing* fanfic you and Nikki wrote during choir right now. Don't show your cringe.

Let's continue.

"Yes, I was an anime fan. A weeb. I grew up watching *Sailor Moon* on UPN Channel 13. Growing up, I didn't have a lot of female-lead adventure shows. I loved Disney princesses like Belle and Jasmine, but I just wanted something more. *Sailor Moon* gave 10-year-old me some amazing female characters that could be my friends and that I could be like. I rushed home to watch *Sailor Moon* because my dad had to record it off TV because I was at school."

Those 7:30 a.m. broadcasts on UPN 13 made it hard for me to catch because I was on my way to school—middle school (a.k.a. the worst).

"I didn't have a lot of friends in sixth grade. I was the new kid. I didn't know how to make friends with people who already had their cliques already set. Watching *Sailor Moon* after school made me feel like the Sailor Scouts were my friends that I would meet after school, and I would join them on their adventures to defeat the Negaverse!"

"And then *Star Wars* was re-released in movies. That was huge deal for millennials. For the first time we would see this cinematic masterpiece in the movies. This was an event for us! I even wore Princess Leia's hair buns to school."

"My mom spent time in the morning styling my hair like Princess Leia's iconic hair buns. She wanted me to be happy. She knew I didn't have a lot of friends. She knew I had bullies and mean girls. And she knew I would throw down ... like Leia ... if anyone crossed me."

"I was different from everyone else. And I was okay with that. I liked who I was and I liked the things I liked. I never understood why it was a crime to enjoy *Sailor Moon*, *Star Wars*, anime, manga, and other nerdy things. They made me happy. Barney the Dinosaur made these mean girls happy, and you would never see me diss their purple dinosaur." I hoped they were picking up on my sarcasm.

"Anime conventions helped me connect with my people. My parents were hesitant at first thinking Anime Expo would be a sexy party with ninjas, but so as long as I had a 4.0 GPA, they would let me go to conventions. I aced all of my classes just so I could be with my people."

"My first Anime Expo I saw so many people in costume. And I was just in the registration line. I saw three people dressed as the heroines from *Magic Knight Rayearth*, and we couldn't stop talking about it! I never felt weird or awkward. In school, I was always picked last, and I was afraid to talk to people because I was really shy. I was afraid of being judged. I'm not even inside the con and we're gushing over our favorite CLAMP series!"

"In short, anime conventions saved me. I had events I looked forward to. I was inspired to dress up as my favorite characters. In class, I would write in my notebook who I wanted to cosplay next: Cardcaptor Sakura in her cat outfit, Sailor Mars, Utena.... I couldn't wait for my next convention. At school, I really had nothing to look forward to other than leaving and graduating. Yet, with Anime Expo and Ani-Magic around the corner, I always got hyped for that!"

Prologue

"Conventions were a safe space for kids who were bullied, queer kids who had to stay closeted from their parents and school community, and this was the place where they could be themselves even if it was for a weekend. This was our space. This was our time."

I gently paused to conclude my sentiments. I didn't know how much time I had, but I felt that focusing on the fact that conventions were a safe haven for marginalized teens would inspire some hope.

And in the back of my mind, I also wondered, were my references to *Revolutionary Girl Utena* and *Magic Knight Rayearth* going over their heads? These were my childhood icons.

The drama teacher asked, "Any questions for our guest?"

"What's your favorite anime?" a student asked.

"That's a good question. I have a lot, but I'd have to go with *Sailor Moon*." I pointed to my *Sailor Moon*–inspired cardigan from Elhoffer Design.

Cheers came from the audience.

"But if you want to take graduate courses in anime, I recommend almost any movie by Satoshi Kon. That dude is a master of cinema. Period."

Another hand went up.

"Do you like *My Hero Academia*?"

"Who doesn't?! Froppy is my favorite. I go to children's charity events dressed up like her. All the kids love seeing *My Hero Academia* characters just as much as Spiderman."

A few oohs from the audience.

"A lot of kids like *My Hero Academia*. And I don't blame them. It's an awesome show! You can learn a lot about heroism and life lessons through it."

And another hand went up.

"Have you experienced any kind of drama at the conventions you go to like the drama in our play?"

I let out a deep breath. This wasn't the time for the 100-yard stare.

"I've seen a lot."

I didn't know how to answer this question thoroughly. I ran panels about convention horror stories. Which one should I tell? Which one was safe to tell an audience of high school students and their teacher?

"When you get young unsupervised teens all together in the same place and time, what do you think is gonna happen?" I smirked.

And yet, I'd also witnessed drama in my twenties and thirties.

"Do you have an Instagram?" another student asked.

"Yes, but I'm on social media for the love, not the likes. This is more of a hobby to me. A very fun hobby that's kept my downtime busy for the past 20 years!"

"Can we take a cast photo with you?" asked a student.

The theater teacher herded all the costumed students together for a group photo. I did my best Asian girl peace sign and vintage girl curtsy in the photo.

Inspiring kids. It's what I do.

"Thank you!" the students said as we started to tag and share our socials.

The theater students wrapped up their tasty Mexican dinner and went on to perform the second act.

The play had ended. All the kids seemed pretty confident that *Geek!* was going to go great with the local audiences.

I went into the parking lot. I began to start my Honda Accord and figure out what playlist I was going to listen to during the long drive home.

I started to think about that one question that one student asked: "Have you experienced any kind of drama at the conventions you go to like the drama in our play?"

Drama.

Conventions.

LOL. XD

I helped a friend sew her *Gundam* outfit for a cosplay contest hours before we were onstage.

I was randomly roped into a cosplay contest on more than one occasion.

I went to an anime convention in the desert that looked like the sketchy hotel from *Manos: The Hands of Fate.* This was a Reddit horror story waiting to be told.

I have seen a grown hairy man dress up as the femme fatale Faye Valentine from *Cowboy Bebop.*

I lost friends. I gained some of the best friendships ever.

I was getting ready to pull out of the school's parking lot. I tuned into Spotify. I looked up James Taylor and listened to "Fire and Rain," reflecting on memories: crushing over voice actor Kirby Morrow, having a seat at the unofficial queer kids dinner table at Anime Expo, the first time I glomped someone (and they liked it), starting my blog about anime conventions, convincing my parents to let me go to an anime con in Chicago and not telling them that I was rooming with 10 other people ... these were some of the best experiences I ever had.

1

I Didn't Know That Was an Anime!

I had my eyes glued to the TV. Another episode of *Maple Town* was on. I had my Patty Rabbit and Bobby Bear toys with me as I anticipated a new episode of *Maple Town* on Nickelodeon. This was a simple story of Patty Rabbit moving to a brand-new town and befriending all the furry townspeople. It was a mix of *Anne of Green Gables* and *Little House on the Prairie*, but all the characters were cute anthropomorphic animals that lived in the cottagecore world of Canada. And boy howdy, did I have the toys! I had the schoolhouse, Patty Rabbit's house, the cars, the fuzzy dress-able figures. This is the earliest franchise I remember ever being a fan of. And I was still in kindergarten.

What I didn't know back then was that *Maple Town* was a 1986 Japanese anime called *Meipuru Taun Monogatari*, or *Maple Town Story*. As a kid in single digits of age, I had no idea this was from Japan. Nickelodeon in the 1980s showed a lot of children's anime during their afternoon block of children's programming—*Maya the Bee*, *Lil' Bits*, *Grimm's Fairy Tale Classics*, and *The Noozles* were just some of my earlier memories. Yet, I didn't know those were straight from Japan. I knew there was a different vibe to them. The characters' eyes were wider, their expressions more dramatic; the animation was more pastel, dark moments even darker than most Saturday morning cartoons that I would watch. Even in the dancing princesses episode of *Grimm's Fairy Tale Classics*, the monsters looked more like they were out of *He-Man* than a Disney princess movie. They were scary, ferocious, and I thought the princesses and the hero were not going to make it. I thought the princesses were going to be torn to shreds and not make it home by daylight. It was definitely something different. Yet, I did not know these pieces of children's media were anime from Japan.

My brother, younger than me by four years, also discovered a show that he really liked. At the age of about four, he was enamored by the wild world of *Speed Racer*. My younger brother loved toy cars. My mom thought about renting *Speed Racer* when we were at our local video store. My brother and I sat patiently in front of our family room's TV. We heard the opening notes of the classic theme song. It was a simple theme song with very simple lyrics: "Go Speed Racer, Go Speed Racer, Gooooooo!" Before the show even started, my brother and I were singing it. Of course, my brother loved the fast cars and the capers Speed would find himself in. My mom kept renting more *Speed Racer* tapes to keep us occupied. It was then we were invested in the Racer X story, and we wanted more. Sadly, the rental place only had five tapes. My mom had exhausted their stock. Luckily she discovered that MTV was playing *Speed Racer* at midnight, and, when she could figure out how to work the VCR timer, she would tape episodes.

We didn't have DVD or Blu-ray box sets that you could just pick up or a streaming service to keep the attention of my brother and me. Back then, you had to put in some extra legwork to watch anime.

Sure, I had a lot of things I liked. My dad introduced me to *Star Wars* via *Return of the Jedi*. "Look! The Ewoks. They speak Tagalog!" he said. The furry teddy bear race that saved the galaxy spoke my culture's language. It was interesting, but I would continuously rewatch this movie all the time on our laserdisc collection. We would later see the special editions in theaters. My mom had us watch *Alien* because, she said, "It's a nice movie. It's not as scary as *Temple of Doom*." My brother and I were traumatized by hearts being pulled out in the movie that had the kid from *The Goonies*. Of course, I had my Saturday morning cartoons and Disney. Disney had princesses, but the villains and animal characters called more to me. Saturday morning cartoons like *Jem and the Holograms* kept me intrigued, but the cartoon about the all-star girl group and their punk-ass Misfits rivals was immediately pulled off air. I caught it in its final rerun. Sure, Saturday morning cartoons had some female characters, but they were sidekicks or didn't really resonate with me as the characters from *Jem and the Holograms* did.

I collected toys like Barbie and the Littlest Pet Shop. I still played with Barbies at the age of 10. I wasn't really interested in dating boys. I still thought they had cooties or whatever deterrents we gals made up to justify not interacting with boys. I wanted to be a Barbie collector and have a ton of dolls like Mr. Smithers in *The Simpsons*. He looked happy having a wall of plastic princesses surrounding him. I wanted that happiness as an adult. Yet, Barbie collecting was an expensive hobby for a 10-year-old. I didn't think I could afford a Bob Mackie designer Barbie with the allowance I got from my chores. No way my parents were going to let me drop $100 on a Barbie!

In the sixth grade, each of my nerdy gal pals was a passionate fan of something. A classmate had a huge collection of *Lion King* trading cards and merchandise. She would show it off from time to time. I tried to figure out my thing, the fandom I could embrace (and my parents' wallet could finance). Okay, maybe *Pocahontas*.... I liked the raccoon and the pug. Nah, there was too little merch featuring the plucky raccoon or snooty pug. I had a huge collection of *American Girl* books ... but I felt I was aging out of it. I loved reading about history, but again, like Barbie, American Girl dolls and their clothes were a luxury. *Animaniacs*? I collected the comics and the trading cards. I liked that there was more than just Dot. I liked the grumpy Slappy Squirrel and the Broadway belter Rita the cat. I knew every word to every original song that was put to *Animaniacs*—including the parody of *Les Misérables*. How about comics in general? Barbie comics were cute but were more of a slice of life with the occasional jewelry robbery that the plastic princess had to stop. I was slowly growing out of the love triangle that was Betty, Veronica, and Archie. I liked our friends from Riverdale, but I just wanted something more. The 12-year-old me was looking for something that leaned into girlhood but wasn't condescending, that was proud and celebrated femininity in a way that was accessible for middle-school me. It was the fall of 1995 when—suddenly—I found the fandom I was looking for.

2

Setting the VCR Timer by Moonlight

I babysat Audrey May, a beauty pageant princess who lived down the street. She was a few grade levels lower than me. We carpooled to and from our K-8 private Catholic school. I would watch her after school. Like any kid that discovered something profound, Audrey May told me about a show that she stumbled across one morning on UPN 13.

"...and I was watching this show where these three girls used magic against these three witches," the eight-year-old I was babysitting babbled on. I nodded, pretending to pay attention to some Saturday morning cartoon show I would have probably grown out of.

"...and then one of the girls used bubbles as a weapon, one of them used her fingers as a gun, and then the main one used her tiara and the witches turned into moon dust!" my pageant princess client continued. "Yeah, that's sounds pretty cool!" I nodded off, pretending to pay attention. "And I'm going to Target to get a Sailor Mars doll because she's so cool!" Yeah, I remember collecting toys. Toys are for kids, right?

I was 12 and doing what most '90s gals did in entrepreneurship— babysit. Babysitting the neighbors' kids was all right to me. I'd let them boast about their 100 percents on tests, how their parents were going to get them the latest trendy toy, how they had TVs in their rooms, and all I had to do was make sure they didn't get into trouble and I didn't accidentally say an "omg" because strict Catholic parents wouldn't let you take the Lord's name in vain.

This particular pageant princess would eventually turn me into the Moonie that I am today. It was this conversation that changed my life. I found my fandom. *Fandom* wasn't really a word back in 1995. You probably said to friends, "I'm a fan of This and I'm part of the official fan club. Check out my fan club button I got in the mail!" or you were known as the dreaded "Trekkie." In 1995, *Lion King* was a big deal if you were a kid.

2. Setting the VCR Timer by Moonlight

Hamlet with lions was all the rage. I was always impressed by my class-mate's *Lion King* collection and their deep-dive knowledge into *The Lion King* movie. I wished I could feel that way about some form of media.

As a 12-year-old middle schooler, I liked a lot of things, but I didn't consider myself hard-core into *Animaniacs*, American Girl, Barbie dolls, or slice-of-life comics like *Betty and Veronica*. I was growing out of *Nancy Drew* and *Goosebumps* books. I was debating if I should still be into the doll col-lecting hobby. Twelve-year-old girls in my middle school were growing out of it and trading their Barbies for after-school sports, *Seventeen* magazine, and gushing over boys. I was terrible at sports, and I was the last to be picked for a team during PE. I didn't really care about crushing over boys, but I had a lot of friendships with boys because we would bond over our casual interest in video games. I was one of the few girls who had a Nintendo 64. It was easy for me to talk about Mario and friends with the guys.

My middle school attempted the year-round calendar. We had an ear-lier start of the school year, but it also meant longer fall and spring breaks. Once we happened to have fall break in October. It was a habit that I was up at 7:00 a.m. I wanted to check out the latest syndicated episode of *Lit-tlest Pet Shop*. Yet, that *Sailor Moon* show my babysitting client was talking about was airing right after. With nothing better to do, I continued eating my breakfast cereal of choice and anticipated what this *Princess Gwenevere and the Jewel Riders* knockoff could be and how much my IQ would suffer as I watched it. After all, I was 12 and had it all figured out. I knew what was cool. I knew that girly things were for babies, not preteens.

Seven thirty in the morning Pacific Standard Time.

I heard a peppy valley girl voice on the television.

"Today on *Sailor Moon* ... an evening with Tuxedo Mask is cut short when Queen Beryl's evil servants come looking for the lost imperium sil-ver crystal. The crystal that will shape the destiny of the entire universe. Will the Negaverse snare it for their own? We'll be right back and I'll show you!"

Ooh ... a jewelry caper, a ballroom dance, a princess in disguise, a gent in a tuxedo that's giving me *Phantom of the Opera* vibes? Okay, Moon Brat ... you got my attention. Suddenly ... the theme song. "Fighting evil by moon-light, winning love by daylight." Dramatic guitar riffs, a melody reminis-cent of a song from *Jem and the Holograms*, and a team of five heroines that looked really badass. I was sold. And wait ... there are two cats in this?! Cats are the good guys?! None of the *Tom and Jerry* evil and villainous cat trope?

I was eagerly watching through the episode and was intrigued by the

15

ballroom caper. Would Princess Diamond be the moon princess they're looking for? I was so intrigued by the romance and aesthetics of the episode—heroines who embraced the girly-girlness of being a tween set in the backdrop of a romantic ballroom intrigue. Dances with mysterious men in tuxes, demonic possession, and a talking cat? As I've said, I was sold.

"The real moon princess would have been expecting me," said the talking black cat.

Wait ... there's an ongoing storyline? It doesn't revert back to the status quo? I gotta follow this like a daytime soap? Okay! Let's not miss an episode!

The Nephrite and Molly arc followed. I was devastated when Nephrite died at the hands of Zoycite and their trio of minions. The final shot lingered on Molly in tears as the Sailor Scouts mourned. And while the trio of minions were defeated, the story still ended on a sad note. "Was he really dead?" I thought. "Are they going to bring him back?" I wondered. I haven't seen anything like that done so dramatically—especially something for kids to be entertained at seven thirty in the morning. This was when I knew *Sailor Moon* was something more than just your average '90s kids show. I kept watching and holding on to each moment.

I knew from the episode where Nephrite died that this was not your Marvel or DC stuff where you could just write a character back to life. Nephrite was not coming back. A few episodes later, we also got to see Molly handle her grief and loss as part of the main story. Normally, in children's entertainment, an episode about grief and loss would be "it's time for a special episode of...." Yet, Molly's story and conclusion fit in organically without taking the overall story to a pause. So, anytime anyone mentions that *Sailor Moon* is best without filler episodes, they tend to forget moments like these that let us grow and move forward even with secondary characters.

Fall break was coming to an end. I would miss my 7:30 a.m. rendezvous with my new friends, Serena, Amy, Raye, and eventually Lita. I had the VCR timer set to 7:30 a.m. must-see TV on UPN Channel 13 each weekday morning. I had something to look forward to coming home from school. At least I could keep up with my new favorite thing.

Commercials for the *Sailor Moon* dolls would pop up during commercials. I needed these "adventure dolls." They weren't fashion dolls. No, that's Barbie stuff. Audrey May got herself a Sailor Mars doll, and she would bring it with her anytime I had to babysit her. I loved the changeable clothes and brushable hair. I knew I needed to have them all!

2. Setting the VCR Timer by Moonlight

I ended up going on an errand run with my mom to Target. And there it was in the toy aisle for $7.99 plus tax—the six-inch *Sailor Moon* dolls released by Bandai. They were half the size of a Barbie. They were petite fashion dolls wearing their Sailor Scout uniforms. They had tiaras and transformation wands, and they had their respective gloves and shoes painted onto them. Sailor Mars and Sailor Venus called to me the most. I took home Sailor Venus even though we had not gotten to her debut episode just yet. I loved my Sailor Venus doll and eventually saved my allowance to get Sailor Mars. I aced several math tests and did some extra book reports to get the rest of the Sailor Scout squad. I had my *Sailor Moon* dolls posing pretty while my Barbies and Disney princesses were making their way to retirement in the attic.

I was also crushing over *Sailor Moon*'s cast of beautifully drawn characters. Tuxedo Mask was my first male anime crush, or "husbando." Yeah, I knew he belonged to Princess Serenity, but I couldn't say no to a gentleman in a suit and top hat. Yet, in addition to Tuxedo Mask, I ended up crushing on Malachite. Yeah, I knew Malachite had a thing for Zoycite, but I couldn't say no to those platinum lush locks and a dapper gent in uniform. And there was Mina (a.k.a. Sailor Venus). Oh wait.... I had an anime girl crush? Better to bury those thoughts, keep them shut out. I didn't want Catholic guilt to flare up.

3

Sailor Moon Is from Japan?!

And there was this thing called the Internet that was starting to take shape. Our household was fortunate to have dial-up access. In 1995, we only had one desktop computer. We had the family computer situated in the living room shareable by all four of us. My dad was an early adopter of whatever was new tech. We had a modem and a phone line, and we weren't afraid to use them. A few beeps and congested noises, and our family computer was able to access the World Wide Web.

During fall break, I decided to search the web for "Sailor Moon." There wasn't a Wikipedia back then, but for those who knew, there was Hitoshi Doi's simple website highlighting '90s magical anime and his Japanese voice actor (seiyū) database. His website for *Sailor Moon* was a sensory overload. Remember, I had only seen the North American dub and I wasn't aware of the world outside of the Queen Beryl story.

Wait ... there were more Sailor Scouts?! I loved Sailor Uranus's boyish features and Sailor Saturn's sad girl vibe. Wait ... there's more story?! More villains? There are HOW MANY episodes?! There are lost episodes that never aired?! They did WHAT to the series finale?! This show is still airing in Japan?! There's a comic book? Can I find the comics in English?! I had to know more. Going through Hitoshi Doi's website when I was in the sixth grade was absolutely mind-blowing.

And there were more *Sailor Moon* websites to check out. While most of them felt like they were a copy and paste of Hitoshi Doi's *Sailor Moon* website, there was Ken Arromdee's *Sailor Moon* frequently asked questions (FAQ) website. This extensive and detailed frequently asked questions guide to *Sailor Moon* listed all the cuts made in the North American adaptation and what we had missed. This FAQ also provided series trivia and what was to come. After devouring every word and committing every word to memory, I was, at the age of 12, a walking and talking *Sailor Moon* expert. I was a *Sailor Moon* "otaku," or super fan.

The Japanese insult "otaku" was reclaimed by Western English-speaking fans to mean "anime fan." The Japanese context meant "house," as in "one who does not need to leave the house and maybe needs to touch grass every now and then." In other words, you wouldn't tell an elderly Japanese person at the grocery store that you were a proud otaku. Utilizing this term was up for debate in this community. One side did not want to appropriate the term that was more associated with an insult and the other side wanted a term for fans of Japanese animation.

And then I discovered the online meeting hub, alt.fan.sailor-moon. Online community hubs where fans of one thing or another could find one another were known as "newsgroups." I did not post in these newsgroups. As a 12-year-old, I was too shy and too cautious to post on these fan groups, where the average age was somewhere between college age and my dad's age. I mainly lurked and read discussions about *Sailor Moon*. It surprised me that a lot of straight men in their twenties were into the series as much as I was.

And wait ... there's more anime that's just like *Sailor Moon* that I might like? Shows that cater to girls that have girls at the forefront doing awesome things to save the world? Where can I find *Magic Knight Rayearth* here in the states? Hitoshi Doi's fan-run database of magical girl anime opened my eyes to animation beyond the world of Saturday morning cartoons. I was ready for something new and something that called to me. Shōjo anime was what 12-year-old me needed—seeing girls close to my age embracing girlhood, growing up without abandoning the childish things they loved, a main cast of girl-led teams saving the world—this was relatable and inspirational all at once. Seeing a team of girls with different personalities, living their day-to-day lives with worries and anxieties a tween would face, and saving the world was what I was lacking in those Saturday morning cartoons. There was no token girly-girl in a mostly male team. This was girl power at its best.

Unfortunately, *Sailor Moon* was taken off the air after a year of broadcast. Low ratings were the reasoning. Seven thirty in the morning in the Los Angeles area was tough to watch live, especially if you had to get to school by eight o'clock. Online efforts were made to bring back *Sailor Moon*. One such effort was "Save Our Sailors" (SOS). This online petition drew tens of thousands of Moonies, as we *Sailor Moon* fans are called, to bring back our beloved show and to also bring in more episodes. The grassroots movement also was convinced that if Moonies bought strawberry flavored Pop-Tarts on a single day in December 1996, maybe *Sailor Moon* could go back on air. The rationale was that since strawberry Pop-Tarts were heavily used during commercial breaks when *Sailor Moon* aired, it would bring attention. This was considered a "pro-cott": buy as many strawberry Pop-Tarts in hopes that this would garner attention to DiC to bring *Sailor Moon* back to American households. We did get *Sailor Moon* reruns back on USA network during their Cartoon Express daily block, but there was no news of new episodes coming to North America.

During this time, I took matters into my own hands to watch the rest of *Sailor Moon*. I live in Southern California. There was the Torrance Mitsuwa Marketplace a few minutes from us. They had the *Sailor Moon* manga! I knew that the manga would be different from the original, so I had to pick up every volume in Japanese because I wanted to experience *Sailor Moon* in manga form, even if I didn't understand the text. It had pretty photos. I was not used to reading comics in black and white and reading books "the other way around." This was different from the *Archie* comics I used to read. These were novella-sized graphic novels. I didn't think at the time it would receive an English translation. The books cost seven dollars each, and I saved up my allowance to complete the 18-volume adventures of Sailor Moon and her Sailor Scouts ... oh, I meant Sailor Senshi!

Gardena is not too far from where we lived. Gardena is populated with Japanese immigrants and some of the best family-owned Japanese, Vietnamese, and Korean restaurants you'll ever have on this side of the Mississippi. There was a Japanese market in Gardena that had a video rental store, Video Japan. Our household had two VCRs. I could rent the last episodes of *Sailor Moon R* and continue on with *Sailor Moon S*. I could follow along with Hitoshi Doi's episode summaries to get the gist of what was going on. This wasn't perfect, but it would give me access to watching the rest of *Sailor Moon*.

The good news was that *Sailor Moon* was easy to follow. The sailors had a friend or a crush that would end up being the victim of the day. Crazy teenage hijinks happened in between. There was a monster sent in by the Team Evil of the season. With the power of love and friendship, Sailor Moon and the Sailor Senshi do their thing and save the day.

Hitoshi Doi's website was one of the first databases for information about anime, especially magical girl shows. Since *Sailor Moon*'s debut, and subsequently *Dragonball*, the anime presence on the internet started growing more and more. More anime fan sites started popping up. Hence, this led to the creation of Anipike, or the Anime Web Turnpike. This website was a one-stop shop and a collective database of anime websites. It was easy to use—you can find anime websites by series and see, for instance, if the website had a focus on galleries, character tributes, music, or reviews. I was curious to see the section called "Fansubs."

Wait.... I didn't have to rent videos anymore and could get English-subtitled VHS tapes? Fansubs VHS tapes with English subtitles made by fans for fans. This was a labor of love. Before streaming or going into the dark web to watch the latest *Pretty Cure*, you had to find an online fansub distributor. You would pay about $36 via money order (online payment like PayPal or Venmo did not exist then) to get six VHS tapes of what you wanted. The general courtesy rule was to remove an anime title the moment it got an official American license and distribution. I keep this section of Anime Web Turnpike in mind now that I know where to find anime beyond televised syndication or getting the Japanese raw VHS tapes from the local Japanese rental store at Mitsuwa.

When I was in eighth grade, our cable service had expanded. Included in our cable service was an up-and-coming channel called Cartoon Network. After school, Cartoon Network would have something called Toonami. Before Toonami defined a generation of Western otaku, the original Toonami lineup had *Thundercats, Johnny Quest*, and whatever random cartoon they had lying around to fill up the airtime. In Toonami's original lineup, there was an anime title that caught my eye; it looked a little older ... kinda like *Top Gun* meets *Star Wars* ... but I was open to anything.

Robotech. This was far from the magical girl genre of the 1990s. In middle school, my brother and I were huge fans of *Star Wars,* thanks to the special edition release and the *Shadows of the Empire* game. I would ditch PE to read Timothy Zahn and Michael Stackpole's *Star Wars* novels so I didn't have to worry about being picked last or bullied. *Robotech* seemed to echo what I loved about space opera. I loved the attention to detail, and you couldn't go wrong with a good-versus-evil-plus-shades-of-gray love story and an amazing soundtrack. It was a space opera with pop music thanks to Lynn Minmay. I liked the variety of female characters: the bubbly pop idol, Minmay; the headstrong, yet vulnerable Lisa Hayes; and the not-sure-how-to-human badass Zentradi, Miriya.

And then I deep-dived and researched more into *Robotech* and its complex history of taking three different science fiction mecha anime (*Super Dimension Fortress Macross, Super Dimension Cavalry Southern*

Cross, and *Genesis Climber MOSPEADA*) and combining them into one singular series to be digestible for an American audience. I delved into online fan sites on *Robotech* and *Macross* that had detailed articles on the history of getting the toys and anime to American audiences in the 1980s. It was the equivalent of taking three tiny children and putting them in a trench coat to pass off as an adult. Coming from the *Sailor Moon* fandom, the history of how anime was brought and localized for Western audiences continued to fascinate me. Even though *Robotech* may have gotten away from the censors with permanent character death, sexual innuendo, and cheap laughs, the editing of the show and rationale of marketing towards Western audiences was an interesting deep-dive read. This was an iceberg I was not ready for. Seeking out information about anime localization and censorship was a research topic that I would always find myself reading about. I never liked doing research papers in school because they were often topics I had no interest in, but having a front-row seat to the days of the so-called Sub versus Dub Wars was intriguing. I can say that I was there! Reading how the original *Super Dimension Macross* had made an impact on anime fandom, I had to track down the original series somehow.

Leave it to good old Anime Web Turnpike to direct me on where to find fansubs, or English-subtitled VHS tapes made by fans for fans. While I was tempted to check out Video Japan for my dose of the original *Macross*, because this was a much more complicated series than *Sailor Moon*'s Monster of the Week formula, I needed something with the English translation now that I knew where to find fansubs. I was going to start with the classic synoptic movie, *Macross: Do You Remember Love* and follow it up with *Macross: Flashback 2012*. The site I got these tapes from also had *Robotech: The Untold Story*, which was a Carl Macek retelling of *MegaZone 23*.

I submitted the money order to get my three tapes from this independent distributor online. The total was $15 before shipping for all three tapes. I convinced my parents to get me a $15 money order to send to someone I did not know online. I had my allowance saved in cash in my *Sailor Moon* coin purse. I didn't know how to get a money order. This was during the days when you could not send payment online, so you had to send payment by mail. You could not just Venmo or PayPal someone right away. You had to either go to the post office or grocery store and exchange cash for a money order to send safely via physical mail. This was quite a gamble waiting for the VHS tapes, especially the first time I was requesting fansubs.

I waited patiently for my VHS tapes to come through the mail. The anticipation was so nerve-racking. I could finally watch the original

Macross, even if it was a synoptic movie that covered most of the story of what I've seen, I was hyped. I carved out one Saturday to watch all three tapes. I went through a rollercoaster of emotions watching Misa, Hikaru, and Minmay go through their love triangle. I cried during the title song, "Do You Remember Love?" I went through a "feels trip" while watching *Macross: Flashback 2012* as these music videos synopsized everything leading up to the voyage of the SDF-3. Even though I was a tween in the late '90s watching *Macross* after its heyday, I immediately became a fan of this franchise.

I needed more *Macross*.

I dived back into the internet to learn more about *Macross*. The sequel series, the alternative universe, and drama CDs were just so fascinating to me. I loved these characters and I wanted to see what legacy they left after their adventures on the SDF-1. I was reading about *Macross Plus* and how it was the most expensive anime produced at the time. The animation looked impressive, and it did in fact look like *Top Gun* if it were an anime. It looked like *Macross Plus* was available for purchase in the United States. And it looked like it was dubbed and not censored either! Getting officially released anime VHS tapes was somewhat of an inconvenience at the time for a middle school student. When it came to buying VHS tapes of anime you faced the choice between getting the anime with the English dub cast or getting it with the original Japanese audio with English subtitles. Each tape would run between $25 and $30. The English dub would cost $25. The Japanese audio track with English subtitles would cost $30. This was before DVDs and Blu-ray giving you a choice. I saved my allowance in eighth grade to get all four English dubbed tapes of *Macross Plus*. I was in love with the AI killer idol, Sharon Apple. She was like a cosmic pop star changing her look every time for each of her songs. Her music slapped. The animation was simply breathtaking. It felt like watching an anime version of *Top Gun* with Madonna as the main villain. And like any *Macross* series, the soundtrack was always key. Sharon Apple's adrenaline-pumped "Information High" was my jam. Yoko Kanno's melodic and electric score became my go-to if I wanted to disappear in my headphones.

And I had to find out where I could get all this anime music. At the time, a new audio format called MP3 had just surfaced. To get official anime soundtracks imported, it would run you between $40 to $50. Also, you had to factor in shipping and taxes from Japan. For a middle school student, that's way too many chores, and I was already saving my pennies for the anime tapes themselves. A lot of times, fans would upload MP3s, full audio, of anime songs onto FTP servers. FTP servers were like an early form of the cloud or Google Drive. Anime fans uploaded MP3s of their music collection to share with their peers.

Our family was one of the early adopters of the brand new cable-based internet. No longer did we have to rely on dial-up or endure the incessant electronic beeps of waiting to be connected via Earthlink. Cable internet was revolutionary. It meant I could download a one-megabyte file in minutes as opposed to an hour. I went crazy downloading all the anime songs I could find and downloaded them all to my music folder. This was before the days of Napster and iTunes. You really had to know which websites were safe to download your anime soundtracks. While this was not legal by any means, this was the most accessible way to find anime music.

It took time for my parents to get used to the fact that I was listening to Japanese music. I had most of the *Sailor Moon* soundtracks on my desktop. I loved that *Sailor Moon* had solo songs (or image songs spotlighting a specific character) that gave more depth to each of the characters. Sailor Mars's "Eien No Melody" and "Fire Soul Bird Love" were tunes that I could listen to for hours. I always liked the image of Rei Hino as an idol pop singer who was a shrine maiden during the day. I was learning Japanese and also learning how to sing in Japanese. My parents weren't comfortable that I was listening to music in a foreign language. Yet, they listened to Tagalog, or F-pop music all the time. And while I did like '90s pop music, anime music gave me something different. It gave me variety. Sure, I liked the Spice Girls and Madonna, but the nice thing about anime music is that it crosses so many different genres. Yoko Kanno's score for *Macross Plus* (and *Cowboy Bebop*) was my introduction to jazz and experimental, undisciplined genres. *Macross*'s music from the '80s was also my primer for '80s Japanese pop (J-pop) and city pop.

We had just gotten a CD burner for our family PC. I was making anime mix CDs so I had something to listen to on my CD player at school. I could disappear into the world of my anime mix CDs during break and in between periods. I could meditate to the sounds of a Yoko Kanno instrumental, let my mind wander to the opening of *Record of Lodoss War*, or pretend I was a pop star to any of the *Macross* or *Sailor Moon* songs I had. It was a comforting feeling.

I was also able to discover new anime with the random anime MP3 files I was downloading. The opening theme to *Nurse Angel Ririka SOS* is the definition of '90s dance music. An intro reminiscent of "Barbie Girl" with a touch of "This Is Your Night," this opening song was '90s shōjo anime at its best. I found fansubs of *Nurse Angel Ririka SOS*, and I found another aspirational and relatable magical girl by the name of Ririka Moriya. She liked helping people. She wanted to be a nurse. At the time, I also wanted to be a nurse. And she was working on that save-the-universe thing too. I even searched the web to find a Ririka Moriya doll. And I did! She was about the size of a Skipper doll. She still sits happily in my curio next to my Disney princess dolls.

I was very happy that I found fandoms that I enjoyed: *Sailor Moon*, *Macross*, *Magic Knight Rayearth*, and *Nurse Angel Ririka* were sources of comfort and escape. It was easy for me to get lost in anime music. *Sailor Moon*'s original Japanese incarnation had hundreds of songs—including character spotlight songs (Sailor Mars always had the best ones—including a cover of Wham!'s "Last Christmas"). I spent a lot of my free time in middle school in anime brain rot—obsessing over my favorite *Macross* pop idol singers, ranking my favorite songs from *Sailor Moon*, creating singable English lyrics for the opening of *Nurse Angel Ririka SOS*, and eventually tracking down tapes for *Macross 7* at the local Japan Video. I was drowning in anime fandom. And I was okay with that.

Now all I needed was the merchandise to show off my fandom to the world.

When *Sailor Moon* (or any anime really) came to the United States, merchandise was scarce. *Sailor Moon* had the dolls, two children's books that served as a series primer, some accessories for the dolls (including the Moon Cycle, Sailor Moon's lunar motorcycle, which she never had in the anime but which was made for an original unaired live-action pilot), collectable cards that you got out of a vending machine at Toys "R" Us, a soundtrack CD that was hard to find, and that was about it. A translated version of the manga or graphic novel wasn't even out in the United States just yet. I was lucky to find the original manga at the local Japanese bookstore. I was lucky to have access to a thriving Japanese American community in my backyard.

My aunt in the Philippines learned that I was a huge fan of *Sailor Moon*. She got me a ton of *Sailor Moon* merchandise from the Philippines. I got the original Bandai Barbie-sized *Sailor Moon* dolls, *Sailor Moon* messenger bags, *Sailor Moon* shirts, *Sailor Moon* stationery, *Sailor Moon* jewelry, and more. I wore my messenger bag to school. I ditched whatever basic backpack I had for middle school. It was all about my red and plaid *Sailor Moon R* messenger bag. A boy I liked in middle school went to Indonesia and got me a *Sailor Moon* pencil case and a Super Sailor Moon pen. He didn't have to, but I couldn't help but feel giddy about this gift. My middle school crush gifted me *Sailor Moon* school supplies! I wasn't afraid to wear my fandom or show it off. *Sailor Moon* gave me a sense of inspiration, and it was nice to finally see a team made up of young girls—close to my age— working together to save the world. I felt that I could also be Usagi's friend because Usagi is a friend to all. It gave me a sense of inner happiness and inner strength.

I was also in love browsing through so many *Sailor Moon* websites outside of Hitoshi Doi's mega database of magical girl anime. I was thinking that I could make a website too. I wanted to learn how. I asked my dad to teach me website coding in the seventh grade. He introduced me to a WYSIWYG ("what you see is what you get") piece of software called Dreamweaver. I also had CorelDRAW for my image editing software. I spent my free time during seventh grade teaching myself how to build a website. I was learning HTML code, image editing, and how to make a presentable website in the spring of 1997. By the end of my spring break, I built my first website. My dad introduced me to the GeoCities free website hosting service. I uploaded all my website files via FTP. And just like that I was a proud owner of a *Sailor Moon* fan site, complete with a hit counter, guest book where visitors could leave their comments, and a small banner in support of SOS, the Save Our Sailors campaign.

I'll be honest. My *Sailor Moon* website was not the most original concept in the world. My website had a star background with Naoko Takeuchi's official manga artwork of the Sailor Senshi in tuxedos. This was just another *Sailor Moon* website that spouted out the same information that you could find on Hitoshi Doi's website. A lot of *Sailor Moon* websites were just clones of one another. I just wanted to teach myself how to build a website at the age of 13. I also started learning about a passing internet trend called "web rings" where websites were connected by this piece of coding to find the next website. I even created my own to join in on the trend!

So here I was ... a Moonie, an otaku, and in my tweens learning how to code, how to make websites, and rockin' some *Sailor Moon* school supplies. I was happy with myself. I was even happy when I found out that a new magazine called *MixxZine* was going to translate the *Sailor Moon* and *Magic Knight Rayearth* manga in a monthly comic anthology. The news broke out on the alt.fan.sailor-moon newsgroup. Even though I had the original Japanese manga, I needed the English version. However, I could finally get the chance to read *Magic Knight Rayearth*, the series I only knew through Hitoshi Doi's website. Just by character descriptions, world lore, and music alone, I knew I needed more magical girls in my life. I knew I had to track issues of *MixxZine* down—my local grocery store carried the independent zine that featured my two favorite magical girl adventures.

MixxZine was an interesting collaboration of four different manga series all in one monthly anthology zine—*Sailor Moon, Magic Knight Rayearth, Ice Blade,* and *Parasyte.* Of course, *Sailor Moon* and *Rayearth* made sense; they were stories about girl power. *Ice Blade,* however, was a very mature and violent yakuza story, and *Parasyte* was alien body horror. At the time, it was not what I was looking for. I skipped on those. Yet, I could finally read *Magic Knight Rayearth.* I had read reviews, plot summaries, character dossiers, etc., online. I could finally read about the adventures of Umi, Fuu, and Hikaru being whisked off to the magical world of Cephiro where they are summoned by the melancholy Princess Emeraude to save it. *Rayearth* was different from *Sailor Moon.* It took ordinary girls from the real world and brought them to a magical realm of fantasy. It was almost like a fairy tale, but we had not one princess, but three heroines with different personalities, coming from different worlds to come together to survive and save this magical world. I was super invested in *Rayearth.* I felt that I graduated from *Sailor Moon* after its end with the last season, *Sailor Stars.* I was ready for the next magical girl adventure....

I was back into reading comics again! And it was finally comics led by tween heroines that embraced girlhood and femininity. These were written and drawn by women who knew what young girls wanted in their escapism and fantasies. It allowed us to be feminine but not sexualized under the male gaze. It allowed us to be pretty, but pretty can be defined in so many different ways. There was no token girl or "the pink one" in a cast of mostly male characters; girls stood front and center in magical girl anime. These stories did not vilify everything cute and girly, instead *Sailor Moon* and *Rayearth* made girlhood our superpower. It didn't speak down to me because I was a young girl, it spoke with me and gave me the girl power I needed. It felt great!

However....

My love for Japanese anime came at a price. While I was fine being a wallflower who liked reading *American Girl* and *Nancy Drew* books before I became an anime fan, the moment I started bringing my *Sailor Moon* messenger bag instead of a plain backpack, decorating my assignment binder with *Sailor Moon* stickers and cards, and carrying *Sailor Moon* branded school supplies, my classmates had something to use against me. Staying quiet and in the background was fine. The moment I showed interest in something I was crazy about, that's when the bullying began. I had finally found something that made me happy, and the moment I started expressing my fandom in my school supplies, messenger bag, figures, trading cards taped to my binder, that's when my classmates found an excuse to further cut me out.

Classmates would tell me, "The monsters should attack Sailor Moon when she's transforming!" Or they'd say *Sailor Moon* was too childish or too girly for a middle school student to be into. I should be reading *Seventeen* and thinking about what boy I should date, listening to the latest in hip-hop, playing an after-school sport, celebrity crushing on either Leo or Kobe, and finding time on the weekends to take wallet-sized glamor shots at the mall. This was what was expected of a tween girl at my middle school. Those weren't my priorities; I wanted to be a Sailor Scout.

I liked *Sailor Moon* because it showed me that girls could and should support one another regardless of their differences. Usagi was nice to everyone—the sailor team consisted of an Ivy League–level genius, a shrine maiden girl boss, a delinquent who loves to cook, and the ditzy wannabe pop star. I hoped to have found these girl friends in real life. I wanted a supportive group of gal pals. Alas, the Catholic schools I attended were Mean Girl Central. No one would talk to the weird anime girl. I always looked forward to getting home from school because I could watch *Sailor Moon* and felt that my real middle school friends were Usagi, Ami, Rei, Makoto, and Minako. And soon after, Hikaru, Umi, and Fuu when the *Sailor Moon* manga and *Magic Knight Rayearth* manga got their English localized release from *MixxZine*. I just wanted to disappear into their stories and live my best middle school life with them, sharing in their everyday schoolgirl worries about exams and romance and saving the world.

And then I got, "Go back to Japan." I didn't know how to react to this in middle school. We weren't taught about racism against Asian Americans. "You like *Sailor Moon* and that anime shit. Go back to Japan." In hindsight, I should have gone to my principal about it, but I wasn't sure if anyone on our staff would have supported me. I was The Weird One. I was happier disappearing in my headphones between classes and having lunch all by myself. I was happier in headphones without the presence of bullies. I had no interest in fitting in. Fitting in would mean having to sacrifice the things I liked about me. I just wanted to be treated with humanity and dignity. You would think Catholic schools would teach this. My classmates, who were taught to love their neighbor, would continue to ostracize me because I enjoyed a foreign media. I felt alone. There was no one I could talk to about my fandom. Yet, in spite of it all, I lived my teen days like a manga magical girl—to be kind to others no matter what and to put joy and love into the world.

My parents started getting concerned because I was socially withdrawn from my peers. After I got into a fight with a girl from school because she thought it would be funny to steal some of my school supplies from me, the principal recommended that I see a therapist. Instead of our principal addressing the bullying issue, getting to the bottom of why the classmate stole my things in the first place, it seemed that I had to fix myself. After several sessions, my therapist concluded that there was nothing wrong with me; I just had an unfortunate situation of dealing with school bullies. I was more grown up and self-aware than my middle school peers (at least that's what my therapist concluded). Yet, I was not sure if that was the conclusion I wanted. I just wanted to be accepted for enjoying anime and to have some human connection with it. And of course, when I was finished with therapy, I entered the same landscape. No school-wide measures to prevent bullying. No punishment for the bullies. Business as usual.

After my last therapy session, my parents wanted to check out a new shopping center down the street. When they told me it had a bookstore bigger than Walden Books, I was excited. I stepped into Borders, and it was heaven for a book lover like me. Not only did they have rows and rows of bookshelves, but they also carried a ton of CDs and DVDs. It's like Walden Books and Tower Records all in one place! I perused the magazine aisle out of curiosity. I found a magazine titled *Animerica*. I had never seen a magazine dedicated to anime and manga. I had to browse through this issue. *Animerica* had articles about anime that was recently brought over to the states, manga excerpts from CLAMP's *X/1999*, convention spotlights, anime reviews, fan art submissions, and more. I picked up the issue and I was taking notes on what anime to check out next.

However, there was an advertisement in the back of the magazine that caught my eye—Anime Expo 1998 in Anaheim, California. An anime convention with people who loved anime as much as I did? A place where I could talk about anime without judgment or fear of being bullied? I could meet friends there? I could talk for hours about *Sailor Moon* with Moonies? I knew I had to go.

4

Anime Expo 1998
Missed Opportunities

It was a Sunday night in July. I had finished watching an *X-Files* rerun. The commercial for the Fox 11 10 o'clock news followed during the credits. "And we have something from Japan that's bigger than Godzilla! More at 10!"

Wait.

It was July.

Did I...?

Did I ... forget...?

The 10 o'clock news began. "Thousands of fans of Japanese animation gathered at the Anaheim Hilton last weekend...."

I had missed it!

I missed what could have been my first Anime Expo.

In my defense, the spring of 1998 was a very busy time. I was focused on high school entrance exams, applying to local private college prep high schools, graduating middle school, and surviving bullying and exclusion. Remembering when Anime Expo occurred was the last thing on my mind. So much was going on in my 13-year-old life.

The news anchor interviewed a manga-inspired Sailor Moon cosplayer about her thoughts on this year's Anime Expo. She talked about her Sailor Moon cosplay on screen while B-roll showed a plethora of hentai, or anime pornography, VHS tapes.

I was still in shock, but I resolved to attend Anime Expo the following year. I would be 14 and would probably have to take my parents and my 10-year-old brother along. I'd figure it out. I had a year to prepare for my first anime convention. After so many years of being brought to car shows at the Los Angeles Convention Center, I was looking forward to going to my first in-person anime fan event.

Part Two. Hey Mom! Let's Go to Anime Expo!

But no need to worry. During the summer of '98, the SyFy Channel introduced me to even more anime! I knew SyFy Channel showed anime on Saturdays, but I always had something going on on Saturday mornings (or I just wanted to sleep in). During that summer, I was introduced to our "Live Action Anime Girl," Apollo Smile. She was our video deejay for SyFy's summer of anime. I was introduced to *Tenchi Muyo* and *Urusei Yatsura* during this time. I video recorded the movie, *Urusei Yatsura 2: Beautiful Dreamer*. It became a comfort movie for my brother and me during the summer. We didn't know much about the background for *Urusei Yatsura*; it was a good stand-alone movie about the concept of time. My brother loved Mendō for his coolheadedness and insane, over-the-top outbursts, and I loved Sakura for her seriousness and investigative behavior, but I also liked Lum for her free-spiritedness and genki girl attitude. My brother and I watched *Tenchi the Movie: Tenchi Muyo in Love* and loved the *Back to the Future* (without the incest subplot) vibes and the characters. We ended up finding the DVD for *Tenchi Muyo in Love* and its sequel, *Tenchi the Movie 2: Daughter of Darkness*. We didn't like the second movie as much as the first movie, but it was our intro to the comedy harem series.

DVDs were a rarity back then. I thought DVDs were the best deal you could get for anime. Instead of choosing between VHS options—the English dub for $25 or Japanese with English subtitles for $30—you could get both for the price of one DVD. I owned three anime DVDs: the two *Tenchi* movies and one of the *Ranma ½* movies that were out at the time. My brother and I really bonded over characters in anime, finding characters that interacted like us.

I may not have had Anime Expo '98, but I knew that between the summer of '98 and the next Anime Expo, I would be an even bigger anime fan.

I entered our local Catholic college preparatory high school. It was essential for any somewhat affluent Filipino family to send their kids to this particular Catholic high school given that the public system in our local area was not a safe place to send your kids. In light of the stories of gang activity, students misbehaving, and teenage pregnancy—the stuff of a strict Catholic parent's nightmare—families with the means to do so avoided the public system.

Ninth grade was a happy year. I ignored my middle school classmates' warnings of "You better not be into that anime shit. They'll hate you." I met a lot of juniors in the marching band who were into *Tenchi Muyo* and *Dragonball*. *Dragonball*, while I was aware of it, just didn't vibe with me at the time. I was all about the shōjo girl power! A lot of the upperclassmen and I

32

became instant friends over anime. I had a choice between seventh-period choir or drama club for my after-school activity. Because a lot of my anime friends were in choir and band, I ended up joining the choir. Choir would always do collaborations with marching band. It meant more time with the juniors and seniors to geek out over anime and manga.

The anime that I really got into was *Cardcaptor Sakura*. *Sailor Moon* fans were ready for the next big magical girl anime. All eyes were on CLAMP's series starring Sakura Kinomoto, whose daily adventures consisted of surviving elementary school and collecting all the elemental cards of the Clow. It was a very simple story, but the art was pretty. I loved the friendship between Sakura and her cousin, Tomoyo. *Cardcaptor Sakura* became my "feel good" or comfort anime. I would watch this after school after a long day. The positivity, pastels, and kawaii factor always put me in a better mood. It made me happy. I could definitely see myself being friends with Tomoyo and Sakura when I was in elementary school. This was wholesome. To this day, I always recommend that my younger nieces check out *Cardcaptor Sakura* as their first anime or manga.

A few senior students introduced me to a show called *Neon Genesis Evangelion*. I could not for the life of me find the VHS fansubs online. Oh right! Once a series gets licensed, a fansub website stops distributing the tapes. It was just legal courtesy. I was a regular at the Torrance Borders. *Evangelion* VHS tapes were being sold for $25 for the English dub and $30 for the Japanese audio with English subtitles. The original *Evangelion* release had two episodes per VHS tape. Normally, an anime would have four episodes per VHS tape. While I did have an allowance, I tallied up how much it would cost me to own the entire series. *Evangelion* ran about 13 VHS tapes. I had to figure out how I could watch this acclaimed series that every otaku I knew was talking about. However! A local comic book store had *Evangelion* tapes for rent. I could rent the subtitled version and then copy it to a blank VHS!

Evangelion was an exploration of being a teenage mess ... with giant robots! To this day, anyone I know who is a fan of *Evangelion* tells me that the first four episodes capture depression well. I knew so many people who initially identified with Shinji. I also knew so many people who were turned off by Shinji; they were expecting a protagonist who was more badass and less nervous wreck. *Evangelion* was the anime that showed me that the medium could explore deeper themes and even be philosophical. I would watch the last two episodes of the final series to draw conclusions. I would read various *Evangelion* FAQs on websites to get different takes on how people interpreted the ambiguous ending. When I finished the *Evangelion* series and accompanying movies, I ended up falling in love with Misato. She was a femme fatale, badass, and had a very intriguing story arc. Like me, she was the daughter of a scientist. My dad worked for NASA's Jet Propulsion Laboratory and was the lead engineer on special projects such as the Mars Rover. She acted as a mother figure—albeit not the most perfect mother figure—to Shinji, but later in life I would realize I would be the mom friend of my group with an Asahi beer in my hand.

Evangelion became my window into experiencing and finding language to describe depression and sadness. I was close to Shinji, Rei, and Asuka's age. I came from a culture and religion where mental health wasn't talked about. While I do recall a lot of happy memories in ninth grade, *Evangelion* would be my framework to describe later on how I would feel as I navigated adolescence. The first four episodes depicting Shinji's withdrawal from the world really spoke to me through adolescence. Episodes where he was hiding in his headphones reminded me of how I would retreat into my headphones to drown out the world. I was looking for a Kaworu to find me so that one day I might be worthy of being loved. *Evangelion* was more than just a giant robot anime; I was just about the same age as the main cast. It would help me later on to describe sadness, depression, hopelessness, and wanting a sense of belonging somewhere.

I was still a magical girl fan. It was the late '90s, and girl power meant something to those of us tweens. After *Cardcaptor Sakura* and *Rayearth*, I was ready for *Fushigi Yuugi*. I was reading about this in *Animerica*. The artwork by Yuu Watase looked very pretty, and I was also ready for a magical girl show that wasn't your typical transformation and beat-the-monster-of-the-day formula. *Fushigi Yuugi*, or Mysterious Play was finally licensed and available when I was in the ninth grade. The comic book rental store didn't have the VHS tapes ready, so I had to save $25 to get the English dub at the local Borders for the first volume. At least this release came with a free trading card that I stuck on my ninth grade binder.

Fushigi Yuugi is *The Neverending Story* meets high school drama, attractive men, nonbinary finery, and adventures in miscommunication in the magical world of Ancient China. Teens my age watched *Dawson's Creek*, but I wanted to know what happened next in *Fushigi Yuugi*. Would Miaka end up with Tamahome or Hotohori? I was a huge Miaka and Tamahome fangirl, collecting any images of them I found online. Early on in my *Fushigi Yuugi* fandom days, I was gushing over Miaka and Tamahome solely from the official manga artwork. I had the Catholic sex education of anything beyond holding hands is a one-way ticket to hell. Yet, there was something about the way Yuu Watase drew Miaka and Tamahome in affection and in states of intimacy that seemed beautiful. I made a mental note to pick up the art book the next time I was at the Japanese bookstore. No way I could save these images I found online on the family computer. The intimacy presented between Miaka and Tamahome was captivating. Yuu Watase's art showed that intimacy between two people was not a dirty or shameful thing. It could be as sublime as a watercolor painting in a shōjo manga.

And then I saw the anime!

I really wanted to like this pairing. I really wanted to cheer for Miaka and Tamahome. I got too tired of the poorly written miscommunication in the Yui, Miaka, and Tamahome love triangle, and the consistent yelling of "MIAKA!" and "TAMAHOME!" got too old by the end of the 50-something episodes of the epic telenovela isekai. By the end, I was Team Tasuki all the way … with evil Tamahome thrown in for fun.

I was still a straight A student. I had a reputation as being one of the smartest kids in the ninth grade. I was never picked last or the odd one out for group projects. I had friends—most of them grade levels above me— with whom I could talk anime. I had my people at school to nerd out with. I didn't feel alone in my hobby. I was doing well in choir earning some honors at the end of the year. I had printed photos and trading cards of *Magic Knight Rayearth*, *Sailor Moon*, and *Fushigi Yuugi* plastered on my high school binder. The summer was fast approaching. Anime Expo 1999 was on the horizon.

9

Anime Expo 1999
Baby's First Anime Convention

Anaheim, California. Best known for tourism, the ever-congested I-5 freeway, and mostly, Disneyland. While Anime Expo had its start in San Jose up in Northern California, when old-school conventioneers think of the best days of Anime Expo, they recall the Anaheim era. The Anaheim era began in 1998, the year I missed out on the con. It was time to make preparations for baby's first Anime Expo. I really did not have any guides or know how to navigate the fandom convention world. I never saw or was familiar with what goes on at an anime convention. The website had mentioned guests, concerts, and cosplay. My only frame of reference was an episode of *The Simpsons* where the characters attend a local comic book convention where those who dressed up get in for free and attendees asked esoteric and trivial questions to celebrity guests.

I was ready to have an open mind. At last, I could see my people! I could see anime nerds who liked the same things I did! It would no longer be just words behind a screen on a website, a newsgroup, or an online chat room. I would get to experience this all in person!

Oh, wait.... I was 14. It was the summer before my 10th-grade year. I didn't think my parents were going to let me go to an anime convention all by myself. I had to think of some way, some compromise to convince my parents to go with me to the event about those cartoons from Japan. Our family was planning a trip to the East Coast later that summer, so I had to be budget conscious. Okay, I thought, I'm 14. The family trip is going to be expensive. What should I do?

A vendors hall–only pass? And it was selling for $10 per person per day?!

Okay, this was the solution. Our family of four—my mom, my dad, my brother, and me—would just go for a day to shop around the dealers hall. I wasn't too familiar with the guests present, save for Mari Iijima. I would have loved to see her in concert in Anaheim, but sacrifices had to be made.

Could I cosplay? My mom wasn't too thrilled with the idea. I decided to just wear a cute red qipao dress I got from Forever 21. Not quite cosplay, but I wanted to wear something that showed I belonged. Back in 1999, anime shirts and fandom flair to wear were very hard to find. There weren't a lot of online stores that sold anime-inspired shirts or flair. Hence, conventions were essential because you could get your anime fix in the vendors hall.

"Remember, we're going to New York in August. Budget your spending," my mom advised as we hopped into the family minivan for the 30-minute car ride to the Anaheim Convention Center. I didn't know what to expect, but I knew I was excited and could only imagine what the dealers hall would have. I was thinking about plushes, dolls, hard-to-find *Sailor Moon* and *Cardcaptor Sakura* merch, pins, lanyards—anything that I could wear to show off my love for magical girl anime.

We arrived and parked at the Anaheim Convention Center. It was the last day of Anime Expo. We picked up our one-day dealers hall access wristbands at the Anaheim Hilton. I was already amazed by the cosplayers we walked past. I regretted not bringing my camera. I saw attendees wearing their Anime Expo 1999 badges—proudly displaying their "fan name" and home city and state on an Anime Expo branded lanyard. While it was exciting to be at my first Anime Expo, I regretted not getting a weekend badge; it seemed like it would have been the best way for me to truly enjoy the event now that I've seen more anime in the past year.

Of course, I had to take my parents and my kid brother along with me. We traveled as a family unit to the dealers hall, which was inside the Anaheim Sports Arena. While normally home to hockey games and the occasional Disney on Ice, this place was an anime fan's shopping mall. This was the first time I had stepped into a dealers hall. The first booth alone maybe had five, 10, 20 things I wanted! Thankfully, my parents were there to keep me from spending all my money. I had budgeted $100 to spend. "This is your birthday present," said my mom.

There were so many chibi plushes of Sakura Kinomoto in all her outfits from the series. I knew I needed Sakura in the cat girl outfit she wore early in the series. Out of all the plushes at the one booth, I ended up taking Sakura in her black and pink cat outfit home. I went to the next booth over. I was surprised they had a Barbie-sized Minmay doll. Minmay was such a huge J-pop idol to me in middle school. I remembered seeing photos of this particular Minmay doll online. I thought I would never see one in person. I had to have this fully articulated Minmay doll among my Barbie dolls and my one Jem doll. Minmay looked beautiful; she wore a red qipao dress, her blue hair was done in an updo, and she was fully articulated for posing. I eyed my mom with a "I know I'm too old for Barbie, but can I keep her?" Mom busted out her credit card, and she was mine. Knowing that this was a rare find, I vowed not to spend too much on our family trip to New York City.

There were a ton of booths selling VHS tapes. DVDs were still a new medium in 1999. I didn't see too many DVDs I was looking for. Neither did I feel like dropping money on the official VHS tapes when I could probably get them at Borders. I decided to skip getting anime home media. I wanted to get things that I could not find at Borders.

I also found a vendor that was getting rid of posters from *Evangelion*, *Final Fantasy*, *Sailor Moon*, *Utena*, and *Ranma*. It was Sunday, and a lot of vendors were trying to offload their stock so they wouldn't take too much with them back to wherever they were going. Because they were on sale, my dad nudged me to get a few of them to have in my room. My room was going to truly look like my anime oasis.

As I was picking up my last item of the con, I eyed a poster for the Satoshi Kon classic *Perfect Blue*. It looked like it was getting an American screening at some Hollywood art house theater I had never heard of. I did see *Perfect Blue* on a bit of a whim. I downloaded the soundtrack online. "Ai No Tenshi" is a cheery, upbeat, bop—something like Mandy Moore or Britney Spears would be singing at the time. I was thinking, "Cool! This might be an anime about the life and times of an idol!" Because I was into *Macross*, I loved the pop singer idol archetype in anime. I was very excited to see something focused on modern-day pop idols. And that's when I learned not to judge an anime by its original soundtrack alone. I rented *Perfect Blue* at the Japanese video store in raw Japanese. I had a website to provide me with the synopsis and summary as I watched. Boy, was I in for a ride and three weeks of nightmares. I saw the scariest movie I have ever seen in my life. I was expecting a fictitious biopic of the life and times of an idol, but what I got was one of the best psychological thrillers I had ever seen. *Perfect Blue* was a different anime; the realism of the character designs and world was so different from the colorful shōjo and dynamic space operas I'd seen. This could have been done in live action, but the animated medium worked for the surreality and questioning of reality. This was the first time I realized that anime as a medium could be an innovative way to tell stories.

5. *Anime Expo 1999*

"If Alfred Hitchcock partnered with Walt Disney, they'd make a picture like this," the poster tagline read. I took a closer look at the Western release poster for *Perfect Blue*, realizing that one of my favorite movies was getting a limited theatrical release. I was very happy that it was getting this type of recognition. A gentleman in a suit donning his Anime Expo badge asked if I had seen the movie. I simply said, "Yes I have! It's my favorite horror movie. The pizza scene gave me nightmares for weeks!" He talked about how the realistic character designs made the horror seem more terrifying. He then recommended that I see it again. After having nightmares for three weeks, I was not sure if I should see the movie again or if I was ready for it. I also doubted my parents would take me to some art house movie theater in Hollywood to watch an R-rated anime with a ton of violence and sexual assault at the age of 14. However, for a moment, I was having a real-life discussion with an anime fan. It wasn't something on a message board where I would lurk through the comments. I was actually having a discussion about one of my favorite movies—until my mom summoned me, anyway. I don't think she liked the idea of me talking to an adult gushing over a movie.

We exited out of the arena into the Artist Alley. The Artist Alley was small, and we looked at a few tables until my strictly Catholic mother felt uncomfortable seeing some of the more risqué pieces. To us, it was our signal to leave and go grab dinner at the local Max's Restaurant. As we were walking to the minivan, my mom kept going off about how little clothing the cosplayers were wearing. In truth, she saw one Mylene Jenius cosplayer who was wearing a thong back leotard. One cosplayer made her go off in a Tagalog-infused rant. Yet, I did see a lot of people close to my age with honest and loving recreations of Sailor Senshi, *Ranma* characters in qipao and Mandarin collar shirts that you could find in Chinatown, a Tenchi Masaki cosplayer with his laser sword—they weren't perfect replications, but you could tell they were made with so much love and effort. I knew that the next year I wanted to go for more than one day and find some way to dress up in costume.

We had our post-con dinner at Max's Restaurant, a Filipino family style chicken dinner (with karaoke!). While my parents were passing around the kare-kare, I was immersed in my English language *Sailor Moon* manga. At last, I had finally obtained the first few collected volumes of the English language *Sailor Moon* manga. I don't remember much from dinner or what songs were crooned on the restaurant karaoke machine, but I was happy with my first Anime Expo, taking home a new doll, a new plush, posters for my teen bedroom, and manga that I could read over and over.

Part Two. Hey Mom! Let's Go to Anime Expo!

Visiting New York City, Baltimore, Washington, D.C., and Cincinnati to see family was nice. I did bring some of my fansub VHS tapes with me in case I was bored and wanted to watch anime. I picked up *Magic Users Club* out of curiosity. It was more of an adult comedy magical girl series, but my immature side of my brain enjoyed the boys love humor and shenanigans the magic club got themselves into. We stayed at my relatives' house in Cincinnati, and the guest room had a VCR. After catching up with relatives by going to touristy spots and being forced into conversation about where I was planning to apply for college, at the end of the day, I would just pop my tape in and just get lost in the magical misadventures of *Magic Users Club*.

I really did like seeing the cosplayers at Anime Expo. As much as my parents did not like what they saw, I have always liked the idea of playing dress-up. I always wanted to make a statement every Halloween during our school costume contests. I was already writing down in my diary what I wanted to cosplay as at Anime Expo 2000, parents permitting: Miaka in her priestess vestments from *Fushigi Yuugi*, Sakura in her pink cat girl outfit from *Cardcaptor Sakura*, and Utena from *Revolutionary Girl Utena*. These were the main three I wanted to focus on. I picked three characters from anime that I enjoyed and that would get some kind of recognition at a con. I figured they were innocent looking enough to let my parents allow me to dress up at a con.

Ninth grade was a wonderful transition year, and it gave me a lot to be excited about in high school. I was doing well in school. I had a pretty high grade point average. I wasn't an honors student, but I was a nerd for world history and literature. Choir took up most of my after-school time. Most of my friends were in choir. I was still the quiet Asian girl in a school uniform listening to Megumi Hayashibara's albums on burned CDs I created. I didn't know a lot of the anime that Megumi Hayashibara was singing the opening song for, but I did make a note to check out *Slayers* and perhaps *Lost Universe*. I was happy.

Tenth grade would change all that. My anime friends from high school had already graduated and went on their separate ways. My reputation would be on thin ice.

6

Escape from High School World

Eighth grade was coming to an end. I was ready for high school. Ready to start a new chapter. Many of us would go on to the local Catholic high schools. I was full of hope that I might meet anime fans at the high school that I would be attending. I was ready to leave middle school behind and maybe find my people. Yet, my excitement was dampened. Ashley, daughter of our church's music director, warned me, "You better be quiet about that anime shit. They'll hate you there." However, I found friends in the marching band who loved *Tenchi Muyo* as much as I did. I met a Japanese exchange student who knew about *Marmalade Boy*. Of course, *Dragonball* was a favorite among most of the boys at my high school. I experienced the usual ups and downs of high school in the ninth grade. I had good grades. I had friends. Yet, nothing would prepare me for the emotional breakdown that was 10th grade.

My memories of 10th grade are scattered as if a mirror was shattered. Each shattered glass piece contains a memory. Fragmented. Broken. But you can still see your reflection, and if you can still see yourself, you survived. I was not looking for head pats or "You're so strong!" What I needed in 10th grade was human kindness and compassion.

It was the night of the culturally funky "Welcome Freshmen Dance." Traditionally, my high school would hold this dance to welcome the brand new ninth graders. There was a Hawaiian islander theme to it. The kids at our majority white and Asian populated school were encouraged to wear their best Hawaiian shirts, matching leis, and whatever fit the theme. Traditionally, everyone at my high school went to this dance. When we had the promise of a karaoke room, I immediately started thinking of what I wanted to karaoke at the dance.

I didn't own any Hawaiian prints. I just had a silky burgundy button-up blouse, a black fitted blazer, and a black miniskirt. I had a gold cross necklace and black high heels. It's what I had in my closet. Wearing

Hawaiian gear felt like wearing a disguise. I would say costume, but costumes are fun. Hawaiian shirts and wearing floral leis weren't my vibe.

I went by myself. I considered myself a member of no one high school clique because I had friends everywhere—choir, chamber ensemble, marching band, and so forth. I wanted to party with them all.

My memories of the Welcome Freshmen 1999 dance are fragmented. There are two main things I remember. I was mostly hanging out with my friends from the 11th grade. Chadwell was one of my friends in ninth grade; he was the token male friend of our gal pal group. He was "the funny one." After the summer, he wanted to achieve "ladies' man" status. He already had a group of gal pals following him around. He was flirting uncontrollably with the girls in the friend group. While I was not attracted to him romantically, his behavior during the dance bothered me. He was purposefully excluding me from the attention. Yet, while this wouldn't bother me, the dreaded "Mambo No. 5" played. When it came to the line "A little bit of Erica..." he then yelled another girl's name in our group. When the deejay played "Unpretty" by TLC, he then pointed to me when the line "so damn unpretty" came up, despite the fact this is a feminist song about saying no to beauty standards. When the deejay played the misogynoir anthem "No Pigeons," he then started singing the misogynistic lyrics to me. His behavior that night caught me off guard to the point where it really started to hurt my feelings. Why was he treating all of my gal pals with flirtatious attention and then making me feel like I didn't belong? I wasn't looking to be flirted with; I just wanted my friend back. I wanted to be treated with dignity. I wanted to be treated like a human being. Seeing this friend slip into a version of himself that was hateful and toxic was disturbing.

I gravitated to another group of classmates. The gym was dark and I couldn't quite tell, but I remember joining in a random dance circle. One of the girls randomly pushed me into the middle. Two boys decided to grind their crotch on me; I tried to get out of there, but one of the girls tried to block me from leaving the circle. Thankfully, I used the power of yelling "I HAVE TO PEE!" to get out of that claustrophobic dance circle immediately. I went into the bathroom to cry for the rest of the night.

When my dad picked me up from the dance, he could tell that I was upset. I didn't know how to explain that a boy was bullying me, my girl friends weren't standing up for me, and I was nearly sexually assaulted at the dance. So I could at least have some silence on the car ride home, I simply said, "They didn't play Ricky Martin's 'Livin' la Vida Loca.'" Yet, my dad knew that was a lie. He kept asking me what happened. I wasn't comfortable saying it because I didn't think he would understand, and I wasn't in the mood to say something because I was still processing what had happened. Instead of silence, he kept asking and asking me. Because of my silence, I was seen as "disobedient." By the time we got home, he thought that yelling at me and raising his voice would break me out of the silence. He even went as far as to tell me that I didn't fit in with the theme of the dance. "You should fit in! At least try!" I just did not want to talk. At that point, any hope of sympathy from him went out the window. This would be the tone of my relationship with my father for the rest of high school.

The night of the Welcome Freshmen dance was pivotal in my high school life. Before, I was just the quiet Asian nerd who liked Broadway, anime, books, and traveling. I was fine with a few friends. Yet, I started losing friends. More boys started making unwanted comments at me. I would walk down my high school's halls and they would start catcalling me and making lewd gestures at me. Girls would tell me, "But they're boys! They do that all the time!" as if I was supposed to accept it. "At least you're not being ignored!"

There was a gentleman in the drama club whom I did like. We had a few classes together. I admired his trivial knowledge of musical theater and genuine kindness. I decided to be bold and admit my feelings. I wrote him a heartfelt love letter and slipped it to him after class. He immediately rejected me. He stopped talking to me. I was sad. I was upset. At the very least, I wanted to have a male ally and believe that not all men were like the ones I had encountered at the high school dance. I wanted to move forward from this episode. Rejection is normal. This is just some slice-of-life anime episode where the shy girl confesses her feelings to the popular guy and gets her love letter torn. However! The main character will find someone better. However, this crush started befriending Chadwell. My unrequited theatre kid crush buying the rumors. I even asked a few guy friends whom I thought I was still friends with to the formal homecoming dance, and I immediately got rejected. I was able to count. I was rejected at least 15 times for the homecoming formal dance. After those traumatic experiences, I was immediately turned off by the idea of dating boys. The idea of asking any boy out was out of the question. It wasn't for me.

I tried to stay focused on school, so I spent time with teachers before school and at lunch. That way, I could avoid being catcalled; I had a safe place to hide. I didn't feel comfortable spending lunch with my old friends after the dance. I had teachers I could talk to and classrooms that I can take refuge in. I could talk to my history teacher about my travels along the East Coast seeing historical sites; I could talk to my English teacher about books I had been reading, and I could talk to my religion teacher about the latest anime I'd been watching. I felt safe finding friendship with my teachers. For the first few weeks of 10th grade, I felt I was healing and I did not need my old friends. I was happier without them. At least for a moment.

I tried to see what I could do to pick myself up. My otaku senior friends from the previous year had already graduated. The otaku juniors from last year who were now seniors were hyper-focused on college applications, college entrance exams, and doing anything a college prep student would do to get into a highly ranked university. It was still the beginning of the school year. The student council and student activities office were taking applications for clubs. I decided to see if I could submit an anime club to draw in otaku at my high school. We could have space to talk about anime, tape trade, share anime music, talk about J-pop without anyone judging us for liking something in a foreign language.... And I could lead this! I made the proposal to our school activities director.

"Anime is too risqué," the activities director said. "We can't have that here. We believe in family values. Anime is a risky topic for a Catholic school." I was devastated that my proposal was rejected. I wanted to see if I could at least create a space for anime fans at our high school to get together and maybe watch an episode of anime or have a classroom we could go to for lunch. I did not have the skills to advocate and to counter their rejection. I could have made a proposal discussing how anime is for everyone and that the anime we would discuss and watch would follow the school rules. I wanted to allude to family friend anime like *Kiki's Delivery Service* and other Studio Ghibli titles. I could have alluded to the values of friendship and heroism I had learned from magical girl anime. Anime, to mainstream audiences and normies, was still seen as cartoons from Japan with animated tentacle porn. I did not take the rejection well. I was doing what I could to protect my reputation at my high school after the incident at the dance. I thought that maybe being a founder of an anime club and having a space for us nerds would have been the best way to repair my reputation after being assaulted and humiliated at the high school dance. I decided to remain isolated, having lunch in classrooms that were open or hanging out in the computer lab checking my email. I thought laying low would be my best strategy. Yet, my reputation only got worse.

While I was having my lunches in classrooms, Chadwell and his friends began gossiping about me throughout the school. My high school was small enough that gossip went like wildfire. Chadwell and his cronies started claiming that I was "easy." During Halloween, Chadwell and his friends asked me what I was wearing for Halloween at school. I said, "I'm thinking about dressing up like Nuriko. They're an anime character with purple hair who's super strong—" Chadwell interrupted, "You're cosplaying from a hentai?! Erica is dressing from anime porn!" he announced loudly at the school lunch tables so that everyone could hear. More teasing and bullying ensued. You would think a Catholic school would stand up against bullying, because if I recall, didn't Jesus say to love one another? Yet, seeing this going down under the watchful eyes of the administration and seeing that the school would not provide me a space to have an anime club, I didn't think I was going to be protected.

I was an immediate target. Chadwell and his friends also started spreading rumors that I was sleeping around with seniors and teachers for popularity and to keep good grades because I was spending my lunches in classrooms. A ton of boys started giving me unwanted advances and fake love letters because they were convinced of Chadwell's lies. I wished the school would do something about it. It got to a point where I had to request that a student in my class be removed because he kept catcalling me in biology. "Hey Sexy!" he would say. "Where are you from? Is Erica an exotic name?" he would ask. I could not focus in class when I had boys randomly harassing me. The teachers did very little to stop it.

My life at home got worse too. My relationship with my father fractured more and more when he and my younger brother took drum lessons. Of course, the first thing I wanted to hear coming home from choir was the loud noise coming from both of them. I had a hard time focusing on assignments and school. I had asked them to practice when I wasn't at school, but they called me "spoiled." Mom wasn't home enough for moral support either because she worked night shifts. By the time I got home from choir practice, she had about two hours to get ready for work. It was at moments like this I wished my brother took the stereotypical role of an Asian boy who plays violin. At least I could focus on my studies to the sound of strings playing something more soothing than a cacophony of undisciplined noise. I hid in my headphones again to the sounds of Yoko Kanno to calm my brain down. My brain was going all over the place during this time. I was trying to pull myself so many times from dark places that my brain would take me. My high school did have counseling services, but after one session with them, I did not think they truly understood me. I did not think this was a good match. The elderly white counselor looked at me like a deer in headlights when I described *Evangelion* and the lessons I learned about depression from the main cast. How was I supposed to explain fandom and anime to them? Being an anime fangirl was a huge part of my life and my identity. Especially in a Catholic school setting? I just wanted to feel safe coming to school. I just wanted to be understood.

Choir was supposed to be my favorite part of the day. This seventh-period after-school class was where I had the most joy. I could have chosen between choir or drama for my after-school class, but I really wanted to sing my heart out. Singing was always my joy. I loved singing even alongside whatever was playing on the radio. I was even happy that our choir also started singing Broadway musicals. My choirmates were also impressed that I could play Broadway tunes on the piano. I was even playing some anime music by ear on the piano!

In ninth grade, Chadwell and I would sing a lot of Broadway songs together—we knew the whole libretto to *Phantom of the Opera* and *Evita*. I had a friend with whom I could nerd out about Broadway musicals! Yet, Chadwell and his gang of mean girls spread the rumors and the gossip went straight to choir. Chadwell even got a few choir members to also bully and exclude me. It was affecting my vocal performance. I would be in tears right before a performance, killing my vocal chords. The thing I loved at school suddenly became survival. I had to figure out how to ignore him and his bullying. And I didn't want to quit choir either because I loved singing. I needed another outlet for my love for singing and performing.

Anime was an easy escape from all of this. I was getting into more and more anime through VHS fansubs and what I could rent from the comic book store. *Lupin III*, *Nurse Angel Ririka SOS*, *Slayers*, *Marmalade Boy*, *His and Her Circumstances*, *Ranma*, *Maison Ikkoku*, *Kenshin*, just to name a few. I would look forward to getting new fansub VHS tapes brought to my door so I could drown out the real world.

Slayers allowed me to escape the real world. It was a fantasy comedy series that was simply all in good fun. The soundtrack was done by my favorite vocalists in anime, Megumi Hayashibara and Masami Okui. The misadventures of Lina and Naga going from town to town and wreaking havoc always made me laugh. I loved Lina Inverse's fiery personality. I wished I could be as outgoing and as spunky as she was. Naga had a memorably evil laugh that I would imitate when no one was around. I loved her voluptuousness and lackadaisical personality. I would later get into the *Slayers* TV series and follow Lina Inverse and company on more misadventures. It was the sweetest escape. I feel like there was still laughter in my heart. And the *Slayers* soundtrack is a banger! I would listen to Masami Okui and Megumi Hayashibara's vocals on the soundtrack to hype me up.

When I felt the world closing in on me, the *Slayers* soundtracks kept me in high spirits.

Marmalade Boy and *His and Her Circumstances* allowed me to live vicariously through the drama and tribulation of high school relationships. After being rejected and objectified by the boys at my high school, I felt it was safer to explore what having a significant other might have been like. I knew I was still attracted to males, but I think I preferred them as fictional animated men. At least they did not outright reject you or think you were undatable. I lived vicariously through Yukino and her relationship with Arima. Both *Marmalade Boy* and *His and Her Circumstances* focused on heterosexual coupling, but the lightheartedness and overdramatic reactions to the smallest things allowed me to vicariously live a normal high school life through the main characters. These resonated with me more than what was on WB and other teen dramas aimed at my demographic. Shows like *Dawson's Creek* didn't really catch my attention. Slice-of-life anime that had studious high schoolers keeping up perfect personas and navigating the drama and shenanigans that come with having multiple cute anime boys spoke to me more.

The one anime during 10th grade that stood out to me was *Revolutionary Girl Utena*. *Utena* can be best summed up as that anime with sword lesbians. *Utena* is a magical girl anime, but not like *Sailor Moon* or *Rayearth*. This was the first unapologetically queer anime I'd seen. While I did see Uranus and Neptune in *Sailor Moon*, I always saw them as pretty side characters. They had cool outfits in their civilian forms. I loved that Haruka flexed her prowess as a Formula 1 racer in the manga, and Michiru was simply elegant and the face of lipstick lesbian goals. And both of them flew helicopters and had a penthouse. They were bougie lesbians who had it all. No one judged their lifestyle. How cool was that? I loved Uranus and Neptune's presence in *Sailor Moon*, but *Utena* was the first show I saw that put queer characters in the forefront.

I related a lot to Utena—I loved her nobleness, her willingness to stand up for others, and her defiance of gender norms. Most of all, she was still a very femme character who aspired to be a prince and saved princesses. If I were to be in any relationship, I wanted to be the noble, prince-like one in it. I admired the twist on fairy tale tropes. I was able to get the series on DVD through a special order through our local specialty DVD and LaserDisc vendor, Ken Crane's of Huntington Beach. At the time we only had the first 13 episodes. There was a licensing issue with the next set of episodes. I found a fansub website that had the episodes that followed the first 13. I had to order them so I could get into *Utena*. The DVD special order took some time to arrive. However, I scrounged my allowance to get the next story, the Black Rose arc. The fansubs arrived first. There was no telling when the DVDs of the first 13 would show up. I proceeded to watch the Black Rose arc. It was a decent stand-alone story, and if you were familiar with the status quo of the world, it was fairly easy to follow. I was already obsessed. I loved the art style. I loved the music. And most of all, I loved Utena and Anthy's romantic friendship. Utena Tenjô was aspirational and I wanted to be like her and have a princess to save.

And then I heard about *Dear Brother*. This title was recommended to me by some random person on an online anime forum because I expressed my love for *Utena*. "If you liked *Utena*, check out *Dear Brother*. Tomodachi Fansubs have the tapes available." *Dear Brother* follows Nanako and the drama that follows her while attending a private high school. She writes about her daily life to a brother type of figure. This anime was unapologetically queer. The episode that got to me was Nanako thinking about an older classmate, St. Juste. You can definitely tell in the direction that Nanako was having a crush on this older femme student. She was figuring things out. Just like me. I wasn't sure if I liked girls or girls and boys. In 10th grade, I was still questioning myself. Boys rejected me, so maybe I was meant for girls instead of boys? I found women attractive, but I never quite acted on it. I just let my crushes be my crushes. Nanako's experiences in *Dear Brother* made my adolescent questioning relatable and valid.

Both Utena and Nanako gave me a safe place to explore and look at myself in the mirror. While *Sailor Moon* had Uranus and Neptune (and they did look pretty!), Utena and Nanako gave me some more depth and dimension to question myself. I knew I was attracted to women since totally crushing on Xenia Onatopp in *GoldenEye*. I wanted both Pierce Brosnan and Famke Janssen (and Izabella Scorupco was pretty cute too!). But was it just silly celebrity crushes? Was I going through something that was simply a phase? I kept these feelings to myself, avoiding any Catholic guilt. I kept myself from questioning who I was. I kept it all inside and thought it would go away the longer I kept it in. Nanako spoke to me about my questioning and made me think it was okay to admire from afar. She gave me permission to daydream about what could have been. Utena spoke to the type of romantic partner I wanted to be if I ever met a princess I liked. And yet, I did not feel the need to come out of the closet immediately. I was still fighting Catholic guilt. I daydreamed that one day I would have a closet full of fanciful dresses and a badass sword in the event I was summoned to save damsels from fuckboys. I could be the chivalrous princess.

7

Online Voice Acting
Fan Fiction Meets Podcasting

We still had the family computer in the living room. When I wasn't watching anime, I would escape from school life by plugging myself into the internet. One day, I was browsing through AniPike. I was looking for more fansub resources. Underneath the Fansub section was a "Fandub" section. "What the hell is a fandub?" I wondered. I was dabbling into the world of "fan dubbing." I found out that a group of *Sailor Moon* fans decided to dub the first episodes of *Sailor Moon S*. This was a complete fan-made production of an English dub for *Sailor Moon*. While I may have been familiar with the world of online voice acting in ninth grade, I was always too nervous to send an audition. Did I have to have a studio? Was recording lines on SoundRecorder on our Windows 98 fine? Did I have to have a special microphone? Or could I use the cheap $10 one that my dad happened to have lying around? I wasn't sure how these productions were handled. I was all new to this. After all, I was sending a file of what my voice sounds like to a stranger on a personal email. Interacting online was always nerve-racking to me.

Also, I was anxious about socializing online. On alt.fan.sailor-moon, I lurked around but never participated in a thread or an online discussion. I would read threads and call it a day. I liked reading anime recommendations and reviews. I liked reading opinion pieces from fandom websites. There was no passive way to participate—no upvoting or hitting a like button. Just nod, smile, or cringe as you scrolled.

But the more I lurked in this anime amateur voice acting community, the more I realized that these were my people. These were anime fans and theater nerds. Most of them were close in age and expressed love for both anime and Broadway. They were unafraid to declare if they identified as gay, bi, or lesbian. It was very heartwarming to see an authentic community of like-minded nerds. Also, this place was free of the anime sub versus dub

49

debates. By this time, it was tiresome to watch older generations of anime fans try to settle which of the two was superior. I was jaded about that discourse. To me, the rising popularity of DVDs was going to shut down this debate. This voice acting community celebrated both Japanese voices and English dub voices. We hated censorship and erasure of minority identities; for those of us who were into fandubbing, we wanted to bring in an authentic English dub version without censorship or bring to light anime that would never be picked up by an American licensing company. After all, many people in the community aspired to be in an English anime dub. We had to play nice to both sides of the Pacific.

As I was warming up to this community, I realized that I could start another life online. I needed a stage name if I were to get started with online voice acting. I was not planning on using my real name online. I needed a name that echoed that of a chivalrous princess.

Victoria.

Victoria was a name I always liked. Regal and elegant. It sounded like who I wanted to be. I didn't have to be the Erica who was bullied and humiliated in high school. I didn't have to be the Erica who would have mental breakdowns and anxiety episodes before a choral performance. I didn't have to be the Erica who was harassed by high school fuckboys. I didn't have to be the Erica my high school saw me as or the afterthought my family thought I was.

Victoria.

And friends could call me Vicky.

It was time to start a new life in the world of online voice acting. Okay, so there weren't a lot of fandubs back in 1999. Back then, it was a much more complicated process without software like iMovie or Premiere. However! This side of the anime community were also making radio plays, or early forms of podcasting in the form of fictional drama. A lot of these radio plays were *Sailor Moon* fan fiction, parodies of existing anime intellectual property, *Final Fantasy* game adaptations, and a few original stories set to an audio drama. This was podcasting before there was a word for it. The main online community of this was all on VARC, or the Voice Acting Resource Community. People would post audition requests, and one would record lines and then submit. I would do this on my weekends when it was quiet. I would audition for almost 10, 15, 20 productions. This was the outlet I needed—it was drama club, but for anime and video game nerds.

"Sincerely, Victoria"

Signing off as Victoria was empowering. I felt I had more control of myself. This online identity was truly me. I was happy. I could indulge and share my love of anime and acting with this community. I was not judged for liking niche things from Japan. And I could finally showcase my love of acting! I was getting cast in *Sailor Moon* fan fiction radio plays and others. I was given a lot of soft-spoken, melancholy roles like Sailor Saturn. I looked for roles that called for soft-spoken, gentle characters. My upper soprano registry allowed me to sound a pitch younger. My normal voice actually sounded deeper than a regular teenager. Most of these were anime-inspired roles, so I had to use a higher pitch.

There were also opportunities for singing roles. A few folks wanted to create English lyrics for existing anime songs and needed experienced singers. Because I was in choir, I took private voice lessons from someone who trained people for Broadway shows. I had to record lines on the family computer. I didn't mind doing speaking roles in the family room with either my mother or brother passing by. I was more self-conscious of my singing voice. My mom would always show me off at family parties for karaoke. If I did well, it was a reflection on her. If I did badly, I was considered a family embarrassment. I had to wait for my family to be out to record singing roles. I was insecure about recording my singing voice with people around. My family would have season tickets to Dodgers games, and I would tell them that I had a project or a test to study for, so I couldn't make it. Instead, I would wait for them to leave and record multiple singing takes.

I had to create a website for all of my online voice acting roles and have a demo posted somewhere. I created a very basic one with the HTML and web design skills I picked up when I made my *Sailor Moon* website. This was the first time I would be uploading my personal photo online. I found one of my eighth grade formal dance photos. It was me in a white empire-waist dress, my black hair done up in the classic dark raven waves of Elizabeth Taylor in her *Cat on a Hot Tin Roof* era—I looked like a Golden Age Hollywood star, but Asian. It was a perfect way to present me to the voice acting community. I did not have to present myself in my everyday school uniform. I could really take control of how people perceived me. I wanted people to see me as classy, mature, with an air of elegance.

The biggest part I ever landed was a *Robotech* adaptation of *Macross: Flashback 2012*. I was cast as Minmay. I didn't have to sing. The music would be replaced by Reba West's original vocals from the *Robotech* soundtrack. However, voicing Minmay for a fandub that actually did get completed was a big deal. I even heard that this fandub was screened at AniMazement in North Carolina. I don't think I ever saw the completed version, but it exists somewhere.

While I was happy to have been a part of completed productions, the downside to all of this was that 90 percent of these productions would not get off the ground. A lot of these would only go as far as the casting process. Very few would get done. The truth was, these were high school and college students who had great ideas but were not aware of the process and time commitment online voice acting really took. As a producer, you not only had to fill a cast, but you were also responsible for scriptwriting, audio mixing, reminding your cast to turn in lines on time, marketing your final product to the community, and building and maintaining a website to host your production. It was a lot of responsibility.

And then I had a brilliant idea.

I had a lot of free time since I didn't have many friends in real life. My weekends were free. I wasn't the person to talk to classmates in between class assignments. I could start my own production of original works. But where to start.... I needed inspiration. I needed something to work with. I didn't want to write some teen love story because I felt I was "too mature" for high school romance. But what if I wrote something spicy, something like a soap opera? After all, the term "soap opera" came from the soap companies advertising on radio drama shows in the 1930s. What if I could write something thrilling and spicy?

I remembered a conversation I had with one of my teachers. It was during one of my solo lunches in the classroom. This teacher was talking about how homecoming festivities reminded him of some drama that went down between the hot, heartthrob teacher and his crazy ex-girlfriend who got too possessive. I went with that concept and came up with a trope-tastic romantic thriller about the secret lives of Catholic high school teachers. Behind the facade of teachers appearing as God fearing, Goody-Two Shoes, there were secrets, lies, and passion. It was my attempt to write a soap opera or telenovela. It was fun coming up with characters to write about, imagining a romance gone bad full of crazy love affairs with twists and turns. I was not writing Oscar-winning work, but my creative gears would not stop turning. I didn't have a full story, but I had vignettes from the awkward meet-cute between the quirky and quixotic girl-next-door teacher and the former-star-athlete teacher and so many dramatic slaps to the face between characters in moments of passion and fire. I even had a beach volleyball scene that I felt needed to be in there just because. I needed to put this on the page.

I wanted to see if I could write a feature-length script and divide it into four episodes. I didn't think it would be original to have another *Sailor Moon* or *Final Fantasy* story. There were so many *Sailor Moon* stories; I even recall a *Sailor Moon*-meets-*Scream* radio play that was asking for auditions. I wanted to take this opportunity to be creative and try something different. I would spend time during lunch and before school writing the script in my notebook. During downtime during class, I would also write like there was no tomorrow. During lazy movie days in class, I would write. I would take those scribbles and type them into Word. I would take every cliché, every trope that I recalled from *Days of Our Lives*, *Passions*, *All My Children* and throw them into this hot mess of a romantic thriller, or whatever it was supposed to be. I had the crazy ex-girlfriend, the bad-boy heartthrob male lead, the main female lead completing this love triangle, and the "good" guy our main female lead happens to end up with instead of the bad boy.

I was able to cast a ton of talented folks in the show from around the world—Seattle, San Francisco, London, Vancouver, Richmond, Detroit, Cincinnati. They would record their lines at home and submit their complete voice lines to me to mix. Working on a production with a team from around the world was empowering. I loved the cast I was working with. And most of these talented folks were anime nerds like me. The wonderment of online voice acting is that all you really needed was a decent microphone, an audio recording program, and a sense of time management. This was a hobby for most of us. None of us were professional actors, but most of us were aspiring to make it big in anime voice acting as English dub voice actors. A majority of those in this community were either close to my age in high school or somewhere in their twenties in college. I made more friends through online voice acting when I started taking a creative leadership role. Actor, director, writer, producer, audio mixer, and businesswoman—I was living my best life online as Victoria at the age of 15.

I told my teachers about this endeavor, and they were impressed. They were happy to see Victoria thriving and living her best life in this online space. I didn't have what you would find in the life of a teen in a Disney Channel original movie. I was living my teen years as an entertainment entrepreneur in uncharted waters of the World Wide Web.

I tried to stay unbothered in after-school choir, but sometime in December, there was a faction of choir led by Chadwell that gathered together to create an anti–Erica secret society. They created a logo, a knockoff of the Eye of Horus. Suddenly, my favorite class and after-school activity had taken a turn for the worse.

When we sang "Seasons of Love," they would call it "Seasons of Hate" and direct it towards me in between sectionals.

The anti–Erica group claimed they were afraid of students who wore leather jackets and trench coats. The Columbine High School shooting had occurred the school year before. Everyone was on edge about school shooters. It also did not help that teachers and students were making jokes about this. "That could be the next school shooter! Teehee!" I would hear whispers in the hallway anytime my classmates would see a boy in a trench coat or a heavy jacket. It felt like instead of our Catholic school community fostering a culture of empathy and Christ-like behavior, it was built around judgment and creating outcasts within our 1,000-student school population.

The choir's anti–Erica club vowed to keep the school safe from potential school shooters. That was what they were telling people. They pinged me as a potential school shooter because I wore a leather jacket over my school uniform. The expensive leather jacket was a gift from my mom to keep me warm during the cold autumn and winter days. I treated my leather jacket as my armor for my chivalrous princess self. When the anti–Erica club was becoming more aggressive, I sewed a rose patch on the lapel of my jacket so I could have Utena's noble spirit with me. Utena also wore a black jacket. She was strong; she was chivalrous. I did not want to waste my energy dueling with these bullies. Their words and petty assumptions about how I dressed were not the end of the world.

If I left the after-school choir, then the bullies would win. I felt pressured to stay in choir because of this. I did not want to let them win. I was going to show my unwavering and unbothered inner strength. I was not going to cry anymore. I knew who I was at the end of the day. I was Victoria, writer and producer of an upcoming romantic thriller radio drama. Although it was a struggle to stay strong during choir, they were nothing to me.

I had a romantic thriller script to write. I had lines to collect. I had audio to mix. This dramatic production about love affairs and scandals between teachers needed to get done. I knew it wasn't my best work, but it was my first production and I wanted to see if I could do this.

My safe space online was a forum called Silent Dreams. This online community was founded by online voice actors who had been in the community for some time. It was the central community hub for anime nerds and gamers from the voice acting community to congregate. The original owners behind the Voice Acting Resource Community, or VARC, had moved on from voice acting to other creative endeavors. Silent Dreams is where we all migrated to for our audition postings and shameless self-promotion. This was where we solicited and answered auditions; it was a space to talk about what anime we were watching and what games we were playing. Silent Dreams had an aesthetic appeal to it: a poetic sounding name, a dreamy color palette, and a beautiful use of anime art embedded within the forum design.

I wanted to go back into web design after having run a *Sailor Moon* website. I was inspired by the websites my friends had built. Most of them were femmes who knew how to code. And it was beautiful coding paired with web design that could be described as poetic. Art from CLAMP and *Sailor Moon* were used to create these website layouts. Paired with a whimsical user experience and viewing, these websites had flowery names— Ethereal Sea, Vitamin Love, Tenrai, DaTenshi, etc., just to name a few. I wanted this website design life.

Given that those of us on Silent Dreams were mostly online voice actors and anime nerds, we built websites to showcase our productions— fan dubs of existing anime, fan fiction radio drama, and original radio drama. While I had built a website to list what fan productions I had been cast in, I felt ready to begin my indie radio drama organization, Scarlet Rhapsody.

It was the early days of web design. Part of that culture involved having a very poetic name for your website. I liked the color red, and my favorite doll in my Barbie collection was a Scarlett O'Hara Barbie in the red evening dress. Rhapsody because I was a musician who played piano and I couldn't think of anything else poetic sounding.

I needed more web space. I realized that I was not going to get a domain name or my own personal dot com anytime soon. For years, I had used GeoCities to host my *Sailor Moon* website. However, it has expanded to my audio production website complete with audition postings, cast listing, character dossier, behind-the-scenes commentary, and eventually, a section where you could download the audio drama. GeoCities, with its limited space and forced banner advertising on the header of the website that would get in the way of aesthetic web design, was not where I wanted to host my production site. I learned of a new free service called RedRival.

At last, I migrated my website to this new service. Scarlet Rhapsody Productions was born. And I, Victoria, was the director, producer, writer, actress, audio mixer, and young entrepreneur at the age of 15. During ninth and 10th grade, I really didn't know what I wanted to do after high school. My depression at the start of 10th grade made my future seem foggy and uncertain. I was not enrolled in any honors or Advanced Placement classes. The type of college my dad wanted me to attend seemed unattainable. UCLA, Berkeley, Caltech, the Ivy League—all of them seemed out of my reach. With the hard work I put into online voice acting and producing a completed romantic thriller by the end of 10th grade, I knew I wanted to pursue a direction in multimedia and entertainment production after high school. The teens my age I was interacting with in Silent Dreams were in the same boat. They also had college aspirations in multimedia and theater. I also met community college students and college students from liberal arts schools I had never heard of. They all told me that it gets better after high school when you're with your people in real life. I only had one reason to attend college—to finally be in a nonjudgmental environment and to be free and creative with like-minded young adults. It was not the prestige of the university or landing a six-figure salary, it was to finally get out of this town and to thrive creatively alongside anime nerds.

However, my voice actor friends were also getting hyped for Anime Expo 2000. Silent Dreams had a section where you could talk about conventions and cosplay. People were posting what they were going to dress up as. I wasn't sure if I was ready for cosplay. I did like Halloween. I did like dressing up. I thought I could request a movie Anthy cosplay for $20, but who was I kidding? I wasn't going to get this done before the con. I was going to wear "normal clothes" just like in 1999. I took note of who said they were going so I wouldn't miss them. At last, I would finally see friends from the voice acting community!

Anime Expo 2000
But Dad, It's the Woodstock of Our Generation!

I remembered the dates this time around.

I had them marked on my calendar.

I had everything all planned out this time.

Anime Expo 2000. June 30 to July 3, 2000. Disneyland Hotel and Convention Center. I would miss the first day and last day of the convention because I was taking chemistry to get my last lab science class out of the way. I would have my dad drop me off at the Disneyland Hotel on Saturday and Sunday. 1 ... 2 ... 3 ... let's go, bitch.

I saved up some money to get Saturday and Sunday badges for Anime Expo 2000. More importantly, after learning from Anime Expo 1999, I would save every dollar I had to splurge in the dealers hall. I was looking forward to adding more *Sailor Moon* dolls to my collection, getting more posters and wall scrolls to add to my bedroom, and snagging kawaii plushes to live my best kawaii life as a high school anime nerd.

I checked the online forums I was a part of to see who was going. Being active in the fandubbing and voice acting community, I saw a thread taking roll call on who was going and who people were cosplaying as. This was going to be my first time meeting people from online. I was both nervous and excited. I would finally be with thousands of people who loved anime just as much as I did. I wouldn't have to feel like I was the one person in my classes who liked "those weird cartoons from Japan with the big eyes." I would get to be with my people, even if it was just for two days in the summer. This would be my first time rolling solo at an anime convention. I had been looking forward to this all year.

But what to wear? Everyone on the forums were already talking about cosplay. I asked my parents if I could cosplay. I had the list of my top three cosplays—Miaka from *Fushigi Yuugi*, Utena from *Revolutionary Girl Utena*, and Sakura Kinomoto from *Cardcaptor Sakura*. However, my parents refused to let me cosplay at the next Anime Expo. My parents barely let me wear my Forever 21 red qipao at my first Anime Expo. After seeing a scantily clad cosplayer from Anime Expo 1999, my parents had assumed that cosplay was some scandalous sex party. They didn't want me to be a part of it, even if my choices were a school uniform that showed as much skin as my Catholic high school uniform. I dreamed of wearing a princely uniform with a pink wig, or a frilly and pink cat girl outfit.

At my first Anime Expo rolling solo, I wore a simple black button-up, beige A-line skirt, beige dress trench coat, and a black beret. I called this my imitation Chanel suit look. I never dressed this posh, but I also wanted to make an impression with the new friends I was about to meet. I looked older and mature. I still have the photo from my first Anime Expo. Twenty years later, my friends thought I was in my early twenties in the photo. They were shocked when I said, "I was 15, and I dressed as if I was going to a job interview at Anime Expo so my parents could let me leave the house."

Weeks before the next Anime Expo, I practiced my introductions, handshakes, and eye contact in the mirror. I never had an opportunity to truly introduce myself to people close to my age. I was always the quiet wallflower. All my adolescent life, I just wanted for people to approach me and engage in conversation. I didn't know how to start a conversation. Do I ask about the weather? Zodiac sign? Thoughts on the upcoming 2000 presidential election? I knew I was socially awkward, but I wanted to meet like-minded anime nerds and make lifelong friendships. I wanted to get it right with a winning first impression. As Anime Expo approached, I kept practicing again and again in the mirror. "My name is Victoria Erica. It's nice to meet you."

"Dad, this is the Woodstock of my generation!" I said as we got into the minivan. We took the eastbound 91 freeway to the southbound 5 freeway to get to our destination—the Disneyland Hotel. It still had the poshness and luxury of the 1960s resort era. Classic lettering, white buildings with balconies that looked over the themed Peter Pan themed poolsides, and an adjacent convention center. It was a very classy and posh vibe for the annual otaku nerd party.

My dad dropped me off at the Disneyland Hotel lobby. I had to walk all the way to the Paradise Pier Hotel down the street to pick up my badge to get into the convention. There already was a long line for the con that went out the door into the parking lot. That was the registration line all right! I ended up spending the next hour waiting to purchase and pick up my badge. But I wasn't alone. I made some friends in line, and they were people close to my age. We spent the next hour waiting in line talking about our favorite episodes and moments of *Cardcaptor Sakura* and lamenting the recent Nelvana adaptation. It was so surreal seeing that *Cardcaptor Sakura*, or *Cardcaptors*, was now a Saturday morning cartoon on the Kids WB! It was the year 2000, we didn't bury our heads in our smart phones to pass the time. We had conversations about fandom and very strong feelings about Western dubs of children's anime and their original counterparts. This was forum talk brought to life! And it didn't sound as hostile as my mind read it! These were the days of Line Con, or waiting in line for an extended period of time, when the person right next to you was going to be your buddy for the next hour or two while you waited.

While in line, I was admiring *Magic Knight Rayearth* cosplayers from afar. I wished I had that amount of skill and confidence to wear something amazing like that, my 15-year-old self thought. My dad gave me his Advantix film camera so I could take photos of my first convention all by myself. I began snapping photos of cosplayers who passed by me while I was in line—also keeping in mind how much film I had left—I was limited to 24 shots and by the camera battery life.

I picked up my badges for Saturday and Sunday and it was off to the Disneyland Hotel right next door. While it did feel strange that Anime Expo was sharing space with Mickey and Friends, I did not mind too much. I enjoy both Disney animation and Japanese animation. However, the tone at the time felt otherwise. This was the era when you had the *Lion King* versus *Kimba the White Lion* and *Atlantis: The Lost Empire* versus *Nadia: The Secret of Blue Water* debates—who copied whom? Who ripped off whom? We also weren't sure if the upper-middle-class families who had planned a Disneyland vacation were ready for the otaku crowd. The hostility between the otaku crowd and Disney fandom was real.

This was also the same year that Anime Expo had to respond to complaints of 18+ material in the vendor hall resulting in adult-oriented vendors having to vacate the premises during the middle of the con. I was oblivious to what was going on because hey, I'm 15 and I was spending this weekend with more than nine thousand anime nerds from all over the world.

I had one guest I wanted to see—Rika Fukami, the voice actress for Sailor Venus in *Sailor Moon* and Myung Fang Lone in *Macross Plus*—both fandoms that I was totally all about. I did not having anything for her to sign, but if I could get a photo with her, it would all be worth it.

Part Three. Finding My People

Of course, I also had my allowance saved up to spend at the dealers hall. I wasn't going to go over budget or ask my parents for even more money.

The Disneyland Hotel in 2000 was a beautiful place. It maintained a lot of the retro 1960s resort-style architecture, tiki-themed dining, and a cavern of waterfalls. I loved this location. I regretted not cosplaying from my fandoms. This would have been a beautiful place for *Magic Knight Rayearth* or any fantasy-themed anime! Sadly, the waterfall caverns have been removed. The previous year the venue was the Anaheim Hilton and the Anaheim Sports Arena. There was something special about the Disneyland Hotel and its neighboring convention center. It was very easy to find panel rooms, screening rooms, main events, and it was easy to find my people.

And I found my people when I first stepped into the Disneyland Hotel. A group of cosplayers were just hanging out and were on their way to the voice acting panel. I immediately recognized them as my online voice acting people from Silent Dreams. I admired their cosplays; I was simply in a beige imitation Chanel suit and black beret looking more like a fashionable expatriate from Paris in the 1940s than an otaku. I extended my hand and said, "My name is Victoria Erica. It's nice to meet you." I had never formally introduced myself to anyone. I had never shaken someone's hand as a means to extend friendship. This was awkward, exciting, and new to me all at once. I was just happy that this group of cosplayers allowed me to hang out with them at the voice acting panel I wanted to check out.

Even on the walk to the panel room, I started seeing familiar names and faces. A Southern gentleman in a lab coat and glasses stood in the main convention center lobby. It was my friend Jimmy! He was waiting for our friend, Chibi Pink, to change into *Cardcaptor Sakura* so they could gallivant around the Disneyland Hotel grounds. I knew I had to give him a hug the moment I saw him. Jimmy was like an older brother to many of us in the voice acting community.

I also ran into a few familiar people from the online voice acting community, and I couldn't contain my joy and excitement. I was 15, and the more I was able to meet friends and familiar names from the online universe, the more glee and happiness I had to express. I was fangirling. This wasn't something made up from the internet. I didn't have to pinch myself to see if I was dreaming. These people were real. I really felt at home seeing all of them because they were the people I interacted with after school. I was the quiet, weird Asian kid at school who didn't fit in, but here, I felt

Voice actor Jonathan C. Osborne, also known as "Man of a Thousand Deaths," is about to meet his 1,001st death by a high-heeled red shoe at Fanime 2007 (San Jose, CA).

a part of the crowd. I didn't feel I had to hide and or keep my otakudom to myself. For the first time in a while, I was happy.

The voice acting panel was held in the basement level of the Disney-land Hotel's convention center. It was hosted by Jonathan C. Osborne and Brad DeMoss. I didn't think we knew what to expect from this English dub voice actors panel. I just got to the con and barely even looked at the program. I just went with the flow. The only thing I had planned was shopping, making friends, and Rika Fukami. You may not know the names and faces of the characters Jonathan C. Osborne has played, but you definitely have heard his voice in anime. This early anime English dub voice actor was known as the "Man of a Thousand Deaths." At the time, I expected to hear voice actors that headlined anime dubs, but I got to hear Jonathan and Brad talking about background work in anime dubs. Jonathan would talk about how he would improvise dialogue on the spot for background voice acting. He also talked about dying over and over again.

After the panel, we went to dinner at Crocs Bits 'n' Bites, the poolside restaurant at the Disneyland Hotel. We had two separate tables because our party was pretty huge. I was browsing through the menu, looking at the overpriced resort food. There were four of us at the table. I was still hyper-focused on what I was going to order. I didn't want to order something too expensive; I still had my con allowance to work with. "My mom thinks this anime thing is a phase," said Benny, my new friend I met that day from Northern California. "I don't even think she knows I like girls." Benny and I were close in age. I was surprised that their mom let them fly down for Anime Expo. My parents would have had an angry fit if I had even asked to fly out of state to an anime con!

Introduced myself to the chill and cool older boy in our group, "Hi! You must be Vaughn! We have the same birthday—August 8!" Vaughn looked at me weird. I mean ... who introduces themselves with their date of birth? I remember reading up on everyone's public profiles on their personal blogs so I could have something to talk about, to break the ice. After all, I did have a website with my public profile listing my favorites in addition to all the online voice acting parts I had won. I figured any information made public was fair game. Though our conversation starter was awkward, Vaughn and I later warmed up in conversation talking about maybe attending Gay Days at Disneyland and our annoyance with organized religion.

After having a few bites of my fries, I thought about how I had never quite outed myself to anyone. I mean, I didn't think Anime Expo would be the place to come out and admit it. I took a deep breath and just blurted, "Hi! I'm bi!" I had never come out just like that. And like the new kid at school, I awkwardly asked, "Is this the queer kids table?" We all got a good laugh out of that. We started calling ourselves the Queer Kids Table. It was my first time having a meal with friends. It was a far cry from having lunch by myself and in classrooms. I had people to live and laugh with.

This was the first time I outed myself to my peers. My first Anime Expo the previous year didn't allow me to really socialize with other attendees. For the first time, I really felt with my people. We ate our overpriced Disneyland resort fast food talking about our favorite pairings and couples that we shipped. Most of all, we were just talking about the struggle it is to exist as young queer people. I never had this experience before vibing with queer anime fans. We did exist online, but it hits different when you're with them in person. While dinner was turning into fandom brain rot talk, it was a comforting feeling to share this brain rot finally with people who understood me. I would never be able to have this conversation at my Catholic high school. I had expected to nerd out over fandom, but I had not expected to talk about what it was like not to be accepted in our everyday lives. These conversations over overpriced chicken tenders and fries went deep.

I had an hour left of Anime Expo before my dad would pick me up at the lobby of the Disneyland Hotel. It would be best to leave right before the Disneyland fireworks began. Benny invited me to their hotel room just to hang out and relax until I had to get going. They wanted to show me their *Utena* manga collection; I hadn't read the *Utena* manga. I don't recall our local Borders carrying the *Utena* manga just yet. I figured I could kill some time and recuperate before I had to go home. We went into the Disneyland Hotel's Marina Tower, which overlooked the pool. Thankfully, it was the same tower where my dad would pick me up. I plopped on the armchair and began to read Chiho Saito's manga about sword lesbians and unfortunate circumstances as the sun was about to set on Anaheim.

But I couldn't wind down just yet. A few pages into the manga, more people entered the hotel room. My quiet reading time was interrupted. "Are they broadcasting masquerade on TV?" "I don't know if they'll be showing the cosplay contest on Channel 2." I began to see that there were more people coming into the room. Reading adventures about sword lesbians had to be put on hold.

A tall and handsome-as-hell gentleman recognized the name on my badge, and I immediately recognized the name on his. "Robert Black?" I thought to myself. Wait ... isn't he one of the leading men in my radio drama? Is this the same Robert Black with the smooth and deep voice that makes your heart melt? I mean, that's why I cast him as one of the romantic leading men in my radio drama. He was another one of my online voice acting people!

But.... Robert Black never posted his photo online. I only read his voice actor profile on his personal website. I don't remember seeing a headshot. My heart immediately stopped at this face reveal. I could see he was reading my badge name, recognizing "Victoria Erica" printed on my Anime Expo badge.

Before he could say he recognized my name from online, I only had one thing I could think of telling him the moment I laid eyes on his gorgeous visage. I stood up from the hotel armchair. In my best Barbra Streisand à la *Funny Girl*, I let out a "Hello Gorgeous!" No introductions, no formalities. I rushed towards Robert and gave him the biggest, tightest hug and a kiss on the cheek.

This action of intense affection, dear readers, is what we call a "glomp." A glomp is a little bit more than just a tackle hug. One must rush towards a person and immediately wrap their arms around them and hang on tightly.

I looked at the time and my dad was going to pull up to the hotel lobby at any moment. I said my "See y'all tomorrow!" as I exited the hotel room. I had my "Holy Shit! What the hell did I just do?" I was the girl who was always afraid to admit her feelings to someone. I was rejected multiple times in 10th grade by boys. And that happened. Not only had I admitted to someone that I found them attractive, but I had given my first glomp. I didn't know whether to congratulate myself for confidence or to scold myself. I would later find out that glomping, especially without permission, was frowned upon by the anime community.

Either way, my first solo day at Anime Expo went amazing! I had never felt so comfortable around my people. I had never felt so confident to introduce myself. I made friends at the Queer Kids Table when my world outside of Anime Expo had no table for kids like me. And I admitted my feelings to the handsome-as-hell gentleman without hesitation or choking up. I stepped into my dad's minivan from the hotel lobby. We got on the I-5 freeway home. Disneyland started their fireworks spectacular. You could see the display from the freeway. "You're the Inspiration" by Chicago was on the radio, and I was already looking forward to the next day.

Sunday of Anime Expo 2000—this was the main event I was waiting for. Rika Fukami. Star of *Macross Plus* and the voice of Sailor Venus from my favorite anime in middle school, *Sailor Moon*. It was no surprise that my online voice acting friends were also at the same panel. My dad dropped me off at the hotel lobby and I waltzed into the main auditorium of the Disneyland Hotel Convention Center. There was no line to get in, and it was easy to find a seat. And there she was onstage, Rika Fukami. She did a few voice lines as Sailor Venus and also talked about her experience behind the microphone. All of us were just in awe of just being in the same room as one of the original cast members of *Sailor Moon*. After the presentation, we immediately got a selfie with the voice actress.

Sunday of Anime Expo 2000 was mainly our online voice acting clique from the other day hanging out in their hotel room, taking silly cosplay photos, and sharing some inside jokes. I was given the nickname of "sneaky camera girl." I joked that I should make a website about our adventures at Anime Expo 2000. I was having so much fun. I never had a chance to bond with girls close to my age like this—joking around, talking about favorite anime, anime crushes, J-pop, without any judgment.

We all went to one last panel, a voice acting demo panel hosted by a

Japanese dubbing studio. We were able to see a demonstration of Japanese voice actors for a children's TV show doing a live dub. Two of the girls in our group volunteered to go up. It was amazing seeing two people from the online voice acting community do a live dub in front of actual Japanese voice actors.

We went our separate ways in the late afternoon. I did want to check out the dealers hall one last time, and perhaps see the handsome-as-hell friend I had glomped on the day before. Alas, he was nowhere to be found, but I did find so many things in the dealers hall—more posters to add to my bedroom wall and a *Cardcaptor Sakura* diary themed to the Clow Card book.

This was my last day at Anime Expo. I was glad to have made friends, and I really did feel like I was living my best teen years bonding with gal pals and having the confidence to tell someone I was attracted to them, even if it was an unplanned glomp and a peck on the cheek.

Maybe I got a touch too self-assured?

"I should make a website shrine or something about Anime Expo," I said. "Something where I could post my photos and talk about the con." I got my photos developed from the corner grocery store. My dad had a scanner. I was able to put that all to work. I was able to build the website with what knowledge I had from our bootleg copy of Dreamweaver and what basic photo editing skills I had with my dad's copy of CorelDRAW. I divided each section by the two days I attended, preparing for the con, and my final thoughts on Anime Expo. This was a brand new section to my Scarlet Rhapsody website. I wasn't just producing original radio dramas, but I was also blogging about my personal experiences at my first anime convention. I figured it would blend in with the website because I was meeting people from my productions and also learning about voice acting by attending panels and taking selfies with English dub and original Japanese voice actors.

I was inspired to create this website not just by the strong memories I had, but rather, seeing a website called Fansview that was actively documenting Anime Expo 2000. After the con, I was impressed by Fansview's archive of all the main anime conventions of the time. Kevin Lillard, the gentleman who ran Fansview, was updating this website uploading photos and posting convention panel summaries as he was at the con. I was impressed at his level of dedication. I also wanted to document photos and stories from Anime Expo like this. I wanted to share my personal stories.

Part Three. Finding My People

I was so excited to post my photos and my con report. I recalled every detail and feeling I had at the con. I immediately published the Anime Expo 2000 report on my website through the free graces of RedRival's web hosting.

The girls I was hanging out with were not too thrilled about my convention report. I may have gone overboard on the cringe and the fangirling in how I presented reality in the report. I also forgot to run it by my new friends before publishing. I admitted my fault in this. I was so excited to post and share. Then again, I was also 15 and this was my first time really spending quality time and bonding with girls in the online community I was in.

I apologized.

But I still felt bad for acting so rashly.

I fell into a pit of despair. I did what I could.

Yet at the same time, looking at their photos and at their convention reports, I didn't bond with them the same way they bonded together.

I was looking at their shoutouts on their convention write-ups on their personal blogs. My name wasn't anywhere to be found or if it was, it was an afterthought. I felt like I wasn't part of this new friend group. I didn't want the anime world to be a mirror of high school. If I wanted to feel excluded and like I didn't belong, I had my high school for that. I thought things would be different this time. I thought I had gained a group of gal pals. And I began questioning whether this was a community that I belonged in. The world where I thought I could freely be me was crushed. I was not sure where I could thrive and be authentically me. I was listening to "Where Does My Heart Beat Now" by Celine Dion nonstop right after Anime Expo. Where did I belong?

And then two familiar names reached out to me.

Jimmy. Everyone's older brother! The friend I met who was cosplaying as Professor Tomoe. We briefly talked about Anime Expo. "You're that cute girl that attacked me!" he said whimsically. "There's nothing wrong with being a fangirl," he said over iParty, the free voice chat server that online voice actors congregated on. Since then, I have looked at Jimmy like an older brother. To get my mind off post-con depression, Jimmy invited me to dub some *Sailor Moon* clips he was working on. I voiced Sailor Neptune during the reveal of Mistress Nine. I gave my most elegant but defiant line delivery on the family computer. I sent the lines over in just a few takes. Jimmy complimented my soft yet sultry portrayal of Sailor Neptune. I felt like I belonged in the community again. I started submitting auditions again.

And even after I searched for him all throughout my second day at

Anime Expo 2000, Robert Black, my first glomp, contacted me through ICQ, an alternative text chat to AOL Instant Messenger. We got to know each other a little bit more outside of our voice acting hobby. We talked about cosplay contests and our interest in musical theatre as both observer and participant.

He did ask about the glomp at the hotel. Gasp! My heart stopped. I was anxious that he would also have thought of me as a crazy fangirl—in a bad way. I didn't know what to say or how to explain myself. Of all the people I met at Anime Expo, this was the one I most did not want to lose. I didn't want him to think of me as a crazy stalker fangirl. "I'm nice and hyper to everyone," I said on the text chat. In other words, this was my first time socializing with my otaku people. I didn't quite know how to interact. I was on pins and needles waiting for his response. I didn't want to be left on read. "I liked it. It makes you fun to be around," he responded. I had the biggest sigh of relief. He didn't think I was creepy. I was not outright rejected.

"And it was fabulous meeting you. Stay chipper. Positive energy like yours is what the world needs. And yours is too good to lose," Robert said before he logged off ICQ.

I stared at the screen for a moment. I wasn't used to someone saying something nice to me like this. So I didn't lose the conversation, instinct told me to write it down immediately in my new *Cardcaptor Sakura* diary that I got at Anime Expo. "Positive energy like yours is what the world needs. And yours is too good to lose."

His words resonated with me. I felt like I was discovering who I was at Anime Expo. Maybe this was the first step in breaking out of my shyness and anxiety. Maybe I didn't have to always be the quiet schoolgirl wallflower who hid in classrooms. Maybe it was okay to be myself. I didn't know I had this energy until Anime Expo ... and this energy was a good thing. And I also remembered not to glomp others without their permission, of course.

I made adjustments to my Anime Expo 2000 con report to satisfy all parties, even though I probably would not win anyone back. One month after Anime Expo, my report was linked to the main Anime Expo website under "Top Rated Anime Expo reports."

I knew I was doing something right. This was my first con report and to see it featured on Anime Expo's official website meant the world to me after all the drama. When I found out, I played Whitney Houston's "One Moment in Time" to celebrate this achievement. I danced around my bedroom, lip syncing to this diva tune about racing with destiny and victory. It was the small achievement I needed to feel, to be recognized by the Anime Expo community.

I didn't attend Anime Expo 2000 in vain. My report was being celebrated. "Maybe I should do more of these?" I thought. "Maybe I should keep documenting my convention experiences for all the world to read." I thought I had lost friendships at Anime Expo. I had not. I gained two important ones—Jimmy and Robert. Both of them were there for me when I was facing con drama. Both of them wanted me to stay around.

I went back to my *Cardcaptor Sakura* diary. I started jotting down what should be my next cosplay (and I was gonna get these done before the next Anime Expo)—Miaka Yuuki in her priestess outfit, Sakura in the cat outfit, Utena Tenjô, Sailor Mars.... I shouldn't give up conventions. I shouldn't let my despair get to me. I should keep moving forward.

9

Ani-Magic 2000
Where's Lancaster Again?

"Are you going to Ani-Magic?"

"What's Ani-Magic? I never heard of it."

It was risky meeting up with people I had only met online. As a 15-year-old going on 16, I was anxious about meeting teens my age who were just as into anime and cosplay as I was. I met Bianca and Noel through the same online voice acting community. We were surprised we lived in the same neighborhood; it made sense for us to hang out. The three of us loved anime, cosplay, and being dramatic in front of the microphone. That was enough for me.

So when Bianca asked me if I knew anything about Ani-Magic, I didn't have an answer. The only cons I knew in California were Anime Expo, Fanime, and San Diego Comic-Con. As a 16-year-old with a limited budget, no driver's license, and strict parents, Anime Expo felt like the only option for me.

What was this new convention?

"Ani-Magic is in Lancaster."

"Is that Northern California?" I sheepishly asked, not knowing my own state's geography and placement of cities.

Ani-Magic was located in a desert city not too far from Magic Mountain. This was an hour drive from the South Bay. It's one of the cities you pass if you're heading to Northern California. Yet, who puts an anime convention in the middle of nowhere? The Lancaster location puzzled me.

"It's a three-day con. We would be leaving after school on Friday and leave on Sunday afternoon."

And would my strict Asian parents let me have an overnight with friends that I just met online? They were always against sleepovers. Even when I was in elementary school, they didn't want me staying over at friends' houses for my safety.

Yet, I always felt I missed out because I would see images on American television of gal pals having sleepovers and bonding over make-up, gossip, and whatever.

"I'll have to ask my parents if that's ok."

"My mom will be with us. You can let them know we have an adult chaperone, if it helps."

It actually was easy to convince my parents to let me attend my first weekend convention. My parents knew I needed to socialize more and spend more time with friends my age. I think after I came back from the mall safely in one piece after meeting friends online, they were okay with letting me stay with my friends from the neighboring high school.

But what to cosplay? I did not have a lot of costumes. I was envious that my friends could sew. They were honors and serious college prep students, and I couldn't believe they found the time to make their costumes! I was floored that they had a full *Final Fantasy VII* group. And all I really had was an Utena Tenjô cosplay in the works.

So, about that Utena Tenjô cosplay idea that I jotted down....

After Anime Expo 2000, I wrote a list of costumes I wanted to wear for the next year's Anime Expo. I didn't know that my next one would be coming up only a few months after Anime Expo! A seamstress by the online name of Setsuna Kou was recommended to me. Her website was a one-stop shop for all the popular anime fandoms at the time. If you wanted a *Sailor Moon, Revolutionary Girl Utena, Fushigi Yuugi, Magic Knight Rayearth, Slayers*, etc., cosplay, she had it. She was the go-to if you wanted something done.

I decided to have Utena Tenjô be my first cosplay because it was the series that I was in love with. I loved my sword lesbian anime. After Anime Expo 2000, I had completed the series over the summer. I aspired to be like Utena. I wanted to be chivalrous just like Utena. I wanted to save damsels in distress like Utena. I wanted to be a chivalrous princess: a badass, but lawfully feminine. And overall, the series just represented my coming out. This series helped me figure out the kind of person I am and the values I wanted to share. I wanted to save princes and princesses and bring back chivalry to a new era.

Chivalry was nowhere to be found among the boys in my high school. I wanted my first cosplay to celebrate who I was and one of my favorite characters. I had Setsuna Kou's website bookmarked for future reference.

I turned 16 right before Ani-Magic 2000. I tried to throw a birthday party, and I invited people at my high school I thought I was cool with.

First cosplay. This cosplay of Utena Tenjô from *Revolutionary Girl Utena* was commissioned from a seamstress I found online, Setsuna Kou.

Part Three. Finding My People

While I was bullied, I tried thinking of people who had been kind to me. I waited and waited for classmates to show up to my house. My parents ordered a few pizzas and cokes. We had a birthday cake ready to go. No one came. I spent the rest of the day in tears. I remember going back to school on Monday feeling sad that as a teen who had just turned 16 years old, I had missed out on a milestone birthday. Turning 16 was always a big deal whenever I saw it in the media. You had people singing about "Sweet 16." I felt that I had one shot for this. I had missed out.

It was now or never. My parents were anxious about letting me pursue the cosplay hobby.

I asked my parents if I could commission Setsuna Kou to sew my first cosplay costume. I showed them photos from Anime Expo 2000 demonstrating that cosplay was a hobby that people my age also enjoyed. After some convincing and some pity about how no one showed up to my 16th birthday, my parents were ready to cover the cost for my first cosplay.

My mom and I put in the request for the commission, took the necessary measurements, and paid with a money order. We didn't know a local seamstress who could make Utena's main prince-like duelist uniform, but it seemed like Setsuna Kou could get the job done. Many cosplayers went to Setsuna Kou for their cosplay needs. Hence, she came highly recommended.

Almost a month and a half later, my Utena cosplay came in the mail. My mom and I had to make a few adjustments to secure some of the buttons and iron out a few things. But I was going to be Utena, my favorite anime character. I didn't have access to a pink wig that complimented my skin tone, so I just rocked my jet black straight hair. I was simply happy to wear a cosplay at a con.

I was ready for Ani-Magic 2000.

But wait. I had a second costume.

"We need you for our masquerade skit, Victoria."

"What's a masquerade?"

My friends were award-winning cosplay superstars! Masquerade is the cosplay contest where you could either strut down the stage showing off your hard work on your cosplay or perform onstage as the character. Okay, all of us were stage people. All of us were high school theater kids. So what was the catch?

"We're doing Gary Oak's cheerleaders. We need you to be a cheerleader. We'll take care of the costume."

Gary Oak is a character from *Pokémon* who is the rival of the main character, Ash Ketchum. Ash was always taunted by Gary Oak, the kid who always had the upper hand and who had a groupie always following him around. Hence, we would be his groupie cheerleaders. By this time, I already thought I was too cool for *Pokémon*, but hey.... I would get to be onstage.

Noel's mother picked me up after school in a minivan full of Bianca and Noel's friends who were also going to share the room with us.

Lancaster was a long way from Torrance. We left around 4 p.m. and had to fight the usual Los Angeles Friday rush hour to get to the desert highway that took you into Lancaster. It was getting dark, and it was hard to make out the scenery once we got to the desert. We were truly in the middle of nowhere. I didn't know what to expect out of Ani-Magic.

We parked at the Best Western Desert Rose in Lancaster. It was a one-story hotel off an open road. The area was dark and dimly lit. I was glad we had a parent in our group because I was starting to question whether this was the place. Then I saw a "Welcome Ani-Magic!" sign and knew we had to be in the right place. This was a far cry from the Disneyland Hotel's bright colors and posh vibes, lines out the door, bustling energy, and cosplayers roaming freely around the premises.

It was Friday night and we got ourselves checked in. One of my hotel roommates and I decided to check out a screening of *X/1999*, a movie I had been meaning to watch for the longest time. Afterwards, we attended a live riffing and lampooning of the infamous *End of Evangelion*. In what could have been the main room in an Elks Lodge—wooden paneling on the walls, chairs that had seen better days, and the faint stench of rust and age—the hosts poked fun at the mass of confusion that was *End of Evangelion*.

Saturday was the big day! I finally put on my Utena cosplay, and I was ready to step out in cosplay for the first time. I wasn't wearing a wannabe Chanel suit to appear mature; I could at least be me. While my Utena cosplay was not perfect, I was still happy to wear my favorite character. My roommates dressed up as villains from *Final Fantasy VII*. We wandered the convention together and we had comments like, "And it's Shinra with their friend Utena!"

At one point, I decided to wander the hotel on my own. The nice part is that the hotel was a one-story roadside hotel with some conference rooms and a pool. The pool was the central meeting point for all attendees. If you wanted to meet up with friends, you would go to the pool. The pool also had your main events stage and a lot of space to socialize with friends.

Ani-Magic was really small. You could run into the same people over and over again. I don't know how many people attended Ani-Magic, but it felt like it was in the 100s or so. It just felt so different from Anime Expo a few months before.

I went into the small dealers hall, and it was so different from Anime Expo. I was so used to rows and rows of DVDs, plushes, dolls, posters, and animation cels lining the vendor room. Ani-Magic 2000 maybe had two rows of vendors. I did find very rare *Saint Tail* dolls—Meimi and Seira. Meimi is the main girl rockin' a tuxedo dress that can only be found in magical girl anime. Seira is her nun friend. I was a huge anime doll collector then and I knew how rare these were. Suffice to say, after about an hour of carefully looking at the vendor hall, I was already done.

Mari Iijima was also a guest of honor at Ani-Magic 2000. In middle school, I was a huge fan of *Robotech* when it aired after school on Toonami. I would eventually seek out the original *Macross* via fansubs and tape trading. I would eventually seek out the soundtracks through dubious downloading via anime MP3 websites. Mari Iijima is the voice of legendary galactic pop idol Minmay. She was the original Japanese voice actress, and the *Macross* fan in me wanted to at least check out her concert.

In my Utena uniform, I was able to get a front row seat to a live show at the poolside stage. Mari Iijima was a fairly common guest of honor at California anime conventions. This was my first time seeing her live. She got up onstage and started singing some of her original music before switching over to the songs from *Macross* that made her famous. I got emotional hearing the title song to "Ai Oboeteimasuka." I never thought in years that I would have a front row seat hearing one of my favorite songs performed live. It truly was a magical moment. I know my friends gave me flak for attending the concert, but I enjoyed every second of it.

My friends and I rehearsed our masquerade skit for most of Saturday. We had to do a cheer routine for Gary Oak. I wasn't too nervous about being onstage; after all, I was a theater person and I was living for this. It was just an honor to be a part of this. The cheerleader uniforms were simple—pleated skirts with glitter ribbon, glitter tank tops with a "G" to support the true *Pokémon* champion, high ponytails with big bows, and all the glitter we could spare. It was the early '00s, after all.

The masquerade was held at the poolside stage in the evening. As if this were a town square gathering, the entire convention was seated for the masquerade. Not a seat was left empty.

We were towards the middle of the show. We were able to catch some performances from behind the stage as we lined up in performance order. We had a *Sailor Moon* group perform a pop song from one of the *Sailor Moon* musicals, "Knockin' Down Hesitation"; a few Minmays from *Macross* walked on to show off their costumes; Sailor Uranus and Sailor Neptune shared a kiss onstage; and a group of random cosplayers from different fandoms performing an exorcism. In that first Ani-Magic masquerade, we had 14 performances.

And everyone was a winner!

Because the competition was small, all 14 entries got awards tailored to the specific performances. Our Gary Oak and his cheerleaders group got "Best Pimp Daddy" award. What I can best describe about my first masquerade is that it was a cosplay talent show that had a lot of heart. The cosplay contest under the stars was a series of unhinged skits. However, we were there to have fun by the pool with our fellow cosplayers. The best in show went to the most random and manic skits I have ever seen. Hikaru from *Magic Knight Rayearth* was possessed by some kind of demon. No reason. Nothing prompted. It's just how the skit started. All of a sudden, our sweet Hikaru needs an exorcist. Cosplayers from *Gundam Wing*, *Final Fantasy VIII*, and *Suikoden* all came in to perform an exorcism on the magical girl from the CLAMP series. Once all these random characters from these random franchises got together to remove the demon on Hikaru, it all concluded in a dance party where everyone in the skit all bumped and grinded on stage like it was a party and we were all invited and we all had fun.

And then came the masquerade after-party. We tried to cram as many people as possible into one hotel room to watch a video recording of the masquerade. Eurobeat King, a well-known cosplay photographer and videographer, had recorded the masquerade on his camcorder and was taking requests to make copies of the masquerade on VHS for us to take home as an Ani-Magic souvenir. Remember, this was the days when we couldn't watch masquerades on YouTube or TikTok. We all gathered around the tiny hotel TV with Eurobeat King's VHS setup. There were about 20 or 30 of us in the two-bed hotel room. We collectively looked back at what had transpired in the past two hours making commentary on our acts and talking about the makeshift awards we won. I was a wallflower, not knowing many of the cosplayers during the masquerade after-party. But seeing how everyone was bonding over masquerade with laughter and drinks, I didn't feel as anxious or out of place as I would have at a high school dance.

Ah, yes, the Ani-Magic dance.

Part Three. Finding My People

For the dance I changed out of my cheerleader cosplay into the little red qipao that I wore at Anime Expo 1999. I kept my hair in the high pony-tail and added more body glitter. After the incident during the 10th-grade dance, I didn't really care about attending any further high school dances. Being traumatized after the Welcome Freshmen dance was enough to turn me off. However, this dance would be playing anime music. I would be around people I liked being around.

The Ani-Magic dance took place right after the masquerade in one of the conference rooms. "Information High" from *Macross Plus* blasted right on as I entered. I knew I was in the right place. A dance that played anime music, remixes of popular anime, and video game songs? I was so into it! I found a group of cosplayers who also entered masquerade and joined their dance circle. This was better than any high school dance I'd been to—the music was better, the people were much friendlier, and we were all dancing to the sound of Sharon Apple on a cool autumn night.

Sunday meant packing up and getting ready to go. I wore Utena again since it would only be a few hours until Noel's mom drove us back home in her minivan. I wasn't looking forward to the lengthy drive back to the South Bay, but I wanted to have one last look at the convention. As I was walking by the poolside in my Utena cosplay, someone pointed me out. "I remember you! Come over here!" It took me a while to figure out who was calling me. Mari Iijima?! The voice of Minmay?! The person who is the heart and soul of the original *Macross*?! "Yeah, come have a seat and join us!"

I was 16. I had been a fan of *Macross* since the eighth grade. Minmay was one of my favorite anime characters. I had memorized all of Minmay's songs. And Minmay deserved better than Hikaru. Mari Iijima remembered who I was and invited me to join her at her poolside panel! This was just a surreal moment. I asked for a photo with her, and she kindly agreed. I told her I would be back because I had remembered something.

I rushed over to the dealers hall because I remembered there was a *Macross: Do You Remember Love* poster. I immediately scrounged what-ever dollars I had left to get the poster. I ran back to the poolside to see my idol one last time before I left. "Can you sign this?" She only had a ballpoint pen with her but she happily agreed. "There you are, Victoria!" Another familiar voice. It was Bianca with Noel. I had lost track of time, and it looked like we were leaving the con. The van was packed and ready for departure back to the South Bay. This moment of meeting one of my idols was one I would always remember.

9. Ani-Magic 2000

Anime Expo 2000 had reached close to 10,000 attendees. Ani-Magic 2000 had way fewer than that. Ani-Magic 2000 had maybe 100, or at least that's what it felt like. But that wasn't a bad thing! Much of Ani-Magic's appeal came from the fact that there was this general consensus that Anime Expo had gotten too mainstream. Ani-Magic had a reputation for being known as the local "camp cosplay." While cosplay has always been a staple of conventions, Ani-Magic truly did value their cosplay convention goers. Masquerade would continue to be a poolside main event. Ani-Magic even encouraged the decoration of hotel room windows. And it was so much easier to find friends and meet creatives in the anime world.

I would not appreciate Ani-Magic until much later in life. At 16, I left the con with the memory of meeting Mari Iijima and a signed poster of one of my favorite anime movies. It was my first masquerade. Yet, I admitted that I missed the larger convention feel, especially since I'd enjoyed spending an entire day at the dealers hall at Anime Expo.

After the two-hour drive, my friends dropped me off at my house. They would later go on to have dinner at Denny's.

After Ani-Magic, I scanned the photos I took on my Advantix camera. I wrote a day-by-day report for my website. I added the low-resolution scanned photos to the report. It took me about a week to carefully curate and review the Ani-Magic 2000 convention report. Once it was uploaded, Revell Walker, the convention chair, complimented my report, liking the use of an autumn theme. I titled each day to The Eagles' "Hotel California" because Ani-Magic really was off a dark desert highway. "I love the hotel theme," Walker said. I was on a roll with my con reports. I was going to keep documenting my convention experiences.

My third year of high school introduced me to Nikki and Hera. They were in the ninth grade and unapologetically into anime. Their obsessions were *Gundam Wing* and *Fushigi Yuugi*. I met Nikki and Hera through seventh-period choir. I was in 11th grade, and I was happy to know that I was finally making friends at my high school. While I didn't have a lot of friends in my class, I was really warming up to the ninth graders who were open about their anime obsessions.

My third year of high school was mix of focusing on academics so I could get into a decent state school, waiting for VHS fansubs to show up in the mail so I could keep up with *Gundam Wing*, gushing over *Gundam Wing* fan fiction and fictitious pairings with my new gal pals in choir, and spending my time after school with the online voice acting community. College applications were the following year. Junior year was crucial in maintaining my straight As. I knew I would have a unique admissions essay given that I'd written, produced, and acted in online radio dramas. Yet, there was another piece to it—the SATs. I was never a good test taker, and I knew this would be the piece that would likely hold me back.

Fanime would be the next convention that I was scheduled for. I figured I could also sneak in a college visit to San Jose State or Santa Clara University since my parents did not want to make the trip up anytime soon no matter how many times I begged to go on a university tour. Maybe I could take some time in the morning to visit them? San Jose State seemed to have a decent media studies program, and it was close to many performing arts venues.

I touched base with my friends from Ani-Magic. It seemed they had plans set for Fanime. Their hotel room was full, and I was on my own for crash space. They would have offered me a ride up, but I'd be on my own with my room situation. I knew this likely wouldn't fly with my parents. My parents would prefer me to room with people they somewhat knew. Fanime was the same weekend in March as the next SAT test date. So I felt that I had priorities set and I was giving up Fanime for something bigger. I ended up scheduling and registering for the March SAT date.

After school was spent anticipating the next batch of six tapes of *Gundam Wing* fansubs. I would continue watching anime after school, the moment I got home from choir to just let myself mentally relax and unwind. And when I was not watching anime, I was working on my next radio play. It was another original story. This time I was focused on something bold, something Oscar-worthy—Vietnam veteran returns to San Francisco and falls in love. I think that's what the Academy would have wanted? I was focused on having this magnum opus completed by my senior year. Maybe Francis Ford Coppola-senpai would recognize me?

I secretly lamented missing out on Fanime, but it was the best thing to do. I wasn't sure if my friends from Ani-Magic wanted me around with them the entire weekend. I kept asking if there was something wrong with me. Why couldn't I keep friends? But I knew there wasn't anything wrong. I would socialize with my online voice acting friends on iParty on a nightly basis. I would get my homework done, record whatever lines I needed for radio dramas or fan dubs, and then see what everyone was up to.

Anime Central. Arlington Heights, Illinois.

A lot of my voice acting friends were based in the Midwest, or had the funds to travel to Chicagoland. I was intrigued by Anime Central and how everyone was excited for it. I met Sora, a fellow online voice actor

A Fanime 2005 (San Jose, CA) attendee wearing matching cat ears and tail; even if you did not have a full cosplay, you could still express yourself with accessories.

my age. We had the same worries about college applications and admissions tests, and we loved the same anime. I had found someone to talk to about the insanity that was the ending of *Utena*, someone to theorize with about what we thought had happened. Sora and I also became tape-trading friends, copying VHS tapes so we could also be caught up with the animes we had been meaning to watch. Sora and I instantly became best friends through our nightly voice chats on iParty.

And then I had mentioned that I cosplayed as Utena. Sora was sewing her own Anthy cosplay. I was impressed that someone as busy and as academically focused as I was had time to learn how to sew and create a full cosplay. We would always talk about how awesome it would be if I could travel from the Los Angeles suburbs to Anime Central in Chicagoland and we could cosplay as Utena and Anthy. It would be nice.

Anime Central was in mid–May. It was January, and I aced all my finals, maintaining my straight As.

iParty started having more conversations about Anime Central. Friends started talking about cosplay plans, entering the cosplay contest, figuring out what the hotel room situation was going to be, coordinating traveling. I was excited for my friends who were going. But I couldn't feel a sense of missing out. "We wish you could join us, Vicky!" "You would have a lot of fun with us, Vicky!"

I had only gone to Anime Expo and Ani-Magic prior. For Anime Expo, I went in with no plans and not expecting much. Ani-Magic did require coordination for masquerade and travel. The difference was that I was genuinely wanted. Friends wanted me to be there and wanted to include me in plans.

My friends were also thinking about running a session on online voice acting—how to get into it, what you need to get started, the basics of building your website with your contact info, how to send auditions online via ICQ, etc. I was asked to be on a panel on online voice acting. I had never done a panel at a con. I'd only been attending for less than a year. But I had an idea to convince my parents to let their 16-year-old fly out to an anime convention in Chicago.

Also, being a speaker on a panel could also help boost my college applications. My parents didn't think I had enough extracurricular activities (though I had piano, drama club, and choir), and if I convinced them, they would let me go.

I didn't even look at the guest list for Anime Central. What mattered to me was that I was wanted, I was included in discussion of plans—cosplay groups, a panelist for a session, and now, the cosplay contest. I was excited to cosplay with Sora as Utena and Anthy. I would get to be on a panel talking about what I loved to do. And entering another cosplay contest with a nonsensical skit? Sign me up!

Then it came time to convince my parents.

"We have family in Chicago. You could use it as an excuse to visit them?"

"I'm on a panel about online voice acting and producing online radio dramas. It's gonna look great on a college application!"

"I got straight As last semester ... can I go? Please?"

I tried convincing my parents. Ani-Magic was easy because they knew I was staying with local friends with one of their parents staying in the room. I was updating Sora anytime I asked my parents if I could go to Anime Central.

My parents also knew my social life was mainly spent on our family computer in the living room hanging out in the iParty voice chat. They had heard conversations, and they were aware that the voices on the other side were friends close to my age. They knew they were safe.

Two months before the con, my dad had bought airfare from LAX to Chicago O'Hare. He booked a hotel for himself close to the con and close family. It took a while for my parents to understand that these were my only friends. I would take two days off from school for my Anime Central adventure.

I broke the news on iParty that very day. I was going to Chicago. I would get to see Amy, Poli, Regan, Sora, Rasha, Penelope, and Jimmy. I couldn't believe it. I didn't think it would be possible for my parents to let me go to an anime convention in Chicago. I would forever be thankful that this even happened.

May 11–13, 2001—it was time for Anime Central.

But what to cosplay? I finally had the permission and airfare to go.

After meeting Mari Iijima at Ani-Magic 2000, I decided to cosplay as Minmay at the end of *Macross: Flashback 2012*. She wore a white dress with a white floppy hat as she was about to embark on the SDF-3. You only see her in this dress for a few seconds. I loved the vintage and elegant feel to it. Minmay starts off in *Macross* as a bratty, self-centered idol. Yet, you see her grow throughout the series, and this outfit I felt was reflective of her maturity and development.

I had my Utena cosplay that was ready to wear. Sora had agreed to be the Rose Bride to my Utena. We were going to frolic around Anime Central as anime's most popular lesbians of the time. I was so excited to finally do a cosplay collaboration.

Part Three. Finding My People

Lastly, I had Mahorin from *His and Her Circumstances*. I was into this strange slice-of-life high school anime by Hideaki Anno—the same insane auteur who brought us *Evangelion*. Mahorin was a secondary character. I didn't think my parents would let me wear a wig then or spend that extra expense to cosplay as Yukino, the main character in her cropped short brown hair. So I opted for Mahorin, the cold-as-ice classmate with long black hair. The cosplay was easy to pull off—my middle school skirt still fit me, blue tie from JCPenney, white button-up from my high school uniform, and a black cardigan.

My plans were simple, but I was ready for Anime Central.

10

Anime Central 2001

A Mad Scientist
Hosts a Beauty Pageant

"It's not a full flight. We can bump you up to first class," said the attendant at LAX. It was early Friday morning. My dad and I were up bright and early for our flight to Chicago. We were very lucky to have an upgrade on our three-hour flight to the Windy City.

My dad had a hotel room in the Chicagoland suburbs. I would be staying with my friends at the main hotel, the Sheraton in Arlington Heights. My dad had rented a car to drive around while he visited family in Chicago. He dropped me off at the Sheraton. I was up in the air earlier in the day, and then I was ready to run a panel on online voice acting and production in the afternoon as soon as I got there.

My dad made sure I was checked into the con. He went to the short registration line to pick up and pay for my weekend badge. This is the best reward I could have gotten for having straight As in 11th grade.

I checked out the program guide to see where my friends were. Obviously, they were getting ready for our panel. There was a series of meeting rooms right by registration. I walked over to where our panel was taking place. I immediately recognized my friends all dolled up in cosplay! "Vicky!" they shouted! I froze for a moment.

Anime Expo 2000 and Ani-Magic 2000 quickly flashed through my mind. At Anime Expo 2000, I was a tourist in a wannabe Chanel suit hoping to make friends at my first anime con. At Ani-Magic 2000, I felt like I was just tagging along for the ride. But it was a fun ride! It was at this moment at Anime Central that I realized that there were friends who wanted me to be there, who were looking forward to seeing me after all these months of scheming and plotting on iParty.

Before I knew it, I was covered in hugs. Everyone I had met online through our shared interest in anime and voice acting was showering me with affection and a chorus of "Vicky!" What may have seemed like a few seconds felt like a lifetime of the embraces that I never had. I felt welcomed. I felt wanted. This was not just words on screen anymore. This was not instant messenger or an online chatroom. This was real life.

The panel before us was just letting out. We were ready to start. We may have had a quick five-minute debrief right before the start to see what we were going to talk about. I took time on the flight to organize notes and an outline just in case we did not have one. This was my first time participating in a panel, so I had no idea what to expect. I only attended very few panels at anime cons, and most of them were voice-over guest spotlights.

It was a small conference room with the capacity to hold 20 people. My friends and I were seated at a long table up at the front of the room facing the audience. We had microphones. I had my notes on 3×5 inch index cards. All of us were up there—Elodie, the girl who was the baby of our group; Jimmy, my friend from Anime Expo who was best known for dubbing random clips from *Sailor Moon*; Poli; Kim; Sora; and me. We introduced ourselves to the audience—who we were, how long we had been participating in online voice acting, and what online productions we were running. We weren't sure what direction we should go after introductions. Elodie, our moderator and the baby of the group at the age of 14, pointed to me because I had my notecards. My notes were based on creating original online radio plays and the number of hats one had to wear if one wanted to pursue this side of online voice acting—writer, producer, director, line editor, music mixer, marketing, and so forth.

I will admit, the panel went in all sorts of directions, but the most memorable part was Jimmy recalling the time he wanted to go into voice acting. At a college party, he had a few drinks and thus began to impersonate Nephrite, a villain from *Sailor Moon*. "YOU WILL DIE SAILOR ... MOON!" as if he forgot the main protagonist's name, the audience had a good laugh from the college party anecdote.

To our surprise, an actual working professional voice actor was in the audience. Dressed in jeans, a white shirt, and a denim jacket, Scott McNeil made himself present. This was my first time running a panel at the age of 16, and we had the voice of Duo Maxwell from Gundam Wing in our panel room. Let me tell you—I moderate and host fan panels at conventions like San Diego Comic-Con and Anime Expo. I will get folks working in the entertainment industry who will pop during these sessions at times. Yet, given that Scott McNeil has made a huge name for himself now in shows like *Inuyasha*,

Fullmetal Alchemist, and a few *Barbie* movies, seeing an A-lister in the professional voice acting world in our tiny panel room that only sat 20 was a huge deal for us.

After the panel, all of the online voice actors stood outside the panel room for a group photo. Folks from the community were welcomed to join us. There were about 20 or so of us gathered to take one group photo to commemorate a gathering of online voice actors at Anime Central 2001. It was like we were taking a class photo for our yearbook. Some of us were in cosplay. Some of us were wearing our fandom on our shirts or rockin' cat ears on our heads. We gathered and flashed the peace sign to our friends taking hold of our cameras. What was supposed to happen for a few moments ended up taking up more time than expected. Random people were stopping by to take our photo. As more people saw our group, they also busted out their cameras to take a photo. None of us wanted to be rude and ask them to stop taking photos. We had so many people use the flash on us. I don't remember the flashes at all—I was wearing shades in the photo. What seemed like an eternity came to an end at last. We were getting hungry, and we immediately scattered once the last batch was done. My friends were blinded by the flashes after being mobbed by the Anime Central paparazzi.

And after that red carpet moment of us having all eyes and cameras on us, it was time for dinner. We went back to the hotel suite that Sora had reserved for us. It was a Friday night, so we thought about ordering pizza. One of us would go to the lobby to pick it up. "Vicky can do it! She's the oldest-looking sister out of all of us." Of course, I was 16, but I passed for 22. Our room consisted of girls (and a few of their boyfriends) who were high school students or college underclassmen. While I had shared photos of myself online with my voice acting friends, they had finally gotten to see me in person. I agreed to go down to the lobby to pick up the pizza since I was wearing just a leather jacket, button-up shirt, shades, and dress pants to present myself looking more like a college student than a 16-year-old Catholic schoolgirl.

This was also the convention where I first met Regan in person. Regan was another like-minded theater kid in the voice acting community. Regan was also the first queer person who confessed their feelings towards me. When we met online, we grew fairly close talking about yuri, or women-loving-women anime and our lives as outsiders in our world. We would talk about our favorite ships—both canonical and noncanonical in magical girl and slice-of-life anime. They wrote me a love letter. I was still questioning my sexuality. It was clear we had deep feelings for each other.

Each of us really liked the other and wanted the other to be happy. But I was afraid to take the next step because the Catholic guilt had not worn off completely. I still had to spend eight hours a day, five days a week at a Catholic high school. Whatever free hours I had after school and my extracurricular activities were the times I could be my anime fangirl self, but even then, I barely had time to reflect or think about the kind of people I was attracted to. I had never been kissed or gone on a date! Regan and I spent evenings at Anime Central curled up next to each other, holding hands, and it was wholesome. It was the closest I ever was with someone, and it was nice to feel this warmth and affection even if my high school deemed it scandalous and sinful.

By the time we got the pizza into the hotel room, the topic of masquerade came up. "Oh shoot. I forgot about this!" I thought. My mind was so wrapped up in the panel and getting my notes organized, I forgot about the cosplay contest!

But no worries at all. My friends had it all under control. We took whatever cosplays we were planning to wear on Saturday night and took an existing script that Poli had written. Poli had written a *Final Fantasy* beauty contest radio drama. I honestly forget how the original radio drama script went, but if I can recall the punch line, a Moogle enters the beauty pageant and is the last entry to make their case to win. "Yes, I would sleep with you, KUPO!" was the line to convince the judges at the end to let the furry *Final Fantasy* mascot win a beauty pageant title. It was as chaotic and unhinged as it sounded.

The script had a lot of chaotic energy that most masquerade veterans would frown upon and use as a "what not to do." What started out as a cover of a *Sailor Moon* musical act then went to characters from *Chrono Cross*, *Utena*, *Perfect Blue*, *Star Ocean*, *Corrector Yui*, and *Sailor Moon*. Characters from these shows would be vying for the title of Miss Anime Central. Our host was Jimmy as Professor Tomoe. Mima from *Perfect Blue* would be entering randomly during the contest to advertise Strawberry Pocky. Chicagoland anime fans are crazy about Japanese snacks. What was so common as my childhood snacks from the Seafood Ranch Market was such a rarity in the Midwest that people considered snacks like Pocky gold.

We never wrote the script to have this much crossover from different series. Even the emcee was confused about why the psychological thriller *Perfect Blue* was in the mix of magical girl anime and Japanese role-playing game characters. We happened to bring these costumes with us, and we wrote a last-minute skit based on what we had available.

I would be cosplaying as Utena from her eponymous series. My friend Sora would be cosplaying as Anthy. However, before we went onstage, we decided to take photos of our cosplay. With the exception of the Gary Oak cheerleader skit where I filled in for a part, this was my first time planning a cosplay with someone. Sora had made her Anthy cosplay. I was just impressed that an honor student had this much time to work on such a project. Her red ballroom dress was stunning; she had used a Cinderella pattern to make Anthy's Rose Bride dress. On the other hand, I had hired the legendary Setsuna Kou to make my Utena cosplay. Before masquerade, Sora and I gave our cameras to our friend Jimmy. We drafted him into being our photographer. We only had our film cameras and limited shots available to get these photos right. We found a tuffet by the Sheraton to take our Utena and Anthy photos. And that was my first cosplay photoshoot.

Right before the masquerade cosplay contest, Anime Central also had a Meet the Guests reception. It was like speed dating, but with the special anime guests for ACen. We were very excited to find out that the meet the guests reception had the *Gundam Wing* English voice cast ready to meet fans, sign autographs, and take photos with us on our disposable cameras. We could hardly contain our fangirling! We already met Scott McNeil, and now we met Kirby Morrow, the voice of Trowa, at the reception. We were able to take photos with the guests at the pavilion and have one quality conversation with them.

It was time to check in for the Saturday night cosplay contest. This was my first time going on the main stage. Ani-Magic was a cosplay summer camp with a stage by the pool. Anime Central's main stage was a much bigger deal. Our lines were live, so we were still rehearsing while we waited for our turn. Sora and I would go up as Anthy and Utena once Jimmy as Professor Tomoe had announced that Anthy and Utena were entering Miss ACen as a couple. We would introduce ourselves, say the line "No, we are not lesbians," and then engage in a more-than-just-friends type of embrace.

We were ready for the main stage. We were towards the end of the show. Because we were backstage in run order, we didn't have time to see the entries before us. It was time for Isaac Sher, the emcee, to announce us. Doing his own rendition of *Iron Chef*, he introduced the Miss Anime Central act with the names of all the shows represented. "...with characters from *Chrono Cross, Sailor Moon, Utena, Star Ocean, Corrector Yui ...* and *PERFECT BLUE*? ... It's more anime than you can shake a stick at!" he said.

Part Three. Finding My People

It was our turn to go onstage. Jimmy as Professor Tomoe went up first and welcomed the audience to the first Miss Anime Central. He followed up this opening with an evil laugh. He introduced each contestant one by one. Each of us had a quip or snarky line. "I'm Corrector Yui, but no one knows what I'm from," said Elodie in anxious anime schoolgirl mode. "I'm Jessica De Alkirk and give me money! I like money," said Poli boisterously in front of the crowd. The skit stopped for a moment to let the tragic idol, Mima Kirigoe, cross the stage to advertise strawberry-flavored Pocky. The crowd went wild at the sight of Pocky. I forget how the rest of the skit went, but it was the chaotic mess you would expect for a first-timer's experience at masquerade, but oh my gods, did we have so much fun onstage! There was even a wedding ceremony—featuring one of the artist guests, Robert DeJesus, and his now wife, Emily—during the halftime show, and we were all there to witness it. One of the guests of honor, Jan Scott-Frazier, officiated the wedding. Shortly after the masquerade, we were all invited to the reception to have a piece of wedding cake. We didn't place in the masquerade, but it was a fun way to end a Saturday: eating free wedding cake and sharing the stage with my friends being our best cringey selves dressed up in our favorite fandoms.

Sunday marked the end of Anime Central. I don't recall buying too much from the dealers hall. I spent more time with my online friends taking cosplay photos, hanging out in our hotel suite, and simply wandering around the con. I did peek in the dealers hall once. I didn't have the same shock and awe as I did at my first Anime Expo. The small ballroom had vendors selling dvd's, manga, and plushes. Being in Chicago with my best friends was already enough; I didn't need to spend money on anything else.

I had to leave around noon to catch my flight back to Los Angeles. I was wearing Mahorin from *His and Her Circumstances*, which was essentially my blue middle school uniform skirt, a white button-up, a blue necktie from JCPenney, a black blazer, and black thigh-high socks. It was a simple closet cosplay I mustered before Anime Central. We all checked out of our party suite and began to say our "See you real soon" in the lobby.

The whole time, Sora was documenting everything on her camcorder. She was taking video of all of our memories and said she would give everyone a VHS copy of all the footage she took. She took video of us with our final thoughts on the last day. Because we had partied all night, we were exhausted. I was still feeling fine, but I couldn't help but feel a tinge of sadness and melancholy. My dad arrived at the lobby to pick me up. All of my friends ended up giving me a hug "farewell." I didn't want to leave either. It was an emotional farewell. I never felt so much a part of a community. For the first time, I actually did feel held by a community. It was a peaceful and bittersweet experience all at once. Anime Expo and Ani-Magic did happen, but I felt like a tourist. I felt like I was an observer. I felt like I was still a shy kitten adjusting to a new home. Here, I felt like I truly did belong and that I was wanted in the community. It felt like I was finally home. It took two thousand miles from Los Angeles to realize this.

My dad and I went to the parking lot for the rental car. I also met some familiar faces from California there. "Good to know that we're not the only Californians at Anime Central," said Eurobeat King. I boarded the flight still in my *His and Her Circumstances* school uniform, and I wasn't ready to let reality sink in. I would be coming back to a world in Southern California where I was not so sure I belonged. I felt so much more at home in Chicago with my friends.

I came back on Monday wondering if Anime Central was all a dream. I had friends who were happy to see me. Even walking around the con, strangers in costume would say "Good morning" and mean it. I had gal pals and queer friends who supported me. I had previously thought wholesome female friendships were a fiction fed to me by mass media. I thought going out and having fun was something only popular and pretty girls could do. I just had a great time partying it up in Arlington Heights. When asked in our junior year survey what our favorite place to hang out was, most classmates put down the mall or the beach. I put down Arlington Heights, Illinois. It was just that memorable to me. It meant more to me than being invited to any high school party—I was partying and living it up with the right people.

I spent my waking moments, when I wasn't studying for finals, working on the Anime Central report for my website. Like Ani-Magic, I also themed Anime Central to music. This time around, I themed it to classic jazz standards. Each day-by-day section was themed to a 1940s jazz standard because I tend to associate Chicago with jazz and blues. Within two weeks, after careful review and curation, the report was up. All of my friends gushed at their photos and were flooded with the memories we shared in Arlington Heights.

After the convention, my friends and I were obsessed with collecting photos online from other convention reporters of the time. Fansview, Eurobeat King, Lionel Lum, Sunset Grill, and Obsessed with Anime. This was how we found photos of our cosplay. There were a handful of folks documenting cosplayers, and they ran their own websites. We downloaded all of our photos and shared them on the forums we were on. Those of us who had personal cosplay websites posted them to our cosplay portfolios to show that we did have some documentation of our cosplays.

Some of us brought disposable cameras that had 24 shots on them. We took them to conventions to take photos of our adventures. I had my own film camera, and I had friends take photos of my cosplay so I knew I would have something documented that I could scan and post on my website or share on a forum like Silent Dreams or the various EZBoards my friends ran.

Sora and I started talking about our next cosplay plans. She had a list of everything she wanted to do. She had plans for *Sakura Taisen*, *X-Men*, *Sailor Moon*, *Slayers*, *Fushigi Yuugi*, *Cardcaptor Sakura*, *Gundam Wing*, and countless others. I had a very small list of maybe five or six cosplays I wanted to do. I was limited with my medium-length black hair; I had to keep to characters who had somewhat long black hair. At the time, you could get a cheap wig from Party City. A pink party wig was that hot pink that would clash violently with my tan Filipino skin tone. Sora was working on a *Magic Knight Rayearth* group for the next Anime Central. Sora would be Umi. Fuu was already taken, so, by default, I ended up being cast as Hikaru. This was the final armor version. I had no idea how I would pull this off. Would I hire Setsuna Kou again? Would I find someone my mom knew to figure it out? But not to fear ... that group plan never happened. And I also had other commitments on the horizon. I was not sure if I could afford to shell out the money for a complicated costume that involved armor.

That's right! Anime Expo was in two months!

I didn't put much emotional investment into Anime Expo 2001. I wanted to temper my expectations for 2001. I did have friends from Chicagoland who were planning on attending—at least I didn't feel like I was alone. I joined the Anime Expo online forums to see what people were discussing before the con. This was the first time I joined an online community dedicated to a single convention.

The Anime Expo forums were hosted on an old message board platform called EZBoard. You could plot cosplay plans, join various meetup groups, find out what panels and games were going on, read restaurant recommendations, and also find people who needed more people for a masquerade skit. I wanted to keep myself busy during Anime Expo. I really didn't feel the need to have a dedicated group to hang out with, so I signed up for the karaoke contest. A cosplay contest entry that featured the femme fatale, Lady Une, from *Gundam Wing* was scouting for a victim ... er ... another person to be in contest with them. I decided to volunteer myself for that opportunity. The forums were a neat little place online to find out what was going on with the con and figure out how to meet up with people.

Anime Expo 2001 would be moving from Anaheim to downtown Long Beach. I was hyped about this because my family lived close to Long Beach. I could do all four days no problem since we lived about 10 minutes away from the Long Beach Convention Center. No one knew what to think when Anime Expo was making its move from Anaheim to Long Beach. It was a new location that was going to take some adjustment.

I had more costumes to wear and to choose from this time than during Anime Expo 2000. I didn't have to settle for an imitation Chanel suit to dress to impress. What I had in my closet was simple. I already had Mahorin and Minmay set to go. I had two new outfits to debut at Anime Expo. I was reading a manga by *Utena* author Chiho Saitō. When she's not writing sword lesbians, she's writing a ton of female-lead Danielle Steel–tier heterosexual sexy fun smut. One such title was the World War II drama *Waltz in a White Dress*. I had my junior prom dress. It was white. All I needed to do was curl my hair and I was already the debutante protagonist, Koto!

And for masquerade. Who would Lady Une shoot? I thought it would be funny to go up as Shinji Ikari from *Neon Genesis Evangelion*. After all, it was something easy to piece together from my closet. This was the first time I ever dressed as another gender and presented masculine (as masculine as depressed adolescent Shinji can be).

My tepid feelings about Anime Expo 2001 didn't distract me from doing well on finals and preparing for college applications come senior year. While everyone I knew was being super hyped for Anime Expo 2001, I tempered my feelings going into the convention.

11

Anime Expo 2001
An Anime Convention in My Backyard

I decided to get my badge on day zero, the day before the convention officially started. I wasn't taking any chances. My dad dropped me off at the Long Beach Westin where you could pick up your badge at registration. I cosplayed as Shinji for the sole purpose of picking up my badge. I even made a NERV ID badge to go with my costume so I wasn't just anime-boy-in-dress-pants-and-shirt. I wasn't the only one in cosplay that day. I spotted a *Lupin III* gang and someone wearing a giant purple Chuchu cosplay from *Utena*. Everyone was already getting hyped for the four-day anime festival.

It took me about an hour to get my badge, but I was engaged in good conversations with the people next to me. People who were picking up their badge on day zero were mostly from out of town. I was able to pay for my badge in cash from all the cash allowance I had saved up. For the first time in two years, I was going to do all four days of Anime Expo. And what a ride it was!

I had a few people from Chicagoland I wanted to make sure to say "hi" to and hang out with. I entered the karaoke contest to test my singing skills in front of an audience. I also entered in masquerade—the Lady Une cosplayer had recruited a Duo Maxwell cosplayer and my closet cosplay Shinji Ikari; this was going to be fun. I had things to keep myself busy and commit to so I didn't have to rely on others or a clique. I had a few events I wanted to check out, but having something where I was an active participant got my mind off the drama from the previous year. I didn't have to worry about having a group of friends to hang out with when I had commitments.

This was also the year that Broccoli Studios were holding auditions for the voice of Dejiko from *Di Gi Charat* to sing the English version of

"Welcome" to promote their Los Angeles storefront. So many aspiring voice actors on the forums were expecting this to be their big break. I didn't go for it because I already had masquerade and karaoke planned and it would have conflicted. The announcement was made too close to the con for me to adjust my plans. Yet, I was very excited for my friends who were traveling to Anime Expo for this opportunity to voice the kawaii catgirl Dejiko.

Anime Expo 2001 day one. I woke up early so my mother could put my hair in curls so I could look like Koto, the main dame in *Waltz in a White Dress*. This was an obscure manga by Chiho Saitō. I didn't expect anyone to know what this was from. The point was, I was in a white ball gown, unbothered by drama. After what happened at Anime Expo 2000, I was going to grace Anime Expo 2001 like a queen. My dad dropped me off right outside the Long Beach Terrace Theater. I stepped out of my dad's Ford Explorer and into Anime Expo 2001 in my ball gown.

"Are you cosplaying from *Waltz in a White Dress*?" said someone waiting in line for the opening ceremony. I had barely entered the convention and someone knew what obscure Chiho Saitō drama I was from! I wasn't expecting it! I decided to hang out in line with these shōjo manga enthusiasts. I wasn't planning on checking out the opening ceremony, but I now was! The opening ceremony was a treat—Anime Expo introduced the guests. Among them was Yuu Watase, author of *Fushigi Yuugi*. She had her head down while she sat still in her chair. My new friends and I agreed that she looked sad onstage. We really wanted to give her a hug. The voice actress for Utena, Tomoko Kawakami, showed up onstage. She brought a ton of cheerful energy to the auditorium. We also had an introduction video from Shōji Kawamori of *Macross*. He was showing off his studio in Japan in his introduction. Also, Anime Expo announced that they would expand their convention to have a New York event. Anime Expo New York would debut in fall 2002. I was hoping that I could make it. I would be curious to check out a convention in New York City, especially one in Times Square.

I had so many photographers taking photos of me even though they didn't know the source material. "It's an obscure World War II romance manga," I said. Then again it was the summer of 2001, Michael Bay's *Pearl Harbor* was in theaters, and I had to be careful using the words "romance" and "World War II." I didn't want to discuss the horrors of that movie while trying to enjoy my vacation. I didn't want my first cosplay to ever attract photographer attention to be associated with a terrible movie.

Part Three. Finding My People

As I was waltzing through the Long Beach Convention Center, I ran into familiar faces from Ani-Magic and Anime Central. We were able to quickly catch up and have good conversations on what life was like after the cons we attended. I befriended Lina, an artist aspiring to go into 2D animation. She was also part of the voice acting community. As she was settling down, she made a black and white sketch of me as Koto from *Waltz in a White Dress*.

Anime Expo 2001 drew fewer than 10,000 people. You could easily run into people without having to text or call. There were a few cosplay meetups—the most notable were the *Revolutionary Girl Utena*, *Sailor Moon*, *Fushigi Yuugi*, and of course, the mega *King of Fighters* cosplay gatherings. Or, you could find cosplayers from the same series and have an impromptu meetup on the spot. You would find your convention friends through these methods.

I had the karaoke contest later in the evening. I ended up singing "Idol Talk" from *Macross Plus*. I thought this was an amateur mistake because I picked something simple with lyrics in French, and I wasn't about to sing the explicit lyrics. I knew I had shot myself in the foot, but I performed and moved to the sensual *Macross* song, even if I had to fake it. I knew the judges were marking me down. But that was okay. I still had a good time dancing onstage.

Day two of Anime Expo was me cosplaying as Mahorin from *His and Her Circumstances*. The last time I had worn the outfit was at Anime Central a few months back, so it was associated with the tears of joy I cried as I was leaving my Chicagoland friends. I decided to play it cool as ice like Mahorin. I even ran into other *His and Her Circumstances* cosplayers at the con and we had to take a few photos with our disposable cameras. I had a fun time just wandering around meeting people without having to worry about anything.

When Lina was out of artist alley, we did some wandering and found room parties. We went to one at the top floor of the Long Beach Hyatt. Drinks were being passed, but it was a classy and low-key vibe. I had my first Asashi. These weren't wild room parties. We were talking about Studio Ghibli films and hidden gems of anime. It was a bunch of classy adults in a fancy hotel suite that looked over the Los Angeles Harbor and Queen Mary. I nursed my Asashi because I wasn't really a fan of the taste, but I wanted to play it cool with these cool anime kids. I was really interested in checking out the classic anime these cool cats were talking about. One such particular anime was *The Sea Prince and the Fire Child*. The way this tipsy otaku described it to me was, "Imagine if Studio Ghibli produced their version of *Fantasia* and you get this whimsy version of *Romeo and Juliet* with fairies." Even after that party, it took me years to hunt down this Sanrio-produced anime because it had no domestic release. Yet, this title would continue to haunt me for the next decade because this fairy tale classic was next to impossible to find.

After my first ever room party, Lina and I went to the dance at the nearby hotel. It was anime music galore! Deejays and flashing lights and projections of anime filled the hotel ballroom. Yet, I could only take so much of the smell from sweaty anime nerds raving with their glow sticks at the dance in their baggy Hot Topic trip pants with the many belts. Lina and I were just wallflowers in our cat ears vibing with the anime rave.

The next day was masquerade. Anime Expo had a reputation for having the biggest and best cosplay contest in the country. No pressure at all! Here I was on the biggest stage for cosplay contests. I didn't cosplay on masquerade day. I wore a lovely white Chinese qipao. After all, no more imitation Chanel business threads. I wanted to look and feel like a queen. I was not here to fake anything about me. I wanted to live authentically in this space.

I didn't enter masquerade with the intention of winning. I just wanted to be onstage entertaining a crowd. I met my masquerade team— Lady Une and Duo Maxwell—during our morning orientation meeting for the contest. The basic premise of our masquerade act was that Lady Une was hosting *The Weakest Link* and Duo and Shinji were contestants. Shinji would get shot by Lady Une because that's what Lady Une does—shoot the weakest link from the ranks.

Anime Expo 2001 masquerade was an interesting experience. We had an actual theater to work with. This wasn't some ballroom in the hotel with a makeshift stage and amateur lighting. This was the Long Beach Terrace Theater where Broadway shows were put on. We had an actual stage with actual dressing rooms and an elevator that took us to the main stage! The theater was large enough to hold all of the Anime Expo 2001 attendees.

We had a virtual master of ceremonies, Max, a mecha girl who took up the main screen onstage and was voiced offstage. She was a VTuber before there was a word for it. While innovative for 2001, the audience hated and booed Max. Max would pull the energetic and sugar-coated kawaii anime girl schtick. Yet, a lot of her commentary didn't land with the audience. The audience groaned anytime Max would make a witty quip from the last masquerade skit. Or Max would start dancing on the big screen if there was a dance act onstage. The virtual emcee was way ahead of its time, but the Gen X and elder millennial attendees weren't ready for this early version of VTubing.

Our act came up later in the show. We were able to see a live video feed of what went onstage. We had two *Dance Dance Revolution*–themed acts. Two *Moulin Rouge*–inspired "Lady Marmalade" acts. A *Sailor Moon* and 'N Sync mashup. Mima from *Perfect Blue*. Two *Clover* duo's in beautiful dresses and wings. A group from Japan that went by Uran that showcased *Five Star Stories*. Overall, I was impressed with what I saw onstage.

I don't remember who placed in masquerade, but I made so many friends backstage and bonded with cosplayers I would not have met otherwise. I made friends with the *Angel Sanctuary* group that was after us. I also made friends with the Team Rocket group. I mentioned to Iris, who was cosplaying as Jessie from Team Rocket, that I was still in high school and was considering applying to University of California at Irvine. UC Irvine seemed to have one of the top theater programs and a solid film program. I wanted to be somewhere where being creative was celebrated and where weird people thrived. Iris was a current student at UC Irvine. We had a good couple of hours together backstage while waiting for our turn. Iris was telling me how important and how freeing it was to thrive in your hobbies in university and how people were much more accepting of people being into anime and cosplay. Applying to college actually sounded more appealing to me. Beyond Iris sharing how she made her crazy Jessie wig, which seemed indestructible, and telling me about her past masquerade experiences performing as Team Rocket, Iris and I really bonded backstage. She became one of my cosplay mentors. Yes, you can enjoy cosplay while being a thriving full-time student at a prestigious university. As I was figuring out what to do after school, it was helpful seeing older cosplayers doing well and still finding time to enjoy conventions. I also met Yaya Han backstage. She overheard a conversation I was having about what I wore to Anime Expo that year. "I remember *Waltz in a White Dress*! I read that manga!" she said. She was cosplaying as the Red Queen from *Miyuki-chan in Wonderland*. Before we went onstage, we just gushed over the obscure Saitō historical drama. I admit, I was a fan of Yaya Han when I saw her *Angel Sanctuary* and *X/1999* cosplay. Both cosplays had such intricate details, gothic beauty, and sheer elegance that I aspired to have in my upcoming cosplays. I was rooting for her group's skit!

My plan of taking Anime Expo 2001 as it went without worrying about meeting up with people or worrying about how other people would think of me worked just like that. I had a memorable evening of being shot onstage by Lady Une as the crowd laughed and cheered at the death of Shinji and the corpses of Duo and Shinji were dragged offstage by Anime Expo masquerade staff.

It was the last day of Anime Expo and I was wearing the Minmay cosplay I had worn at Anime Central. I did one final round across the dealers hall and picked up the *Sailor Moon* musical dolls for my *Sailor Moon* doll collection. That was my big spend at Anime Expo: a set of the Outer Senshi in their musical outfits for $100. I took a lot of photos on my Advantix camera to supplement my convention report. I went through about four rolls of camera film to capture cosplays and photos with friends. I wanted to continue my Anime Expo "top convention report" status.

I also had my first creepy fanboy experience at Anime Expo 2001. The online voice acting and anime community wasn't short on questionable personalities. I was hanging out in the hotel lobby waiting for a friend. Someone offered me a seat in the lobby. I didn't want to decline the offer. I needed to sit down. At the time, I had braces, and I would always wear my glasses at conventions unless I was getting my photo taken. "I think girls with glasses and braces are cute," he said to me. He was clearly older than me. And he randomly spouted out, "And Nuriko from *Fushigi Yuugi* ... he ain't gay." He proceeded to provide his reasoning why. I let him talk but ignored what he was saying. I really had no time to be hit on or hear a homophobic rant about one of my favorite characters. I had to remove myself from that situation. "Sorry, I have to meet up with someone." I didn't want to cause a scene; I just wanted to get out. And that was baby's first convention creeper story.

I went into Anime Expo 2001 with low expectations, taking things as they came. I didn't look for fun. The fun came to me. I had time on day four to attend Takumi Yamazaki's voice dubbing workshop where you could dub a scene from an anime and get feedback from the legendary voice actor himself. We were dubbing scenes from *Vandread*. I leant my voice to the character of Meia in this practice session. Takumi said I needed to relax more. I wasn't used to the style of dubbing where you had to match lip flaps. Keeping up was pretty hard. I had to figure out how to relax but keep up with the lip flap movement. This was difficult to keep up with. I was not used to this style of dubbing. It was like karaoke on Dante Must Die mode.

At the end of the convention, I was also happy to learn that my friend Bianca from Ani-Magic and my first masquerade act got the singing part of Dejiko for the Broccoli auditions. I was so happy that the person who drafted me into my first masquerade skit finally was gonna make it big as a voice actress in anime.

A lot of people complained about Anime Expo 2001's Long Beach location and how spread out it was. The convention center, Hyatt, Renaissance, Long Beach Terrace Theater, and Westin all hosted the 10,000-person convention. People were complaining about walking around too far. I was one of the few people who actually enjoyed Long Beach. I liked the ocean breezes and just the joy of having Anime Expo 10 minutes away from my house. A lot of veterans of Anime Expo do not recall having a positive experience, but as a teen finally able to explore this convention and make some meaningful friendships, I had the best of times. I even thought about asking that Duo Maxwell cosplayer in our masquerade group out to the Sadie Hawkins dance, but he lived too far from the South Bay to attend. Oh well.

Of course what was waiting for me after Anime Expo 2001 was my senior year of high school.

12

Class of 2002
Cat Ears and School Uniform.
I Can't Stop Me

I had to have some careful planning for my senior year. I wanted to make time for all my senior extracurricular activities—playing piano in chamber ensemble and seventh-period drama club—while finishing senior year strong academically. I ended up getting a lead part in the drama club's fall play. I was cast as a person who was diagnosed as neurodivergent trapped in juvenile detention. It included a heart-wrenching monologue and I was ready to make people cry. I could finally put all that time spent in online voice acting to use onstage. Yes, this was my time to shine. I was looking forward to making the audience shed tears. Because of our show schedule, I had to let Bianca and Noel know I wasn't going to make it to Ani-Magic 2001. After Ani-Magic 2000, I did not feel a reason to go back unless there was a guest who compelled me to go like Mari Iijima of *Macross* fame. However, after having positive experiences at Anime Central 2001 and Anime Expo 2001, I wanted to go and yet, I wanted to focus on this lead part I got for the fall play. I opted to cancel plans for Ani-Magic 2001.

Yet, it didn't mean I could totally nerd out during my senior year of high school. By this time in high school, I was unapologetically an anime fan. I didn't care if my classmates thought it was "cartoon porn from Japan." I didn't care if my teachers thought it was "risqué things we can't have at Catholic school." I had classmates in the literary journal club talk down on anime. We had freshmen and sophomores who were really getting into anime because of Toonami and submitting anime-inspired art to the literary journal. The upperclassmen board of the literary journal would start talking down on these entries and would shut down any anime-inspired art. It was clear that the bougie kids at my conservative high school had a disdain for anime and anime fans. I never could tell why. I did not want to think about it too much. I didn't care though. I loved my niche hobby. Being anyone else or pretending to be anything other than a whimsical magical girl felt false. I did not want to be another Asian teenager with a Honda Civic. I'd rather pretend I was a chosen magical girl who was going to save the world with the help of her cat and she would ride off into battle (and school) on a winged horse like Pegasus. I had a creative mind. I had a wild imagination. I was going to have the confidence of a main character my senior year of high school. I was going to be the truly authentic me. I was going to live my best life in my senior year. No apologies.

I decided to brave the Welcome Freshmen dance, the dance where I was harassed and humiliated. I was planning to get back to that karaoke room. I went to a vintage consignment store and put together a Hello! Project–inspired outfit. I wasn't going to wear cheap Hawaiian or tiki fashion to the dance. I was going to go all-in on J-pop vividness and whimsy. My mom dropped me off at the dance. "I'm proud that you're being you," she said. I only had one thing planned that night—sing "Love Machine" by Morning Musume at karaoke. I had the CD with me. I had the lyrics memorized. I ended up singing it and got a rousing applause afterwards. No one knew what I was singing or what it was from, but for one night, I was able to share one of my favorite J-pop acts with my classmates whether they liked it or not.

And I didn't stop there. I was planning on living it up during my senior year. I didn't think I was going to the homecoming dance because I didn't have a date. Yet, at the last minute, my mom found some family friend to set me up with. For my 17th birthday, I asked my parents if I could commission a Princess Mars cosplay from the same seamstress who made my Utena cosplay, Setsuna Kou. Sailor Mars was one of my favorite Sailor Senshi. I had long black hair and bangs just like she did. All the Sailor Senshi would have a princess form at the end of the *Sailor Moon* manga series. My new Princess Mars cosplay was sitting in my closet for most of the fall. That is, until the homecoming dance.

I wore my red Princess Mars dress to the dance with my date, Oliver. I still think the reason why my mom had set us up was to prove to Oliver's mom that he was straight. We spent most of the dance killing it on the dance floor; he really knew how to salsa. I was wearing this red empire-waist dress while most of my classmates were wearing either black or white. The Class of 2002's colors were red and black. Princess Mars was all about being fiery, fierce, and true girl boss energy. It seemed appropriate to radiate red to show class pride and, above all, Moonie pride.

12. Class of 2002

Also during homecoming week—I wore my Utena jacket to school with my black uniform dress pants. After all, school colors were black and gold. I would not have done this the year before. I was an anime fangirl, and I was going to show it. I may not have had friends at high school, but it was my last year. I was going to live it up in style. A photo of me as Utena exists in my high school Class of 2002 yearbook.

I may not have gone to Ani-Magic, but there were small events that Bianca and Noel invited me to. Broccoli had a storefront opening in Los Angeles with a Kunihiko Ikuhara meet and greet. I was pretty hyped because Kunihiko Ikuhara directed my favorite seasons of *Sailor Moon* and *Revolutionary Girl Utena*. I ended up wearing my Princess Mars cosplay to that event. A few people from Anime Expo hosted a Christmas party in Fullerton called Condensed Milk. I wore my closet cosplay Wolfwood from Trigun to that event. All events allowed me to get to know my local otaku community. My friends from ninth grade had graduated and may have moved forward from anime, but I knew I wasn't alone in Torrance: I had friends with whom I could celebrate my otaku pride.

Staying in contact with convention friends in the early days wasn't as easy as exchanging business cards or scanning a QR code with your socials. In the early '00s, you had platforms like LiveJournal, Blogger, or EZBoard to stay in touch. There was no central hub. You kinda had to know everyone's online alias to follow and stay in touch. You had to make sure you had a pen and paper to jot down a new friend's email address and AOL Instant Messenger name. We followed each other to stay in touch and to keep up with one another's lives in between conventions. This wasn't a numbers game to see who had the most friends. At first, I had a Blogger account. I made my own website layout and added coding to have a comments and interactive section. I tailored my Blogger design theme to Madonna's "Take a Bow." My Blogger account was another personal website—I would journal about my daily life and my favorites were listed on the right-hand panel so new friends from conventions could get to know me.

And once the community began migrating to LiveJournal, I continued my blogging shenanigans over there. My first username was soletta_orihime from Sakura Taisen. I had a basic LiveJournal account with a handful of custom icons to match my mood. I could use tags to let people know what my interests were. I could also make private posts for my friends' eyes only if I wanted to make things more personal. I could even mention what song I was listening to when I posted so people could gauge the mood I was in as I composed a happy, introspective, or emotionally fraught entry.

LiveJournal, AOL Instant Messenger, and EZBoard were the methods I used to keep in touch with friends after conventions. LiveJournal was a platform for talking about my daily life as a high school otaku nerd in cat ears, AOL Instant Messenger allowed me to text with friends in real time, and EZBoard told me where all the upcoming cosplay get-togethers were.

The more I began to socialize in the SoCal cosplay scene, the more I got interested in cosplaying. I didn't consider cosplay a hobby. I considered convention-going my hobby. Cosplay was just a way to enhance the experience at the con. Cosplay was the add-on. Cosplay was the bonus. Cosplay was the icing on the cake. Most of my cosplays were closet projects or commissions. I was hoping to have the opportunity one day to learn how to sew. For me, it was time. Senior year was defined by college applications: I identified colleges with robust media studies programs, theater programs, and anime clubs and focused on my essay about online voice acting and writing and directing my productions. I had a shit SAT score, but damn could I write. In one draft, I wrote about my experience with the online voice acting community as a 15-year-old director, producer, writer, voice actor, and business person and how it tied into my career goals of going into entertainment production. In just one draft, I impressed a lot of my teachers, admissions readers, and scholarship committee members.

I thought to myself: Should I create a separate identity for cosplay? I had Erica the Catholic schoolgirl. I had Victoria the girlboss writer, producer, actress, and director of the voice acting world. Victoria sounded a bit too plain after seeing all the cosplay names that were popping up. It was common for non–Japanese folks to adapt a Japanese or anime-inspired online handle. At the time, it was seen as common practice since we were all anime fans and we were taught to never reveal our real names online, especially if we were minors. Plus, I liked the idea of being immersed in a new identity in a space outside of real life.

I came up with the online name Nadeshiko Gatsby. Nadeshiko was synonymous with a simple, quiet elegance. It was also the name of a flower. I wasn't just another Rose or Daisy. I just read *The Great Gatsby* in 11th grade, and I was in love with the aesthetic and sounds of the Jazz Age. My cosplay persona would be defined by demure beauty with the sounds of a vintage gramophone. Every cosplay forum I was on, I signed off as Nadeshiko Gatsby. The vibe of the cosplay community was different from the voice acting community. We were still theater nerds who wanted to take it to the next level, but the cosplayers I met came from all walks of life—university students, researchers, high school students, retail workers, etc.

I attended a few local cosplay events. Anime Expo hosted a post-convention summer in Orange County. We also had an event called J-Con that celebrated the January birthdays of local cosplayers. It was held in Little Tokyo at Curry House—it seated all 30 of us. This was the first time I really got to meet other cosplayers in my area outside of a convention. We were all cosplaying at Curry House. I wore a very last-minute Yuri cosplay from *Wedding Peach*. It was just my high school uniform with a red ribbon added. I already had some red in my hair. So why not? I met my Team Rocket friends from Anime Expo's masquerade again. Iris, the Jessie cosplayer, was asking me how I was doing on my college applications. I excitedly told her I had received four acceptance letters from California state universities. She was very excited for me. Of course, being that this was Curry House, I had my first taste of Japanese curry. I was enamored. I didn't know where to find a Japanese curry place in my neck of the woods; most of the Japanese places specialized in sushi and udon. This immediately became my favorite restaurant in Los Angeles. Anytime I was near downtown Los Angeles, I made sure to go there for dinner—one tropical iced tea and menchi katsudon at very spicy.

J-Con was labeled as a "Who's Who of the SoCal Cosplay Scene." Yet, I didn't see it that way. I was a high school senior who just wanted to meet other cosplayers and nerd out over anime and manga outside of an anime con. And I didn't want to wait for the next Anime Expo to do so. I didn't want to wait another six months to be in my happy place and indulge in anime. We ended up singing karaoke at the nearby Japanese mall. This was my first time going to a karaoke place with a private room. I was so used to the Christmas parties my parents took me to where everything was set in a living room and you had to change the laserdisc if you wanted to sing a different song. This place had Japanese songs; we sang L'arc-en-Ciel, Hikaru Utada, and Ayumi Hamasaki. Yet, to take a break from J-pop and J-rock, we busted out the occasional 'N Sync and ABBA. While I was happy I had my voice acting community in the online universe, it was nice to have cosplay friends in my own backyard all over Southern California.

I found ways to add cosplay to my daily life. Every day I wore my school uniform. Why not add cat ears to it and carry around a cat plush with me to pretend she was my magical cat friend? You would call this a cringe era, but this was an era where showing off my anime pride was also my mental armor. It was my protective bubble. I wasn't going to be afraid of being who I was. I did not have to be the shy girl who hid in classrooms. I could be the me I liked seeing at anime cons—Victoria, the girl in the white ball gown getting her photo taken covered in eleganza and beauty. Every morning, I put on my school uniform—black pleated skirt, white button-up, black cardigan, black knee-high socks, black Mary Janes—and topped it off with a set of black cat ears.

At one point during senior year, I wore my hair in two buns like Chun-Li in *Street Fighter* because I thought it would look cute with my school uniform. While most Catholic school students lament wearing a uniform on a daily basis, I rocked that pleated skirt and white button-up, invested in black thigh-high socks and a cardigan, and lived my best anime main protagonist life. I wanted to bring that energy to every day. I wanted to write my own shōjo story in my last year of high school. I was gonna live my best life in a school uniform and cat ears. I didn't want to have to hide who I am.

The more invested I got into the local cosplay community in Southern California, the more I was shifting from auditioning for online voice acting projects and discovering and learning more about cosplay. I was reading and catching up on Fansview with every new con Kevin Lillard was visiting each weekend. I was learning about new cons across the country each week—Katsucon, Ohayocon, Otakon, and more. Kevin would capture as many cosplayers as he could. I loved seeing them all. The joy of Kevin Lillard's photos is that he took photos of everyone and made a clear effort in doing so. It didn't matter if you were a beginner or a seasoned cosplayer, if you thrifted or raised the sheep to make your fabric, Kevin took everyone's photo. He showed that everyone could cosplay. It was encouraging for a newbie like me seeing cosplayers of all skill levels. I didn't feel alone in sourcing many of my cosplays from my closet. The pictures gave me inspiration for my next project.

It was through religiously checking Fansview every weekend that I learned about more out-of-state cons. I learned about Katsucon. A few of my Chicagoland friends attended Katsucon in the Washington, D.C., metro area. I was excited whenever I saw Kevin capture their photos. Otakon was the other large anime convention in Baltimore. I was persuaded to check it out, but I wanted to wait until I had more financial freedom outside of the allowance and maintaining a high grade point average to check out one of the best anime conventions. My friends from Anime Central were also singing Otakon's praises. I knew that had to be my next convention once I had the money. Fansview was my mirror to fandom nationwide.

I loved seeing everyone's cosplays and the articles Kevin was posting during the convention weekend. You felt like you were there even if you were at your computer in the comfort of your home.

And I discovered cosplay-specific websites online. There were two prominent ones—American Cosplay Paradise and Cosplay Lab. These were databases where you could keep track of your cosplays and what conventions you had worn them to. Most seasoned cosplayers at the time created their own websites and invested in their own domain names and had bulletin board communities through EZBoard where they could build communities and discuss cosplay plans. If you didn't have time to create a website, you could create a free account on either of these websites and you could create your very own profile under your cosplay alias. You could organize all your cosplay photos over at American Cosplay Paradise. Cosplay Lab was a very helpful resource, but they only allowed one photo per cosplay entry. A lot of us used the same strategy to circumvent this rule: make a digital collage of several cosplay photos into one image to upload.

"Are you going to Anime Central this year?" Sora, my Chicagoland cosplay partner in crime, asked.

I was wondering about that too. At the time, I was also interested in someone I had met at Anime Expo 2001. He had the good looks of Russell Wong from the film adaptation of *The Joy Luck Club*. He was soft-spoken, albeit on the shyer side, and both of us were generally into the same fandoms. We liked CLAMP, and I was curious to learn more about fighting games and he was my guide to it. His name was Mark, and we had made plans to perhaps finally go out on a date at Anime Central 2002.

Did I have to burden my parents again by asking them to send their daughter across the Mississippi? At least now my parents knew that conventions were my weekends of fun. Anime Central 2002 would be my second overnight convention. I made a case to my parents: I did get accepted into four out of the five universities I applied to. I had finally accepted my admission to Sonoma State University. After writing about my experience with the online voice acting community, I ended up getting a scholarship that would cover the cost of attending. Getting a scholarship to cover the cost of my education meant a lot to me. Federal and state financial aid was out of the question. My family was middle class. My parents had a decent income. My brother and I were attending private Catholic schools. However, the cost of going away to university—moving from the South Bay to the San Francisco Bay Area—would be a financial challenge. I wanted to leave my hometown to get that university experience. I wanted a change of pace and scenery. I felt I had reached the end of my South Bay era. I was ready to trade beaches and sunshine for redwoods and morning fog. At least I could be cozy in my leather jacket and beret. This dream would cost my parents approximately $20,000 per school year for a state university education. Even with their income, any financial aid or support would help. Sonoma State had an anime club. They had a communications major and a theater minor where I could be a wild and crazy creative college student. Sonoma State was in Rohnert Park, an hour flight from home. I could finally be independent. More importantly, I had survived senior year. And it was much easier for my dad to be sold on going to Chicago since we had done it the year before.

And just like that, my dad booked us round-trip tickets to go to Chicago. I would be returning to Anime Central at the end of April.

13

Anime Central 2002
Ever Wonder What a Gundam Does in the Hangar?

I was so hyped to see my Chicagoland friends again. We would be reprising our online voice acting panel. Sora and I agreed to cosplay as Princess Neptune and Princess Mars from *Sailor Moon*. I had a few new cosplays to bring to Anime Central.

Bianca and Noel introduced me to *A Little Snow Fairy Sugar*. This was a cutesy children's anime focusing on the adventures of fairies in and old world European town. It felt something Nickelodeon would have shown back in the 1980s: family-friendly and cute. Senior year was stressful: keeping up good grades, completing college and scholarship applications, and enduring the usual high school drama and ennui. To escape all that, the saccharine magical girl anime *A Little Snow Fairy Sugar* became my comfort anime. I liked Pepper because she had dark hair and glasses like me. I then learned about the "meganeko," or the glasses girl archetype. These characters were shy, kind, strong-willed girls who typically had dark hair and wore glasses. The best part was that these characters kept their glasses—they didn't need a makeover to change who they were. The glasses were a part of who they were. This archetype really resonated with me because as a glasses wearer, contacts were consistently suggested to me by my peers. And anytime a fictional character in Western media wore glasses, she immediately needed a makeover to be accepted by the world. I actually did like wearing glasses. I always felt that they were a part of who I was and that I did not need a makeover to change me.

My next cosplay plan for Anime Central 2002 was Yomiko Readman from *Read or Die*. This was a relatively new anime that I discovered at Anime Expo 2001. I had everything in my closet—the skirt, button-up, tie, and vest. Of course, it was the thick black glasses that made the cosplay truly be Yomiko Readman. Sora was working on a masquerade skit for Anime Central–Anime Showdown: *The Slayers* versus *Sorcerer Hunters* with Jimmy coming back as Professor Tomoe to host the standoff between the two fantasy franchises. Sora needed an extra person who could be from a random anime to play the part of the frustrated scorekeeper. I volunteered my Yomiko for this part.

I brought my Princess Mars cosplay that I wore at the homecoming dance. At last, I could finally be my favorite Sailor Senshi in a princess dress at a convention! I didn't really bring many costumes to Anime Central. I just wanted to have a good time with my Chicagoland friends again. I had not seen them in a year.

Anime Central would be in a new location—Rosemont, Illinois. The Hyatt in Rosemont was a luxury hotel, so different from the simple Sheraton in Arlington Heights. When you stepped into the Hyatt, you were surrounded by hanging gardens. It was almost like you were stepping into a fantasy. You were stepping into a palace with hanging plants all around you. An anime convention in a luxury resort!

We ran the online voice acting panel again on Friday night. We were given a bigger room. Our format was much more organized and we covered about the same content to an audience that was four times the size of what we had in 2001. I wore a vintage little black dress for this presentation. While I do not recall much from the panel other than that we had the same panelists as the previous year, I do remember that we had a young Laura Post in the audience. Laura Post would eventually join the online voice acting community. She would then go on to be cast as Ahri in *League of Legends* and Queen Nehellenia in *Sailor Moon*.

Anime Central 2002 was also my first time having a date at the convention. I met Mark at Anime Expo 2001. He was wearing a black suit from some CLAMP anime I couldn't figure out right off the bat. As it turns out, a lot of men in CLAMP anime and manga wore suits. In high school, I had a thing for gentlemen in suits. There was something about the maturity and elegance behind it that was different from the blond, spiky-haired skater boys of Torrance. We kissed our "see you soon" on the last day of Anime Expo. It was spontaneous, and after that we had immediate attraction. I had found out he was going to Anime Central, and we decided to finally have a date at the convention.

I was in my Pepper cosplay and we were holding hands as we ambled through the dealers hall. We went out to dinner and went out to the main dance. Even my mom knew we were dating, and she was okay with me dating a polite Asian American gent. My dad was staying at the main hotel in case I needed anything, but I was rooming in a giant suite with my best friends from the voice acting community. The suite had almost 15 people, but it fit us comfortably. We had two queen beds and two couches, and a lot of us—including me—who were okay with sleeping on the floor.

Our group was also in masquerade, so Sora and I were slaving away at the final pieces of her Wing Zero from *Gundam Wing* cosplay. The story of the masquerade skit was that characters from *Sorcerer Hunters* and *Slayers* would face off against one another onstage with Professor Tomoe hosting this battle. The prize would be Wing Zero from *Gundam Wing*. The punchline was Wing Zero dancing to disco at the end of the skit. I would serve as Sora's handler as the stressed-out stage manager, Yomiko Readman, so she could get across the stage in her clunky Gundam mecha suit cosplay.

Sora and I were at the dining room table in the hotel suite getting last-minute parts and pieces of Wing Zero together. I was learning the basics of how to sew at the same time. While Sora was stressing out, I was calm. It was our call time to the stage, and we were waiting in line for our turn. Between stressing out and last-minute rehearsals, I made sure Sora was staying hydrated in her Wing Zero cosplay.

We were near the end of the line for the cosplay contest. There were more than 80 entries for the masquerade. We were entry number 70. We went onstage, and Team *Slayers* and Team *Sorcerer Hunters* each did their thing to show up the other franchise. However, to my surprise, when I went up, the audience started cheering for Yomiko Readman. "The Paper!" several voices from the audience yelled. I didn't know how popular *Read or Die* was. I had only heard about this direct-to-video anime at Anime Expo 2001! I couldn't believe people knew what I was from! I had such a small part and I wanted to support my friends in the cosplay contest even if our skit was a little silly. I had no idea that I would be getting so many cheers for being onstage for several seconds.

"Ever wonder what a Gundam does in the hangar?" I yelled over the "The Paper!" cheers. Sora got into her best John Travolta stance and started dancing to "Staying Alive" to end the masquerade act.

I had not gone in with any expectations, but my team felt down in the dumps when we didn't place in the contest. There were a lot of fun skits that year, such as the Anime Central mascots advertising the importance of hygiene, mecha Godzilla, and a huge *Cardcaptor Sakura* group. The show really stepped up the craftsmanship and creativity game compared to the previous year. Even from the audience, I was floored at the level of cosplay now entering masquerade. People were really stepping it up. However, even with that, performing in masquerade was an honor and award in itself—I got to perform onstage with my best friends and we got to work up the crowd.

I wore Yomiko Readman again on the last day of the convention since it was an easy cosplay to wear on the flight back. I got to spend time with my best friend and went out on a date with someone who liked anime as much as I did. It was a good con.

At the end of the con, Sora said, "Hey.... I'm thinking about going to Anime Expo...!" And my friend Poli asked, "Are you going to Anime Expo? Because I'm thinking about going too!"

More of my Chicagoland friends would be going to my hometown con. Sora and I were seniors in high school. Anime Expo 2002 would be our last summer before going to college. I could not wait to spend the summer after high school with my best friend.

The last weeks of senior year seemed to last forever. I was finally hyped for Anime Expo. I had more friends from Chicago coming along.

I attended my senior class events for formality's sake. While I didn't feel bonded with the Class of 2002, I showed up. I was a wallflower in a turtleneck sweater and short skirt during the senior luau. I resented my parents telling me I should dress according to the Hawaiian theme. They wanted me to fit in more. To be honest, I was looking forward to playing *Dance Dance Revolution* and the new *ParaParaParadise* machine at the mall arcade afterwards. I learned about *ParaParaParadise* at Anime Central. Someone had brought the controllers for this hand motion rhythm game set to *Super Eurobeat*. So when I found out that our local mall got a *ParaParaParadise* machine, I had to get to it every chance I got.

I attended senior prom without a date, but that was okay. I dolled myself up in the most 1930s old Hollywood glamour red carpet realness. Who needs a plus one when you're the spectacle on the red carpet? This look was inspired when I found out that our prom was being held at the Millennium Biltmore Hotel, the original home of the Academy Awards. I needed to look the part. And there I stood in a white dress that draped to the floor and a feathered headdress that screamed Folies Bergère, a mask decked in glitter and rhinestones in one hand. It wasn't cosplay, but I sure felt dolled up for an occasion.

The end of senior year meant the ritual exchange of yearbooks—"See you real soon," "Have a nice summer," and the occasional "Have a nice life."

In my high school yearbook, one of the yearbook staff members took a photo of me cosplaying as Utena during homecoming week. It was a candid shot of me not looking at the camera looking as valiant and noble as Utena. It looked like I was about to take on the student council in a duel vowing to protect my Rose Bride. I signed "I will be a prince!" next to the photo the yearbook team took of my Utena cosplay. Utena was not the only cosplay photo in the Class of 2002 yearbook. Earlier in the year, I was voted "Most Memorable." It always caught me off guard because I never considered myself popular. I was the weird girl who wore cat ears with her school uniform. Yet, next to the title of Most Memorable was me in my Princess Mars cosplay. I was dolled up in red carrying a long-stemmed rose looking regal, my eyes looking away from the camera to a future unknown.

Grad Night was at Disneyland, and I didn't have a clique to hang out with. I played "Ave Maria" at our senior class's send-off liturgical mass. And then we were on our way to the happiest place on earth. I was sitting by myself on the hour-long bus ride over. I had my CD player playing *Para-ParaParadise* music to get me hyped for the night. I did not plan to spend Grad Night with anyone. I rolled solo. I met kids from other high schools. I introduced myself as Victoria from Chicago. It was like I was living my life as Victoria in the real world. It felt empowering to claim the night for myself rather than being unhappy with classmates who didn't want me around. I was even getting all eyes on me when I was playing *Dance Dance Revolution* at the Starcade in Tomorrowland. And yet, on the bus ride back to campus, we drove by the freeway exit to the Long Beach Convention Center. I was feeling melancholy. I wanted to spend this night with my online friends from the voice acting community. I said to myself, "July…. I promise you … everyone…. I'll give you all the warm hugs you deserve." I wanted to be with my friends again. I could only take so much of being someplace where I was not wanted. I could be voted Most Memorable, but I still was not happy.

14

Anime Expo 2002
Like American Graffiti but Anime

I had a much more robust cosplay list for Anime Expo 2002. For Halloween, I had my mother find someone to make me an Eva Friedel from *Memories: Magnetic Rose* costume. Yet, we underestimated how much fabric we would need. It didn't have the "wow" factor I had anticipated. But, I wanted to represent one of my favorite anime movies, *Memories: Magnetic Rose* and have an opportunity to sing the operatic aria of "Un bel dì, vedremo" from *Madame Butterfly* on the spot. I spent a good month teaching myself the song so I could prepare to wear this at Anime Expo. The red opera dress really called to my aesthetic—pure eleganza, a romantic touch of red, and Old World beauty. And I could even use my natural hair for this cosplay!

Of course, Sora and I reran our Utena and Anthy cosplays. I also needed another cosplay for my 18th birthday party on day three. I decided to go with Nadeshiko Kinomoto from *Cardcaptor Sakura*. I was cast in a *Cardcaptor Sakura* fandub as Nadeshiko Kinomoto because of my soft-spoken and sweet voice. Nadeshiko is Sakura's mother, so I could pose with any *Cardcaptor Sakura* cosplayers and call it a family picture. This *Cardcaptor Sakura* production actually did go forward. CLAMP has this thing where they like to draw their characters in a multitude of different outfits. I had my mom find someone to create my Nadeshiko cosplay. I had a Sakura Kinomoto doll that I could carry with me; Sakura was wearing a white and pink dress complete with angel wings. It matched perfectly because I was also wearing angel wings. I also bought wings from the local costume store to give Nadeshiko a much more angelic touch. I mean, she was a dead character, but she was always presented as looking angelic.

And the last cosplay for Anime Expo was my day four cosplay. That was easy. Princess Mars from *Sailor Moon*. I wore Princess Mars to my senior homecoming dance and to Anime Central. I had always wanted to wear a *Sailor Moon*–related cosplay at Anime Expo because there were a lot of *Sailor Moon* cosplayers. The early '00s brought in a lot of folks cosplaying from the *Sailor Moon* musicals. Sora would go as the *Sailor Moon* musical version of Sailor Uranus. She commissioned her Sailor Uranus from Setsuna Kou. The musical versions were special because they were much more ornate versions of the typical Sailor Senshi outfit. They were embellished with sequins and beads. Skirts were fluffier and the outfits seemed to pop. Cosplaying from the musical was en vogue if you were a cosplaying Moonie.

Sora and Poli from Anime Central would be joining me for Anime Expo. I also got word that Lina from Canada would be coming back too. I was overjoyed when my convention senpai, Robert Black, said he would be returning to Anime Expo. I was excited that I had so many friends joining me for the con.

I would be commuting to Anime Expo from my parents' house. Anime Expo was returning to Long Beach. Since Sora and I were entering college the following fall, this was our way to save up some money but make sure we had the best summer ever. Also, what got Sora's parents to agree to send her from Chicago to Los Angeles was that she was staying at my house under my parents' roof. Sora and I made plans not only for Anime Expo but also to go to Disneyland. Since I wanted to be with my online friends at Grad Night, we figured we would go to Disneyland. And since Sora didn't go to her prom, I would find a way to play "Toki ni Ai Wa" from the *Utena* movie so she could have her dance.

And speaking of adolescent rituals, my Uncle Greg kept asking me if I was ever going to have a debutante ball. It's customary for Filipino girls to have a debut once they turn 18. My dad responded, "She doesn't have any barkada." Thanks, Dad. I really needed to be reminded that I didn't have any friends. I had friends online, but I did not have the usual set of Pinay friends who would go to photo studios at the mall and take glamor shots every weekend. I was up all night on voice chat singing karaoke with my friends on iParty. Also, a debutante ball would cost upwards of $3,000. Yes I was on a full-ride scholarship to Sonoma State University, but instinct told me that $3,000 would be better off saved considering that I was moving away for university.

Instead, I suggested to my dad a birthday lunch with my friends from

My best friend, Sora (right), and I at Anime Expo 2002 (Long Beach, CA). We were cosplaying from two different fandoms, but we had fun.

all over the country at Anime Expo. There was a restaurant across the street called the Rock Bottom Brewery. I had gone to this restaurant the previous year, and I really liked their different flavors of pizza. There was something on the menu for everyone. The restaurant could easily accommodate large parties. They also had a unique brand of root beer that they created in-house! I had about 10 or so friends whom I wanted to invite. I would be happier with my 10 closest friends, the 10 closest friends who supported me throughout my crazy life as a fangirl, cosplayer, and online voice actor rather than hundreds of relatives I didn't know.

My dad and I picked up my friends from LAX. Thankfully, we all coordinated to have the same flights arriving and departing. The one guest my friends were so excited to meet was Maria Kawamura. She's best known for being the voice of Naga from *Slayers*. She was the mother of the anime "Ohohohohoho!" laugh. Lina, Sora, and I kept imitating the laugh while we were getting settled at my parents' house. With our evil laughs, we thought we were going to wake the whole neighborhood.

Day one of Anime Expo 2002 was upon us. Lina had more time to hang out with us at the con. This was going to be Sora's first Anime Expo. I was so excited for her. Picking up our badges was not an issue. We missed out on opening ceremonies, but that was okay. Sora and I were looking at panels we wanted to check out, but first, we wanted to dive into that huge dealers room that was the basement of the Long Beach Convention Center.

The fandom vibe of Anime Expo was changing. I saw that more locals were checking out Anime Expo. I even recognized a few friends from high school. At that time, Toonami was taking American audiences by storm. Toonami showed *Gundam Wing, Sailor Moon, Dragonball, Tenchi Muyo, Kenshin*—their programming had truly expanded into different genres of anime. Anime was becoming more and more accessible. It was no longer that niche thing at the video store or on late night TV. Adult Swim was also picking up some steam. Adult Swim brought *Lupin III, Cowboy Bebop,* and *Trigun* to those who were able to stay up late at night. We also had the bonus of uncensored *Gundam Wing*. More and more anime nerds were buying up day badges to sate their curiosity about this anime thing that was taking over Cartoon Network.

The Long Beach Convention Center's exhibit hall was bigger and better than before. Gone was the era of rows of tables and chairs in a large ballroom. Anime Expo was showing off the industry's giants. Pioneer had a huge castle to promote the new *Hellsing* series. Bandai had a booth that showed trailers and had beanbags for anyone who wanted to chill and relax in the area. A.D. Vision's space was like walking into a party. The Texas-based anime company had giant screens showing trailers of upcoming anime and staff on towers firing off the t-shirt cannons.

Anime Expo 2002's dealers hall had more of a trade show feeling than an otaku's shopping mall. It wasn't a bad thing; it just showed you how anime fandom was evolving.

Anime Expo 2002 (Long Beach, CA) line for opening ceremonies. I was cosplaying the opera diva, Eva Friedel, from Satoshi Kon's *Magnetic Rose* in the *Memories* film anthology.

14. Anime Expo 2002

Sora and I were wandering around the dealers hall. It was bigger than ever! We were so overwhelmed at the spectacle that Anime Expo had become that we had to rest up at the Bandai booth with the many beanbag chairs. There's even a candid photo of us on Fansview cuddling as Utena and Anthy at the Bandai booth.

I was hyper focused on advancing in the karaoke contest. I spent most of day one rehearsing "森をぬけて–Born to Love You" from *Mermaid Forest*. I figured that since Anime Expo was four days long, I could meet up with friends on the subsequent days. After all, there was no guarantee that I would make it to the semifinals. I stuck around for a majority of the karaoke contest at the Renaissance Hotel. There were two acts that I actually did enjoy. Someone brought a blow-up doll to serve as a facsimile of Britney Spears. "I would like to dedicate this song to Britney Spears," said the contestant. She sang "The Baka Song" from *Ranma ½* and was throwing down on the blow-up doll like it was the WWE. There was another group that went up and sang a two-part harmony of "Messiah" from *Angel Sanctuary*. And then I found out that I was in the semifinals! Like whoa!

I had two costumes for day two—Utena with Sora's Anthy and Kyoko for the mega SNK versus Capcom annual cosplay meetup. We had more time to seek out friends on day two. We ran into Poli, who was cosplaying from Malice Mizer. She needed help getting into her wings. Sora and I also made sure we had the reservation ready for my birthday party. While my birthday is in August, celebrating it in early July with my closest friends before I made the move to university would be the next best thing.

There was a lot of wandering around Anime Expo on day two. We were supposed to meet up with a friend from high school, Maya, who was cosplaying as Kaoru from *Kenshin*, because she wanted us to join her at the Watsuki panel. Yet, we were running late. Sora and I were hanging out in the lobby and a couple remembered us from Anime Central. They recognized our Utena and Anthy cosplays, and they were surprised to see people who attend Anime Central at Anime Expo. They offered us tickets to the popular Meet the Guests reception!

So, at Anime Expo, there was an event called Meet the Guests. This was a separate ticketed event that would cost an extra $10 to wine and dine with Anime Expo's guests of honor. Sora and I were totally hyped about this. We would get to have appetizers and a cheese platter with Maria Kawamura. We were so lucky to have this opportunity. We were living large and we were barely out of high school. This was the life we were living.

117

Anime Expo 2002 (Long Beach, CA) had an SNK versus Capcom cosplayers meetup. I cosplayed as Kyoko from *Project Justice: Rival Schools* in a cosplay that I pieced together with things from my closet. I happened to run into a Q cosplayer.

We were so lucky to have run into people who remembered us. We scored big with those elusive tickets!

I changed into Kyoko because the SNK versus Capcom cosplayers meetup was right before the Meet the Guests reception. As I was making my way to the lobby, I heard a familiar voice. It was Robert Black! He was trying to get my attention, but it had been two years since we had seen each other face to face. We did stay in touch online, but I was so happy to see my convention senpai again. He was also headed to the reception with the guests of honor. At last, we could finally hang out at an anime convention after so many hours of talking on ICQ.

But first, I had a cosplay meetup to attend. Thankfully, the SNK versus Capcom meetup was steps away from the guest of honor reception. I heard about this meetup from a friend who was one of the people running it. He suggested I cosplay as Kyoko since it was a relatively easy outfit to do. I already had the sweater and short skirt in my closet. My mom, who works at a hospital, hooked me up with a lab coat. I have never been a part of an organized cosplay gathering before. So many people showed up as their favorite fighting game characters. I had to ask random people to use my camera so I could get some photos on my camera too for my con report. As soon as we had our last group pose, I met up with Sora and Robert at the reception with Anime Expo's finest guests at the Hyatt garden downstairs.

I had very little time to spend at Meet the Guests because I was in the karaoke semifinals. Sora, Robert, and I agreed that if there was one guest we all wanted to see together, it was Maria Kawamura of *Slayers* and *Gundam* fame. We indulged in so many appetizers at the reception that we all got our dinner for the evening.

It's very rare to have this interaction with guests at Anime Expo nowadays. People pay more than $100 for a *Love Live* VIP meet and greet and another $100 for floor seats at an idol concert. This was $10 to wine and dine with guests.

Maria Kawamura complimented my Kyoko cosplay. She asked me if I was cosplaying from *Evangelion*. With what Japanese he knew, Robert kindly corrected her that I was cosplaying from *Rival Schools*. I had forgotten that Maria Kawamura played a small part in *Evangelion* as Asuka's mother, who was best known for having a dramatic breakdown the moment she finds out her husband has been cheating on her.

Maria Kawamura talked to us about what it was like working with the legendary Megumi Hayashibara since they played opposites on *Slayers*. They would talk about their food adventures prior to their recording sessions. She gushed about how much she and Megumi were like Naga and Lina in real life.

At this point, I had to leave to prepare for the karaoke semifinals. I would be singing Shina Ringo's punk cover of "I Wanna Be Loved by You" by Marilyn Monroe.

Sora and Robert stuck around to meet another guest, Kōichi Mashimo of the anime studio Bee Train. As the story goes from both Sora and Robert's perspectives, Kōichi was looking to hire people for Bee Train. He said that, to work for Bee Train, all you needed was a passport, a driver's license, and to be in love. Mid-conversation, Kōichi ended up threatening Robert with a spork. We're not sure how that happened, but it was an inside joke that Sora, Robert, and I shared throughout Anime Expo 2002. "Remember when the *Noir* director threatened you with a spork?"

Sora and I spent the rest of the night at the karaoke contest. A boy idol group called Otaku Generation performed one of the songs from *Love Hina* and had a striptease act associated with it. It got a lot of laughs from the audience! We also had USA Musume, a local Morning Musume idol cover group perform in their pastel frilly beach outfits with their producer in a matching Hawaiian shirt and shorts. Someone also did a cover of "First Love" by Hikaru Utada, and I realized I had the sheet music on me for "First Love." Sora and I were very tempted to sing along since this was THE love ballad of anime fangirls who loved J-pop ... and we loved our Hikki! It was a very mellow night enjoying the show. I didn't place into the final round, but I wanted to be supportive of everyone. After the karaoke contest, while we waited for my dad to pick us up, I found an empty piano at the Renaissance Hotel. I took out my sheet music and began to play the chords to "First Love." It was a peaceful and calm way to end day two.

Day three was the big day—I was celebrating My Strange and Unusual Otaku Cotillion. I wasn't really big on having a debutante ball. After all, my dad admitted to my bougie uncle that I didn't have a "barkada," or friends to have a fancy bougie ball with. It was an expectation that Filipino girls from well-off families have a fancy party. I was the only niece on my dad's side of the family, and after my bougie uncle attended his coworker's roommate's uncle's brother's cousin's show horse's daughter's debutante ball, he was very persistent in insisting that I have one too. I just wanted to spend my birthday with my closest 10 friends from across the country who were here for Anime Expo.

Every debutante event needed The Dress. Because I was recently cast as Nadeshiko Kinomoto in a *Cardcaptor Sakura* radio play and I was known for being cast as soft-spoken, sweet, and kind voices, I picked an outfit from the *Cardcaptor Sakura* art book that Nadeshiko wore. At Anime Expo 2001, I wanted to come in looking like a queen. At Anime Expo 2002, I wanted to look like an angelic debutante on my birthday. I wanted to own my 18th birthday. I got tired of what family members thought about how I should look and how my 18th birthday should be. The debutante dress was a cosplay outfit I had custom made. I didn't want to be just any debutante. I wanted to express my love for shōjo manga and anime during my 18th birthday with my

At Anime Expo 2002 (Long Beach, CA) celebrating my debut by cosplaying as Nadeshiko Kinomoto from *Cardcaptor Sakura*. The cosplay was made by a family friend.

best friends from the community. And what girl can say she wore angel wings at her debut?

I told all my friends to meet up at the Hyatt lobby so we could walk together to the Rock Bottom Brewery. Most of my friends came from the online voice acting community. Sora, to keep with the CLAMP theme, wore Umi from *Magic Knight Rayearth*. She was the only one from our original *Rayearth* group who finished the costume. Stephanie, from high school choir, joined us as Duo Maxwell from *Gundam Wing*, her anime husbando, in an outfit she concocted from her closet. It was her first Anime Expo, and we senior kids wanted to show her around. Maya, another friend from high school, wore Kaoru from *Kenshin* in a kimono she picked up from the dealers hall the previous year. Lina wore something from *Cyber*

Part Three. Finding My People

Team in Akihabara. Poli would be in a Malice Mizer outfit. A few of my other online friends joined us, including Allison Rose, one of the first online voice actors who was in the original *Sailor Moon S* fandub that inspired all of us to go into this voice acting hobby.

It was pleasant being seated with all of my friends at the table. I didn't want a grand entrance with some random cousin escorting me to my table. I had all of my online besties from all over the continent with me. These were the people who had supported me the most; I was glad to celebrate a milestone birthday with them. I remember being calm and at peace during my birthday lunch. Allison Rose gave me some soaps and lotion from Williams Sonoma because she knew I was going to Sonoma State in the fall. Stephanie got me a necklace. Robert got me a CLAMP art book because he knew I was a huge fan of the all-girl manga team. The art book featured illustrations from *Wish*. I would later learn that this was their gay *JoJo's Bizarre Adventures* fan fiction if Jotaro was a doctor who fell in love with Kakyoin, but Kakyoin was an angel who fell from the sky. Sora was taking video of the whole party. She had everyone introduce themselves to the camera talking about who they were and how they got into the voice acting community. When we were not eating, we were just having a good time. I was smiling pleasantly because I got to have this day with my closest friends.

Most Filipino girls will have a fancy debutante ball on their 18th birthday. I chose to have a simple lunch at a local brewery with all of my friends all getting to know one another. I got to be with the most important people in my life to that point. The people who made me who I was. They reminded me of what I was capable of, my strengths, and why I was worthy of being loved. I needed them the most while surviving high school. I didn't need 300 family friends I didn't know. I didn't need to learn how to waltz with some random gentleman caller. I was with my friends and that was enough.

A friend gave me tickets to the masquerade for my birthday present. I wasn't planning on seeing the cosplay contest. I knew tickets were hard to come by since people were lining up for it in the wee morning hours. I have never seen a masquerade or a cosplay contest from the audience point of view. I was always performing onstage. Yet, I was very excited to see one of the biggest and best cosplay contests later that evening. It was like going to the opera!

Right after we were done with my birthday lunch, Robert wanted to check out some of the voice acting panels that were happening. Sora, Maya, and I were interested in the Voice Actors Roundtable panel featuring Maria Kawamura and Crispin Freeman. Sora and I may have met Maria the day before, but how often did we get to see her? And she was the guest we wanted to see.

Maria Kawamura showed up to her panel in a lime green kimono with her hair done up. Crispin Freeman followed wearing Alucard from *Hellsing* to promote his new role in the English dub. Maria did a few of Naga's lines and a laugh for the audience and then talked about dancing with a Naga cosplayer at Katsucon earlier in the year. Maria also talked about her Japanese dub work for Western productions. She was also the voice of Tanya from *An American Tail: Fievel Goes West*. She even sang the Japanese version of "Dreams to Dream."

A few other voice actors joined the table. We had Amanda Winn-Lee, voice of the stoic and melancholy Rei Ayanami from *Evangelion*. She was talking about "The Rei Ayanami Sex Tape," which consisted of 20 minutes of silence followed by Rei asking, "Are you done yet?" I don't think I attended a voice actor roundtable that also included the Japanese voices. However, as we were ending the sub versus dub war with the advent of dual audio DVDs, seeing talented folks talking about their experiences behind the booth and their inside jokes was a refreshing change from debating if the original voices or the English voices were superior.

Masquerade at Anime Expo was a huge deal. Every year, cosplay contestants were stepping up their game. We're very thankful to view old cosplay contest videos online now, but before then, all we had were photos from Fansview, Lionel Lum, and whoever else took photos of the contest. The Long Beach Terrace Theater was a beautiful venue to see the cosplay cavalcade. I was in my fancy Nadeshiko Kinomoto cosplay, the angelic debutante.

Sora, Maya, and Stephanie did their own thing. Stephanie wanted to see more of Anime Expo. Maya wanted to watch more anime and wanted to learn more about *Slayers* after meeting Maria Kawamura at the panel. *Slayers* was playing in the video rooms. Maya and Sora ended up binging a few episodes. I was making my way to the Long Beach Terrace Theater for a night at the masquerade.

The show started off with a duo of *Final Fantasy* cosplayers playing anime music on the cello and violin. I did see this string duo around the con busking for spare change playing anime music outside the dealers hall. I learned that they were Ramen and Rice, a cosplay music act from the San Francisco Bay Area. When I saw them live, I was instantly a fan. I wanted to know where I could get a CD of their string arrangements of anime and video game music. A taiko act also helped to open up the cosplay show.

The show was hosted by the epaulet-obsessed Matt Greenfield. He wore a fancy and decorated military uniform onstage. He had the fanciest epaulets. The ADV head honcho kept us entertained from cosplay act to act. Memorable masquerade performances included a rapping Gundam, a Gundam that went onstage and fell apart to "YMCA," a giant robot project made completely from Tupperware, an *Ah! My Goddess!* chorus, *Fruits Basket* hijinks, full-on *Jin-Roh* armored suits, and *Final Fantasy* cosplayers dancing to Michael Jackson's "Thriller." This was an anything-goes sort of show. I was seeing some of the top tier cosplayers from the world compete on the main stage. It was truly a night at the opera. I had my birthday in the daytime, and it was nice to conclude it with a display of the world's best cosplayers entertaining the thousands of us at the Long Beach Terrace Theater.

It was the last day of Anime Expo 2002. Sora and I would soon go off to college. I would be going to Sonoma State. She would be going to Northern Illinois University. I had promised Sora one thing. I would make up her high school prom for her. I didn't have a music player on me, but I sang "Toki ni Ai Wa" from *Utena* to her, and we proceeded to badly waltz in the Hyatt lobby. We weren't even cosplaying as Utena and Anthy. I was dressed up as Princess Mars and she was Lina Inverse.

Maya, Sora, Lina, and I went down to the dealers hall one more time. However, to avoid the line into the dealers hall, Maya and Sora discovered a secret elevator to get in. Skipping the line that wrapped around the building, we ended up doing our final shopping and browsing. We ran into some of our friends on the last day to say our "see you real soon," yet for many of these friends Anime Expo 2002 day four would be the last time I would see them. I wouldn't be going to Otakon that year. Anime Central 2003 was up in the air depending on my university schedule.

Maya, Sora, Lina, and I took one group picture by the *Initial D* display outside of the convention center. This would later be the cover photo for the Anime Expo 2002 TikTok video.

Yet our day wasn't over.

I wanted to take Sora and Lina, the non-locals, to Mitsuwa Marketplace in Torrance. This was the place where I was introduced to the original Japanese *Sailor Moon* manga and rented the original *Sailor Moon* anime. There was a new store in the small Japanese mall called Mandarake that supplied manga, plushies, anime laserdiscs ... and they happened to have a sale that if you filled up a box of manga, it was all yours for $10.

All four of us went buck wild and picked up as much manga as we could. This was otaku Christmas. I was raiding the josei section looking for all the Chiho Saitō manga. Maya was looking for shōnen manga. Sora and Lina were just happy to be in otaku heaven and filling it with whatever they found pretty.

We had four boxes filled with manga. Sora and Lina had to figure out how they were going to take it back to their homes.

We concluded this epic summer with a trip to Disneyland. We also had a few of my local Californian friends join us. Sora and Lina had not been to Disneyland prior and they were in for a treat! And while I made up prom for Sora, my friends made up Grad Night for me. I couldn't have asked for a better weekend to have before starting university.

It was bittersweet saying farewell to Lina and Sora. My dad and I dropped them off at the airport. It was a long week in Los Angeles for Lina and Sora. We gave our hugs and hoped to see each other soon.

Sora did take video of Anime Expo 2002 on her camcorder. She was hoping to create another convention music video as she did with Anime Central 2001 to "Crash and Burn" by Savage Garden. This time, she was going to use "Only Time" by Enya. However, because moving away to college was going so fast, we didn't have a chance to exchange tapes.

Our experience at Anime Expo 2002 was the stuff fond teenage memories are made of. My friends were all with me. I had the best gal pals anyone could ask for. We gave our cringey fangirl selves free rein. Maya was super excited for *Inuyasha* and was covered in all her brand new *Inuyasha* merchandise during Anime Expo. Sora was documenting her first time at Anime Expo and was excited to meet everyone from the online communities we had engaged in. Lina was glad to be back and network with people in the animation industry. And I was simply happy to be with my friends. If our story were a movie, the ending credits would roll to "All Summer Long" by the Beach Boys and you would see our portraits and find out what happened to each of us next. Thankfully, no one died in Vietnam.

15

San Diego Comic-Con
Do I Belong Here?

My collection of convention reports was growing. I was using a free online hosting provider to host my website. I was adding more pictures, more media. I was going to need a website that could hold more content and space for Scarlet Rhapsody. That summer, I registered my domain, www.scarlet-rhapsody.com. Scarlet Rhapsody would be the name of the website. I would brand my convention reports under "Traveling," named after the Hikaru Utada hit of that year. "Traveling" was a whimsical song that took your brain on a whimsical trip. It was the exact kind of journey I associated with conventions. "Traveling" became the name of my growing collection of convention reports. I finally had a credit card, and I wasn't afraid to use it on maintaining Scarlet Rhapsody.

Bianca approached me to ask if I wanted to join her at San Diego Comic-Con for a day. Wait ... San Diego Comic-Con? The OG of all cons?! It was just for a day, and I was curious to check it out. Bianca was in masquerade, and I'd heard great things about the San Diego Comic-Con. I did have time before going up to Wine Country to check out the convention everyone talked about.

Bianca and her friend, John, picked me up from my house early on a July Saturday morning. I wasn't sure what to cosplay as. I had a new Karen Kasumi from *X/1999* cosplay that was pieced together by hitting up a cheap dress store in Carson and a veil that was made from scrap fabric from Nadeshiko. I also had Kyoko from *Rival Schools*. I brought both because I was not sure how well anime would be received.

You see ... most of my fandoms had been Japanese anime–related. My world had been anime-related: pastel backgrounds, expressive eyes, with a city pop vibe. This would be the first time I would be attending a pop culture event with Western focus. I did like *Star Wars* in middle school when the special editions came out, and I liked reading the books. I would even ditch PE and sneak into the chapel to read the Thrawn trilogy. Yet, I vibed so much more with Japanese anime than anything Western between middle school and the end of high school.

It was a two-hour drive from Carson to downtown San Diego. When we parked, I changed into Karen Kasumi to see if that would have any reception. Bianca already had her badge ready for Comic-Con because she was in masquerade. I had to pick up my one-day badge. I stood about an hour in line to buy and pick up my badge. It was a long line, but at least it was moving. It was still early in the morning, so there was no sun beating down on me.

I spent most of my one day at Comic-Con on the exhibit hall floor as Karen Kasumi. I was wondering if I belonged there because I felt lost amidst Western pop culture. While I had a surface level appreciation for much of it, it was too overwhelming and a sensory overload. Wearing an art book version of Karen Kasumi was too obscure for Comic-Con. I decided to change into Kyoko from *Rival Schools*. At least video games tend to be universal.

I did like seeing cosplayers from things outside of anime. One of the pet peeves from my friend group at cons was non-anime cosplay at anime conventions. When Anime Expo worked with the charity City of Hope and the tables the organization set up across the convention in hopes of raising money were manned by *Star Wars* cosplayers, a few of my friends snickered, "Don't they have their own con for that? Why are they here?" A lot of them also questioned seeing Disney cosplayers at anime cons. Of course, this would change within a few months with the release of *Kingdom Hearts*.

San Diego Comic-Con 2002 had significantly fewer cosplayers. There were a few anime cosplayers who braved San Diego Comic-Con. If you were cosplaying from *X-Men* or *Star Wars*, you would get immediate attention. The quality of cosplay at San Diego Comic-Con was unreal. It was as if people stepped out of the movies and rolled up to the convention. This was so different from the mundane garb of school uniforms, suits, karate gis, CLAMP ball gowns and froufrou dresses, and store-bought kimonos I saw at anime conventions. I felt sorry for two *Magic Knight Rayearth* school uniform cosplayers who were wandering, so I had to get a photo of them to make them feel that they were seen and appreciated.

The other culture shock with San Diego Comic-Con was that people would snap your photo and go. Photographers didn't ask permission. This made me feel uncomfortable. At anime cons, the norm was to ask.

It just seemed rude and off-putting that photographers would randomly come up to you, snap a photo, and then leave without saying a thing. Additionally, when I was taking photos for my blog, a few cosplayers from Western media thought I wanted photos with them as if they were Disneyland mascot characters. I just wanted single portrait shots for documentation.

The dealers hall was bigger than Anime Expo. If I had to guess, it was about four times the size. I ended up getting some James Bond merchandise. Also, I had no idea that San Diego Comic-Con was also named "Comic-Con International." I decided to play a game to see if I could find Filipino *Komiks* such as Darna in the dealers hall. How international was the merchandise selection? Alas, no Darna to be found.

After so much walking around, John and I were seated for the masquerade. Bianca would be in a *Sailor Moon*–themed skit where she was cosplaying as Black Lady. It was a *Sailor Moon* skit that was a crossover with Top 40 hits of the time. It was almost like a sequel to the *Sailor Moon*/'N Sync crossover I saw at Anime Expo 2001.

The San Diego Comic-Con masquerade was different. It was held in a huge ballroom on the second floor of the massive San Diego Convention Center. The danger and anxiety of performing at San Diego Comic-Con is that you needed to WOW the audience. You couldn't just show up in a costume and randomly dance onstage or perform in a skit that you made up on the spot the night before. That would not fly here. Comic-Con had a professional feel to it. You could actually get booed offstage if the audience didn't think you were good enough.

There were some very interesting skits—*Star Wars* and *Lord of the Rings* crossover, a random belly dance group, *SpongeBob SquarePants*, etc. It felt like this was anything goes with pop culture or if you had an original design. What stuck out to me the most is that people had long introductions that detailed who and what the characters and source materials were. At anime convention masquerades, intros were simple—character name and source and cosplay performer name.

Don't get me wrong. I loved being entertained. Yet, as someone who loved cosplay contests for the sake of performing in front of an audience, San Diego Comic-Con's stage really made me anxious to ever go up. I was floored and impressed by the level of costuming presented. And the audience was not kind to a few entrants. I recall a few acts getting booed offstage. I recall a few anime acts and how the Western pop culture–centric audience showed their confusion through silence. Despite anime coming to Cartoon Network, anime was still a stranger in this space.

15. San Diego Comic-Con

Thankfully, I was in good company. I was hanging out with some very well-known cosplayers in the community. I was sitting with *Sailor Moon* cosplay group Sailor Jamboree and convention photographer Lionel Lum while enjoying the show. I got to make new friends with these local cosplay legends as we were watching the show.

Bianca, John, and I left as soon as the masquerade was over. We packed up the car and made the two-hour drive back to the South Bay. On the ride home, I began to question if I felt at "home" at San Diego Comic-Con the way I felt at "home" at an anime con. Because I was more into anime media, I felt like a curious tourist. I had a good time at Comic-Con. I liked seeing the massive dealers hall. I liked seeing fandoms of all kinds. I was willing to learn and keep an open mind, but so much of the culture of San Diego Comic-Con 2002 was so off-putting that it didn't matter if I didn't go to Comic-Con again. I didn't like how anime was treated like black sheep of fandom. It just showed me that Comic-Con was not for me. While I liked seeing the cosplays from so many different fandoms, the photography culture was so strange to me. The amount of photographers taking photos without permission felt invasive. A photographer would just sneak a photo and walk away. Had they asked, I would have struck a pose rather than looking off as I was waiting in line for a pretzel. I was not sure if this would be a convention worth my time. At least then.

August was approaching fast. Soon it would be time to make the move from Carson to Sonoma State.

16

Cosplay Community Before Social Media

LiveJournal, Blogger, and the occasional AOL Instant Messenger kept us in contact after the con. LiveJournal and Blogger kept us posted with our day-to-day lives. AOL Instant Messenger allowed us to text back and forth on our personal computers. Mobile phone–enabled texting on the go was not a thing back then among teenagers. I had older friends with mobile phones, but you had to pay extra to call or text. It was not cost efficient back then. To stay in touch, having access to an internet connection and accounts on these services was essential. To text on AOL Instant Messenger, you had to be in front of your desktop computer. I always had a notebook with me to jot down everyone's contact information after the con so I knew how to contact friends when the convention was over.

When it came to posting cosplay photos, we had EZBoard and our personal blogs to share what photos we took of ourselves or our friends. However, digital cameras weren't as common as they are now. We were limited in how many shots we had on our cameras. I was very picky about what photos I wanted to take when I was still using film. Most of it was photos of me with cosplayers whom I admired. Some of us were thrifty and opted for disposable cameras. Disposable cameras would give you 24 photos. I knew friends who bought multiple disposable cameras to capture their weekend cosplay shenanigans. I had a film camera that held 24 shots. I always brought four rolls of film with me to every con so I could get some nice cosplay shots of friends and cosplayers I liked. After the convention, my parents would take me to the grocery store to develop my film. I could get my photos developed within a day. I was always excited to receive my photos and see how they had turned out.

And if we had access to a digital scanner, we would scan our developed photos and then upload them to our message forums and boards or on a website to share with the world. Sometimes, it would take a month to see photos from a convention go up. That's why websites like Fansview were so important. Kevin Lillard would upload his digital photos in real time as the convention was happening. He was one of the early adopters of digital camera work. If you weren't at the con, you would tune into his website and see his work being uploaded on the day of.

And when it came to talking about the convention—if you cheered or jeered it—forums were the way to discuss if you liked or had gripes about your experience. On EZBoard, you could read how people really felt about Anime Expo's long lines and crowd control, their annoyance with the Long Beach location, their personal experiences good and bad. Yet, you didn't read the Anime Expo online forums for constructive feedback, you read them for the gossip, you read them for the drama that was going down. You wanted to read about people's bad con experiences even if the drama was no fault of the con. You just had to make sure you had a bag of popcorn ready while you read.

A lot of our ways to connect were scattered. A lot of our ways to talk about conventions were all over the place. A lot of our ways to collect and document photos were not quite centralized. You kinda had to know who the bloggers and photographers were covering conventions. Yet, during the summer of 2002, a revolutionary website debuted that would bring the cosplay community together: Cosplay.com.

Cosplay.com became the central hub for cosplay and convention discussion. The EZBoards we had personally set up, along with the domains and websites we had created, slowly became virtual ghost towns. We abandoned free web hosting sites like Angelfire, Tripod, and GeoCities and our personalized domains and dot coms to be a part of this centralized website. We had a free space to share our cosplay photos and discuss our upcoming convention plans. Cosplay.com had an international scope. I was only familiar with the cosplayers from the East Coast, Midwest, and California coast because of my travels. I would only hear about popular cosplayers like Tristen Citrine, Honey Chan, Yaya Han, or Jez Roth through convention coverage pieces by Eurobeat Kasumi or Fansview. Cosplay.com brought us all to one place to congregate and interact online.

Cosplay.com allowed us to keep track of our costumes. I could finally have a place where I could post multiple photos of my cosplay. While I did have my website to document and list what cosplay I had done, this was an easier and much more streamlined way to post multiple photos of the same costume providing descriptions. Cosplay.com made it easier to view all my friends' cosplays.

Cosplay.com also allowed you to upload photos taken at conventions. A lot of photographers ended up migrating to cosplay.com to post their photos once they went digital. Plenty of new cosplay photographers also went in this direction instead of opting for a personalized website. This was a centralized way to find your photos online. I still planned on keeping my website as it was so I could have control of my convention photos. I liked the freedom of having my personal website. I still enjoyed designing layouts and themes for my convention reports. I had built a reputation of being the fangirl who writes convention reports themed to music that fits the vibe of my experience. I wanted to keep that reputation as the quirky, musically inclined anime convention journalist. I did not see myself as a cosplay photographer; I saw myself as a community commentator.

Cosplay.com had its upsides and its downsides. I loved that we had a singular place to upload photos, keep track of costumes from all fandoms, and organize cosplay meetups if we were from the same series. I honestly missed the spontaneity of people from the same fandom randomly running into each other, but plotting cosplay gatherings and meetups also did help me prioritize what cosplays to bring to cons. I could go to the Anime Central section on Cosplay.com and look for *Sakura Taisen* or *Sailor Moon* meetups and plan my cosplay accordingly. I felt that I could prioritize my cosplay list far in advance, and it gave me more motivation to know that I would be meeting up with people from the same fandom.

The downsides involved ... well, the ugly side of the community. Cosplay.com's online forums, while a great space to organize cosplay groups, share and gather resources for costume making, and share photos, had forums to discuss topics outside of the cosplay community. If you wanted to share anime memes, talk about favorite movies, share your excitement about the next *Lord of the Rings* and *Harry Potter* movies, it was all in the off topic forums. Yet, the off topic forums also exposed the toxic side of the community. "Serious Discussion" was a forum to discuss just that— politics, current events, personal issues, etc. For context, Cosplay.com was created in a post–9/11 world. Feelings about countering terrorism were divided. I came away from a thread about the impending war on Afghanistan thinking that we cosplayers were ill equipped to talk about geopolitical issues. We didn't have the information from different platforms to discuss political issues. The web was a mess of information. Additionally, it was hard to talk about racial equality; there was a thread about Black History Month and, of course, all the non–Blacks chimed in with "Where's my history month? Shouldn't we all be equal?" It was easy to be silenced if you were a minority. There was also a considerable amount of acephobia, even before the term "ace" was coined. A thread about a cosplayer not really caring for having sexual relations with anyone degenerated into a cis straight male pressuring femmes who expressed the same sentiment to explain why they didn't for sex. Seeing this unfold in real time made me uncomfortable about sharing anything personal about myself online. I felt comfortably open about being queer and open about bullying and exclusion in my real life with the voice acting community. Yet, this was a larger community. I had to keep my personal life on the down-low. I wanted people to see me as a creative community contributor. I had value to add with my convention reports. I had always believed that the anime convention world was a safe place for people who did not belong. Yet, seeing community members express their ugly side online had me second-guessing.

I just then started using Cosplay.com for its functional purpose—uploading photos, sharing photos and convention reports, and checking in if there was a cosplay gathering or meetup at a convention. I was even able to find someone to create my *Sakura Taisen* cosplay on Cosplay.com. I wanted to go with a new seamstress this time. I wasn't on the website for constructive criticism of cosplay that I had not made or had to shop for. I knew that people could get very nitpicky about accuracy. There were Live-Journal communities that had posted unwarranted cosplay critique, and it was not nice at all. Some people were looking for excuses to be bullies in our spaces in the guise of constructive criticism.

Even the early cosplay days were not free from judgment, bullying, or exclusion. My friend group from online voice acting looked down on Sakura Kinomoto and Syaoran Li cosplayers over the age of 12. "They're too old. These should only be saved for little kids." I shrugged. I wanted to cosplay as Sakura in her pink cat girl outfit at a con, but I didn't want to deal with the heavy judgment of my friend group. "Some cosplayers have no shame," a few would say if they saw an overweight cosplayer in a skimpy Faye Valentine–like outfit or any conventionally attractive femme wearing next to nothing. I shrugged it off. I didn't say anything. I felt cosplay was for everyone, but I also did not want to start drama among my friend group. That was the general rule in the cosplay community—keep your head down and don't start drama. Even if you felt you were wronged, stay silent. Don't start anything. Sadly, this was the social norm in the cosplay community. I saw this message repeated on community forums and blog posts and mentioned in conversation at conventions and cosplay meet ups. No one liked someone who started drama.

134

There were public forums that shamed cosplayers. I tried to avoid the energy from those online sites because I did not want bullies to kill my enjoyment of the hobby. I recall one online community that would anonymously roast and speak ill of cosplayers if they did not make their outfit from scratch. People would comment on said public forum providing more negativity than the community needed. A lot of discussions on Cosplay. com would have "Cosplay however you like, but know you'll have more respect if you make your own cosplays." When I was learning to sew much later on after I graduated from university, a friend from the Lolita fashion community asked me, "Isn't part of cosplay making your own shit?"

I didn't have a lot of access or time to make my own costumes. As a high school student, with a limited budget, my biggest projects were birthday presents made by either my mom's friend or Setsuna Kou. Anime clothes were mundane, so I had to use what I could find in my closet or at the cheap dress store next to the Albertsons or whatever Forever 21 had on sale. I didn't think what I did was the wrong way to cosplay. Yet, seeing discussion of how it was preferred for cosplayers to make their own costumes from scratch, even if you just wanted to walk around the convention and just be the character you love, got to me a lot. I didn't think I was anything special because my cosplays were commissioned or found items in my closet or at stores. I just felt another face in the crowd unworthy of any praise. The image of me as a debutante cosplayer from Anime Expo faded. While I admired cosplay creators and seamstresses, it felt very belittling to be told that I was not enough because I hired others to make my costumes or I thrifted parts and pieces from secondhand and vintage stores.

17

Wine Country University

Before moving away to university, I said farewell to the online voice acting community. I was on my way to Sonoma State University. Sonoma State was one hour north of San Francisco in the heart of Wine Country. I wanted to focus my creative production and dramatic performance energy as a theater minor and a media studies major. The online voice acting community was getting bigger and much younger. I left it to the next generation to lead the way for fandubbing, parody dubs, and fan fiction radio plays. After all, I was assigned to a dorm room with two roommates. I didn't think I would have time or privacy to record lines as frequently as I did in high school. I was going to focus on my studies, making new friends, and getting to know the San Francisco Bay Area anime community. Friends told me how vibrant the Bay Area was for anime fandom. I was excited to be a part of it. I made friends at Anime Expo from the Bay Area. I felt I already had a built-in network of support in university. I was told that your university experience defines your adult friendships for the rest of your life. With a circle of nerdy anime compatriots waiting for me in the Bay, I was ready to make lifetime friendships.

I had to pick and choose what cosplays I was going to bring with me to the dorm. I kept it to about five. I wrote down what conventions were coming up. There were a handful of small anime events in San Francisco's Japantown. Of course, I was very excited to return to every California cosplayer's favorite convention in October, Ani-Magic in exotic Lancaster. Ani-Magic would likely be my next convention. One of my friends from the Queer Kids Table at Anime Expo 2000 offered a ride down from Wine Country to Lancaster. Funny enough, my first anime convention in university would have me taking a road trip back to Southern California.

My dorm wasn't like most university residence halls. It was a full-on apartment-style dorm with plenty of closet and storage space. My roommates gave me the coat closet to store all my cosplay things. I could store my garment bag, a few wigs, and my suitcase. My section of the dorm room was covered in anime posters and wall scrolls. I had a few anime figurines on my desk. I had my small collection of DVDs on my bookshelf. I was happy to be able to claim my nerdy space in the dorm room that I was sharing with two people who didn't mind me showing my otaku side.

I also needed a job to support my expensive hobbies of convention going and cosplay. Before I even stepped on campus, I interviewed for a food services job at Sonoma State. I was offered an assistant cook position at the quick service campus restaurant, The Commons. I learned how to make gourmet wraps, soups, salads, cake, and burgers, and enjoyed a steady flow of part-time income. And as a cheap college student, I could not say "no" to free food. I dined on Greek wraps and potato salads on days when I did not feel like having university dorm food.

Sonoma State had a predominantly white student body in the early '00s. When picking colleges, I did not take diversity into account. I didn't think it would matter at the time because I figured everyone who went to college had an understanding that equality and diversity is important. After all, didn't you have to learn all that in high school at one point or another? You would eventually learn that everyone is equal and all that stuff. Boy I was naive! I knew I was wrong the moment I set foot in the "No Place for Hate" club meeting. "I'm tired of people having to call my family racist. Some of us were actually nice to our property during the Civil War!" said a white freshman. I had to peace the hell out. I didn't feel comfortable that Black folks were still deemed as property by people my age. No one called them out for it.

I became an active member of the anime club and Asian American Students Association. I was happy to know that a few people on my floor were into anime. Shelly, my roommate, was into *Gravitation* and *Inuyasha*. She didn't consider herself a hard-core otaku; she just enjoyed anything cute. Momo was all about creating fan art, boys love, gothic Lolita, and J-pop. I also met Layla, a freelance writer for *Animerica*. I was surprised! Someone from *Animerica* was a student on my college campus. I was happy that I was surrounded by anime nerds. The first semester, I ended up dating two different otaku gents. I was happy that the dating pool in university included anime nerds who loved anime as much as I did. My high school didn't have any of that! I dated Ronan, who was really into live action role play and started the LARP club on campus. He also attended San Diego Comic-Con cosplaying as Captain America. I had no framework of Marvel at the time. Ronan also introduced me to anime music videos. He had a whole folder on his desktop dedicated to anime music videos. While I had seen a few anime music videos at anime conventions, this was an entire library of anime music videos I'd never seen! His favorites were comedy anime music videos from *Trigun* and *Cowboy Bebop*. Many of our date nights consisted of watching anime music videos into the early morning hours.

I started dating Eddie from English class. He was also an anime nerd. We had met during a freshmen bonfire. We would spend time after our classes watching *Kenshin*, *Trigun*, *Cowboy Bebop*, and *Hellsing*. I wasn't really into the more masculine, seinen titles. He introduced me to a lot of anime that I would not have discovered otherwise since I was drowning in magical girl and josei anime throughout most of my teenage girl life at that point. This relationship did not last; Eddie dropped out of university after his first year.

I also befriended two Japanese exchange students who loved *Evangelion*. Because Sonoma State was a very quiet campus and Rohnert Park was a sleepy town, what we did for fun was community service. I was happy that I had friends with whom I could practice my conversational Japanese.

By 2002, VHS fansubs were nearly a thing of the past. I didn't even have a VCR player in my dorm room. My new laptop had a DVD player, so I could play the DVDs I had. Getting unlicensed anime meant you had to go on the internet and "sail the high seas." You could pirate anime online. There were early attempts at peer-to-peer sharing of anime. You could try to download anime via Kazaa or LimeWire, but you had to be careful as some anime titles were labeled incorrectly. My roommate wanted to download *Inuyasha*, but the file ended up being something more adult in nature. There was mIRC, but it was complicated to figure out how to download anime on this chat platform. High speed internet in the college dorms encouraged the circle of otaku to download series and burn them on compact disc. We would then exchange anime by means of copying compact discs and labeling them in black Sharpie pen.

There was also an air of elitism directed to broke students who could not afford to acquire anime by official means. "Anime is a privilege, not a right." I remembered wanting to find episodes of *Fruits Basket* a day or two before the license was announced. I wanted to see if I liked the main cast before committing to a cosplay group. When a license was announced, it could be a while before the DVDs would hit store shelves. I was called out on an online forum to support the Funimation release. I never liked this implication that anime was only for those who could afford dropping $30 for four episodes on a DVD. What about cash-strapped young people who had finally found a piece of media where they saw themselves? Anime became more and more attractive to queer kids as more boys love anime was gaining popularity. While toxic themes and characters in *Tokyo Babylon* and *Gravitation* were not the best representation for queer characters, it was still something for us queer kids to watch; even scant representation was better than none. We could be angsty with our favorite boys love characters.

However, torrenting ended up being huge for anime fans to download English fansubs to watch from the comfort of the laptop or desktop. Torrenting anime from websites became a game changer and was the standard way of obtaining full series of anime. This was how I finished watching CLAMP's *Chobits*. This was a different experience from popping in a DVD or a VHS tape in your living room. Anime became a much more personalized viewing experience in front of your laptop.

Also, my cosplay friends pointed out that you could get anime DVDs from Hong Kong at a fraction of the cost, though you might have to suffer through some bad English grammar in the subtitles. You could find these Hong Kong "imports" in any Chinatown or anime convention or buy them via eBay. This is how I eventually completed watching *Fruits Basket*—one bad subtitled line at a time. Kyo, the boy who turned into a cat, was named "Cat." Of course, these "imports" from Hong Kong were not official releases. These were bootlegs that started popping up all over the place in the early '00s. Thankfully, the anime club at Sonoma State also had their CD trading faction. We all had our binders of anime CDs to share amongst ourselves. This made consuming and obtaining anime possible for me as a broke college student with a minimum wage food services job.

I really appreciated that Sonoma State University had a lively anime community. This was a far cry from high school, where if you were nerdy about something, you would immediately be deemed "different." One of our favorite things to do was watch anime music videos we discovered through file share services. If we found a really neat anime music video, we would watch it on a Friday or Saturday night before our Adult Swim get-togethers. Since I had so much anime digitally, I toyed with the idea of making anime music videos. I was a media studies major. I wanted to just test run Windows Movie Maker to practice my video editing skills. I took episodes of *X/1999* featuring my favorite character, Karen Kasumi, and set them to Madonna's "Like a Prayer." I showed this off to my anime nerd friends, and they were impressed with what I had made. I admit, there was not much to do in

Sonoma; it was rural Wine Country, after all. It's not what you would call a college town. To do anything exciting or cultural, you would have to go into the city of San Francisco. I spent one night making that "Like a Prayer" anime music video. I edited the video in less than three hours. All of my friends had movie editing software on their laptops whether it was iMovie or Windows Movie Maker. We all started taking the anime we had downloaded and creating our own anime music videos to show off to each other. They weren't perfect. We still had the subtitles present and some editing cues were off. Yet, we had a lot of fun making these as a way to bond and share our favorite moments in anime through our favorite songs.

I think my favorite anime music video I ever created was Britney Spears's "Lucky" to *Perfect Blue*. I finally saw *Perfect Blue* with English subtitles in university. I no longer had to follow the raw Japanese with the summary or second-guess what was going on on-screen. I found a version of *Perfect Blue* online that did not have the subtitles layered onto the movie. I proceeded to spend a week editing the Britney Spears song about the price of fame to the psychological horror anime about a pop idol's identity crisis. My university friends were impressed, and my cosplay friends were floored by this skill I had. "Are you going to enter this at a contest?!" a friend asked. It never crossed my mind to enter an anime music video contest. I think I'd only seen one contest anime music video contest, during Ani-Magic 2000, and I saw the winners at Anime Expo 2002 during masquerade halftime. I was always impressed by the editing and the mixture of emotion and choice of songs that further enhanced these animes. I didn't think my skills were anywhere near those of these anime music video creators. I then thought about maybe entering "Lucky" at a future anime convention. Either way, I was starting to feel confident in my editing and media skills. I had not even taken a production class yet. I was still in my first few months of university. I was happy that I was getting support for my creative endeavors from my friends. This time, it was friends in real life. That feeling really hit differently. I felt I was already succeeding in the major of my choice and I had found my people in university—content creator otaku.

And while I had friends who were into anime in university and an in-person community I could mingle with, I still felt excluded by a lot of my classmates. It was then I started seeing that I was a Person of Color and also, not The Perfect Asian. I was Southeast Asian: I had darker skin, a much rounder eye shape ... and I didn't have the qualities of what was deemed The Perfect Asian. My roommates and peers looked down on me because I didn't know how to cook. I was still learning how to cook at my restaurant job. In high school, I didn't have time at home to learn how to cook because my mom made the kitchen her domain. Momo even looked down on me for heating up instant ramen the first week of school. "You're not going to live by ramen alone!" she scoffed. I just wanted a quick bite. I was even judged by Shelly for heating up Campbell's soup for dinner; she told me it was processed and unhealthy. I didn't need a lecture from either of them. This poor college student just wanted to eat to survive. And after all, my mom sent me a care package of canned soups. I just wanted a simple soup at the end of a long day as we were approaching the colder winter months.

I took an Asian American studies class at one point at Sonoma State. I just wanted to learn more about myself and how I fit in with American society. My experience as a minority at Sonoma State prompted me to take this course just to better understand why people were treating me the way they were. It might be a one-time elective, but it was for my own love of learning. I figured since I was in university, I might as well take advantage of this moment. I then learned of the "model minority," how Asian Americans were perceived as being the minority for other people of color to look up to because they were succeeding so well in the United States above all other persons of color. However, it was a myth. It was made to pit Asian Americans against other persons of color. When my peers saw that I was not a Perfect Asian who fit the model minority mold, they were disappointed. I didn't know how to cook and clean like a perfect housewife. I got Bs, but I wasn't a bad student. I was just seen as a disappointment. I was so confused about how Asian Americans were supposed to act or how we were supposed to fit in. I didn't question my identity until university when I started to see that I was the minority, not one of many Filipinos at my Catholic high school.

I talked to my white boyfriend at the time about my identity and why other Asians and non–Asians were treating me differently. I was learning how to cook with my restaurant job. I could make a tasty wrap and a simple burger. It was a marathon, not a sprint. I didn't like this expectation that was put on me by my peers. "Your identity doesn't matter," said my cis white boyfriend. "Stop trying to impress others. You are you and that's what makes you special." While he might have had a point, my Southeast Asian identity was still a part of me and I did not like being seen as less than. I took a Japanese class to fulfill my foreign language requirement and also because I wanted to take Japanese anyway. "Are you trying to impress your Asian friends?" he asked. No, I wanted to learn Japanese outside of "super kawaii," "ohayo gozaimasu," and "baka."

Part Four. Anime Going Mainstream: Everything Changes

I didn't hide my otaku-ness in university. My dorm room had my anime posters. I had a *Sailor Moon* lanyard for my ID badge, when I had an IT job the second semester of my first year, my laptop background rotated through different anime images. It could be *Sister Princess* one day or *A Little Snow Fairy Sugar* the next day. I may have been watching more masculine anime, but I was still all about that kawaii magical girl life. I attended the weekly anime club meetings. Sometimes I wore my cat ears to feel more like me. I knew where I could feel at home. As my university days continued, I began meeting more people, making new friends—most of whom were like-minded anime fans. I felt like being an anime fan was a requirement for friendship just so I could feel understood. Anime fans back then knew what it meant to be an outsider and a supporter or member of the queer community.

It came time to plan for my event schedule. I was working a steady part-time job in food services. I was getting Bs in my general education courses. I had planned a few one-day Bay Area events, and I did want to return to Ani-Magic and Anime Central.

Ani-Magic would be a carpool from wine country to Lancaster. Anime Central would be flying from San Francisco's airport to Chicago O'Hare. I planned for two major overnight conventions per semester. Thankfully, Anime Central's May date did not interfere with finals. I would then return to Anime Expo the summer after I was done with university.

The problem with Wine Country is that it is pretty far removed from San Francisco. There were buses, but they didn't run often. Or they didn't drop you off at a convenient stop. As a first-year university student, I did not have a car on campus. And because of my issues with anxiety, I did not even attempt the road test for a driver's license. I had to rely on others to get to the city for events.

I took a high school teacher's advice to not schedule classes for Friday since Thursday was the party day in university. It was easy for me not to miss any class. I was pretty excited for Ani-Magic. I wanted to see everyone again after my One Epic Summer of 2002. It would be cool to see both my Bay Area and Los Angeles area cosplay friends. I was picked up at 3:00 a.m. at my dorm, and we began the eight-hour road trip to Lancaster on that familiar dark desert highway.

We got on the road to Ani-Magic. I was in a huge battle van with six or seven other cosplayers. I learned that Ani-Magic had added a few more events. One of them caught my eye—Cosplay Revue. It was a cosplay talent show. It was different from masquerade. Inspired by the showmanship and theatrics of the anime *Sakura Taisen*, Cosplay Revue was a showcase of talent by cosplayers. It focused more on performance than craft. No need to create your own cosplay from scratch, it was all for entertainment and fun. It was right up my alley. I ended up entering singing "Cha Cha Cha" by Akemi Ishii.

We got to the familiar Best Western that I remembered from high school. At last, we were at what the cosplay community called "Camp Cosplay" in the middle of the Palm Desert. I was wearing my nightgown with a denim jacket over it with my hair in braids. We got to our room, where I had floor space this time around. Vaughn, a veteran of the Queer Kids Table, also roomed with us. He let me have some extra fabric to serve as a blanket. Vaughn and his friend from Denver would be wearing *Cardcaptor Sakura* cosplays. They cosplayed as Toya and Yuuki, one of my favorite pairings from the show. They both invited me to join them as Nadeshiko Kinomoto. It was nice to run around the con as mother and son.

I didn't have much in terms of cosplay with me. I had brought Nadeshiko, Yomiko Readman, and Karen Kasumi. I wanted to keep it light since I didn't have a lot of my cosplays with me in my dorm. Cosplay Revue took place at the same poolside as the cosplay contest. This was a Friday night event. What wowed me about this show was seeing the event organizer Tristen Citrine's Las Vegas–style *Sakura Taisen* showgirl cosplays. I knew of *Sakura Taisen* after watching a few of the direct-to-video anime, but I never got myself entirely into the fandom. Thankfully, Tristen Citrine hosted a *Sakura Taisen* panel the very next day so I could get to know more about the fandom. Cosplay Revue concluded with all performers singing "Fly Me to the Moon." It was a magical night.

I just remember Ani-Magic 2002 having a much more lively vibe to it than my first one in 2000. In 2000, I wasn't sure what to make of it. I was not used to small cons. Yet, it was easy to sit down and catch up with friends and their new significant others. It was also relaxing to organize a private cosplay photoshoot without worrying about being in line for the next panel or event. Ani-Magic was also known for having Western English dub voice actors as guests of honor. While Anime Expo did highlight English dub actors, they were never listed as guests of honor. It was common to see Scott McNeil roam around the pool in his denim and cowboy hat.

Ani-Magic 2002 also was a huge party con. I remembered the Anime Expo 2001 room party I went to when I had my first Asahi. It was just anime film enthusiasts talking about rare hidden gems. It was not anything too wild. Ani-Magic 2002's nightlife was drunken debauchery, people jumping into the pool, people stuffing the hotel hot tub, and Lord knows what.

A found item cosplay of Yomiko Readman from *Read or Die* at Anime Expo 2004 (Anaheim, CA). All elements to this cosplay were found in my closet.

Ani-Magic also had a swap meet. On the day of the swap meet, I wore Yomiko Readman from *Read or Die*. I had someone come up to me and tell me that I had Yomiko Readman's spirit. It was one thing to look like the character, but quite another to also be told that I possessed the essence of her character. From that point on, I felt that Yomiko Readman was the cosplay I was best known for. It was the best compliment I could have for a simple closet cosplay. I planned to wear her again for Anime Central.

Ani-Magic was a chill convention where I could follow up with friends after the madness that was Anime Expo. I appreciated the hang-outs by the pool and taking photos in the Japanese garden. After attending a few conventions that took place in large convention halls, I was starting to see what cosplayers saw in Ani-Magic when I first attended in 2000. This was a cosplay oasis; this was the end-of-year party. It was so easy to find friends without having to use phones or walkie-talkies. Everyone was centralized at the pool to chill or at the Japanese gardens for photos.

Our travel party journeyed back to wine country. However, our battle van had trouble on the road. We would not be able to make it to wine country until the next day. I felt bad for the people in our vanpool who had flights to catch from the Bay Area. I talked to my parents about the breakdown and they thought it might be best to fly from LAX to the Bay Area, but it seemed we were in good hands. Our driver was a AAA member. AAA gave us a complimentary hotel room. We dubbed our adventure "Middle of Nowhere Con" or "MON Con."

And I got back to campus safely the following night.

And then a few boys asked me about Yaoi-Con in downtown San Francisco later that month.

Okay, as a queer young adult, I never got into Yaoi. I was more into WLW or Yuri. At the time, the Yaoi or fujoshi community had a bad rap. It was characterized by a paddle-wielding 14-year-old fangirl who could not keep her hands to herself. I could not get into it because I felt the community was objectifying queer people. The rampant misogyny also got to me because a lot of times there would be intense hate towards female characters who would "get in the way of the ship." My male friends just wanted to check out a local anime con. They had never been to one. So we went to one day of Yaoi-Con.

I ended up putting together a Nicholas Daniel Wolfwood cosplay. It was simply a dress suit I already had in my closet. I just had to find cross cufflinks to paint white with white nail polish from the local pharmacy. This wasn't my first time presenting masculine in cosplay. I did look pretty hot for a slender built pretty boy. Yaoi-Con was in Japantown. We didn't buy badges because we felt $60 was too expensive for a small con where we were just gonna be there for a few hours before driving back to Sonoma. We were more intrigued by the prospect of exploring Japantown. This was my first time exploring Japantown in San Francisco. The bookstore, the many restaurants, the gift shops, the crepe place, the Italian-Japanese fusion restaurant with manga filling up the walls! I experienced sensory overload. My friends and I ended up dining at one place that had tempura, sushi, and udon. This was my first time really trying Japanese food for myself. At anime cons, we would just have the overpriced burgers and hot dogs at the convention center. I fell in love with Japantown. My Yaoi-Con 2002 report was basically a foodie's guide to Japantown.

And then I found out about the annual Cherry Blossom Festival. I had heard about this event since I was in high school. I saw it as THE main event for cosplayers in San Francisco. The Cherry Blossom Festival was a parade that had cosplayers march from San Francisco City Hall to Japantown. I loved seeing Eurobeat Kasumi and Lionel Lum's photos from this event. It seemed so cool that the Japanese American community acknowledged anime fandom. It would also mean going back to Japantown and eating all the tasty food. Sonoma lacked any kind of culture. The idea of going out for Asian food meant going to Panda Express. As someone who grew up in a community of family-owned restaurants, I needed access to tasty food again.

Yet, no car and no direct access to BART meant I could not go. I felt really sad that I couldn't make it. Yet, I had to focus on other projects and the upcoming Anime Central.

Since Ani-Magic 2003, I had been obsessed with *Sakura Taisen*. I found a character that I liked the most. I had to narrow it down to one. *Sakura Wars* had such an amazing cast of characters. While it was primarily a steampunk mecha anime, I liked the theatrical side of it. I liked that these were stage actors who also went to battle in steam-powered robots. I ended up choosing Soletta Orihime. She played piano, she had a tan complexion like me, and I could use my natural hair. Above all, her dress ... that was the dress in which I wanted to waltz up into Anime Expo 2003. Every Anime Expo, I felt that I had to one-up myself by arriving in a fancy dress. Cosplay.com had a feature where you could find folks from whom to commission your costumes. I wanted to try someone different. I hired Amethyst Angel; her prices were great for a starving college student and her quality was just amazing. I ended up hiring her for more cosplay commissions.

Alucard from *Castlevania* graces the San Francisco streets at the annual Cherry Blossom Festival parade.

I test ran Soletta Orihime at my university's formal dance. My college boyfriend also decided to nerd it up while wearing a suit with Kuroneko-sama from Trigun pinned on his shoulder. I received a lot of compliments that night. I was ready for Anime Central.

And as I was finalizing my travel plans, Maya Okamoto, voice of Soletta Orihime, was announced as a guest. In my tradition of meeting a Japanese voice actor at every con, I made it a point to attend the Meet the Guests reception and attend any panels she was on and to wear Soletta Orihime as often as I could. While Anime Central was my hangout con with Chicagoland friends, my friend group would slowly start changing in 2003.

San Francisco to Chicago was nothing. It cost me $177 for a round-trip flight on American Airlines. I pre-registered early on so I could get the cheapest badge price possible. It would be at the same place—Rosemont Hyatt and Convention Center. I would be traveling to Chicago solo for the first time. I admit I was nervous doing this, but I did it anyway.

Anime Central 2003 would also be the first time I would be using a digital camera to take photos. I would finally make the transition from film to digital. No longer would I be limited to the 24 shots on a roll of film. I could take almost unlimited shots (or whatever the memory card could hold) of cosplayers and Fanime. Going from film to digital was a game changer for my Scarlet Rhapsody blog. I no longer had to scan photos; I could just upload them.

I was not rooming with Sora this time. Sora was rooming with her anime club from Northern Illinois University. I was rooming with folks I had befriended in the voice acting community. Although I was no longer doing online voice acting, I still had good friends from there. I was excited to see them again. It was almost like a high school reunion after one year of being so focused on university life.

Anime Central 2003's highlight was dressing up as Soletta Orihime in her red and black ball gown. I so wanted to meet Maya Okamoto. Not only did she voice Soletta, she also played Soletta in the *Sakura Taisen* musicals. During the Meet the Guests reception, I first went to Yoko Ishida's table. Yoko Ishida was a singer who had a Para Para dance tour that year. Sora had seen her live at Anime Expo a few months prior. I picked a few of her CDs that had anime cover songs. We talked a lot about '80s J-pop and what inspired her.

I wasn't nervous meeting Maya Okamoto, but I was starstruck. I had this cosplay commissioned in hopes that I would meet her and that we could get a photo of us together. I didn't have any Soletta Orihime

At Anime Central 2003 (Rosemont, IL) cosplaying as Soletta Orihime from *Sakura Taisen*. Maya Okamoto, who voiced Soletta Orihime, was a guest at this event.

merchandise on me to sign. I think my DVDs were still at my parents' house in Southern California. Yet, it was pleasant meeting one of my idols. We had photographers snap photos of us as voice actress and cosplayer.

Part Four. Anime Going Mainstream: Everything Changes

I also saw that our friend dynamic at Anime Central was dissipating. Sora was having drama with people in her room and putting out some fires. As she was occupied in her peacekeeping duties, I started to notice something. A lot of my friends and I had different interests. We were starting to grow apart. There was no voice acting panel to run in 2003. Some friends were part of the *ParaParaParadise* dance squad for the convention rave. Some friends wanted to attend voice acting panels and demos. I had guests I wanted to meet and cosplay photoshoots set up. It was clear that 2003 was not 2001. I don't even think we had dinners together. We were going our separate ways. It was time for me to retire from Anime Central. As I flew back to San Francisco, I made the decision not to return in 2004 and maybe hit up Otakon instead. I remembered my voice actor friend and convention senpai, Robert Black, saying nothing but good things about Otakon and that I should check it out some day. I had to move forward to new horizons.

Summer was approaching. I made a statement on my LiveJournal that because of the finals schedule for my second year in university, I would not be attending Anime Central in 2004. I would be planning for Otakon instead. The budget afforded by my job at the university restaurant only allowed me to attend maybe three major conventions per year. I finally had to face the harsh truth. There would not be another Anime Central 2001 or another Anime Expo 2002. I had to focus on the present and embrace a new era of growing up and the mainstream's flirtation with Japanese pop culture in the 2000s.

13

New Friendship Circles

Anime Expo 2003 was on the horizon.

However! I had an unexpected invite to check out Fanime 2003. I was not planning on Fanime 2003 in Santa Clara in Northern California. I had already been back in Los Angeles after my university finals in May. I was already enrolled in a community college's Japanese class. My budget was set for Anime Expo 2003.

And then came Todd.

A mutual friend introduced me to Todd. Our friend thought we would make a cute couple. Both of us were fun-sized Asians who loved anime and cosplay. I was going through a Hong Kong cinema phase in university. My library had a ton of Hong Kong movies I was renting out. Todd and I liked the same movies from Stephen Chow comedies to John Woo gun operas. Fanime 2003 was our mutual friend's attempt for us to get together.

I decided to go to Fanime 2003 with the intent to spend time with friends. I had friends coming up from Southern California and I wanted to spend time and get to know my Bay Area cosplay friends much better. Opportunities to attend San Francisco events were limited because of my rural university's lack of proximity and transportation to the city. At last, I could finally get some time with cosplayers whom I had admired from afar and with whom I had exchanged many a text message conversation through AOL Instant Messenger. Maybe we could become closer friends once started hanging out in real life? Maybe a few of them actually did live in rural Wine Country and I could finally get a ride to the big city cons?

This would be the first Fanime and first major Bay Area anime event that I would be attending. I was so excited to finally have Fanime coverage for my website. At last, I'd have my Fanime blog post alongside Anime Expo and Anime Central. I was too nervous to apply for media credentials. My website was not as robust as Lionel Lum's, Eurobeat King's, or Kevin

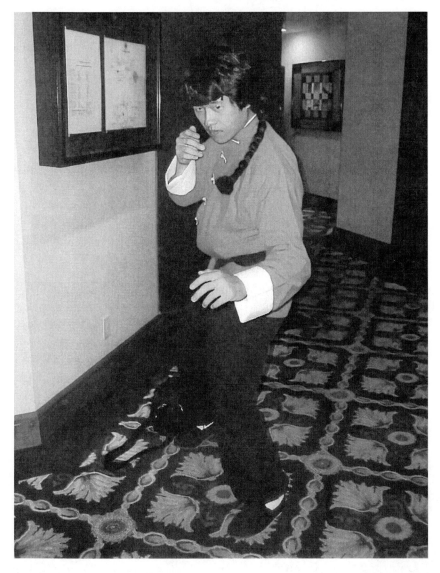

The titular character from *Ranma ½* gets ready for Fanime 2003 (Santa Clara, CA).

Lillard's coverage. I was still a poor college student who scrimped to save for both Anime Central and Fanime.

I planned my cosplay on the lighter side. I brought Karen Kasumi, Nadeshiko, and Soletta Orihime. I had worn these outfits before, but

18. New Friendship Circles

I would also be showing off my cosplays to anime nerds in the Bay Area whom I had adored from afar. Todd had made attempts to match with me so we could pair up in cosplay. I was happy to have a cosplay partner who wasn't too far. We already had cosplays that could work together. Todd was also a closet cosplayer; in other words, he pieced together things in his wardrobe to create a canonical version of a character. And if he didn't have the parts and pieces, he would go straight to Goodwill or some thrift store. Most of his characters wore suits, so it was nothing complicated on his part. At Fanime, we really hit it off. We began to date during the convention.

My first Fanime, the event that takes pride in their "by fans for fans" mantra, happened at the Santa Clara Convention Center. I stayed with a Bay Area friend from Chinatown, Ace. Ace and I hung out during the few times I visited San Francisco. He would always make time to see me and take me to the best Chinese restaurants and bakeries in the city. Through Ace, I met his cosplay buddies—Nando, Moo, Anna, Vilay, and Dez. We all had sushi at the convention hotel to get to know one another just a bit

Stopping by the Gaia Online booth at Fanime 2005 (San Jose, CA). I spun the wheel and won the coveted Kiki Kitty plush!

more. And when we were not having expensive hotel sushi, we would go back to the hotel room and have a favorite convention delicacy—coffee pot ramen. As a university student, I had stocked up on instant ramen. If I needed a quick bite, I would take a pack of ramen, use the coffee pot to get hot water, pour it over in a bowl, and serve with chopsticks. While this may not be recommended by any nutritionist, this is how we starving otaku got by during our weekend parties.

The Bay Area cosplay scene was a vibrant one. I forget whom I wanted to meet specifically, but I ended up making new friends through every cosplay meetup, gathering, or casual conversation in the dealers hall. The Fanime 2003 event I remember most was the CLAMP cosplay meetup. *X/1999* was a big thing in the early 2000s given that the new anime had been released. I rocked my Karen Kasumi and met other people who were obsessed with CLAMP's end-of-the-world melodrama. My new friends and I talked about shippings, ending theories, the possibility of the manga ending, and prospects of cosplaying from *X/1999* in the future. From this point forward, I would be joining a ton of CLAMP cosplay meetups as either Karen Kasumi or Nadeshiko Kinomoto. Attending a CLAMP meetup was important.

My first Fanime was the perfect way to celebrate surviving my first year of university. And as my Southwest flight touched down at LAX, one thought loomed: "Anime Expo is in two weeks?!"

There was no doubt that veteran Anime Expo attendees hated the Long Beach location. The event was spread out and there was too much walking around. By this time, most of my friends who regularly attended Anime Expo had quietly quit convention and cosplay to pursue other interests. They would focus more on investing in the likes of San Diego Comic-Con or just finally quit conventions and cosplay. A few had expressed that anime had gone too mainstream after Toonami brought it to a wider audience. Ten thousand folks at Anime Expo 2002 was too much for them to handle. I would see newer faces during Anime Expo's second run in Anaheim. Anime Expo would continue from 2003 to 2006 at the Anaheim Convention Center and its neighboring hotels. This wasn't the late 1990s Anime Expo. No one was ready for Anime Expo's growth spurt.

Sora and her friend CardCaptor Will decided to tag along with us. Maya from our Anime Expo 2002 squad got us a room at the Sheraton. With my date from Fanime, Todd, we had a pretty good group for the hotel. This would be my first time staying overnight at Anime Expo.

Sora, Maya, and I tried our hand in the first ever AX Idol. This was

Cosplay personality CardCaptor Will gallivanting around the park at Fanime 2003 (San Jose, CA).

a voice acting contest inspired by *American Idol*. *American Idol* in its early incarnation was a singing competition on the lookout for the next pop star. However, what drew people into watching *American Idol* was the snarky and brutal judge, Simon Cowell. Simon was known for tearing people down if he did not find them up to his standard. We did not know that bullying contestants was a main part of this show going in. From the perspective of the contestants, the first AX Idol was designed to humiliate contestants for entertainment.

Sora, Maya, and I were just hyped that this would be like entering the karaoke contest but taking it to the next level. There were two divisions to AX Idol. There was a singing contest and a voice acting contest. Winners would have a chance to work with a voice acting agency. Because I had made it to the semifinals at karaoke the previous year, I thought I had a shot. Even if I did not win, at least I wanted to make some great relationships with the judges to maybe have an opportunity to do voice acting at a later time. Maya and I were based in Los Angeles, after all. If Sora made it through, we would figure out a way for her to make her voice acting career work in Los Angeles.

On the day of the competition, Maya went onstage and was immediately torn down by the panel of judges. I remember her righteously ranting at the stagehands and fellow contestants. I went onstage and performed a song from an anime, but the judges wanted me to do something more Broadway sounding. However, the rules indicated that my vocal selection had to be from anime. I was so pissed off at this that I threw a diva fit backstage. It was not my most glamorous moment, but had I known, I would have prepared something else. Sora saw each contestant being torn down— one after another. When it was her turn to go onstage, she declared in true Taurus fashion, "I'm only wasting my time. Fuck this." She gracefully left the stage.

However, this event did not define Anime Expo 2003 for my friends and me. This was the first year that Anime Expo hosted a ballroom dance. I had a new Karen Kasumi dress made for this. I commissioned Amethyst Angel to create this piece for a special occasion. It was in the style of a slimmed down red evening dress that looked like it came from a 1950s perfume advertisement. A big red bow on the back evoked Marilyn Monroe in "Diamonds Are a Girl's Best Friend."

Even before I met Todd, I was very hyped that Anime Expo was hosting a fancy dance where I could rock a ball gown. A few of my Anime Central friends and I were envious that a few conventions were getting ballroom dances inspired by the *Final Fantasy VIII* ballroom scene. The simple cut scene—Squall in his fancy uniform and Rinoa wearing a beige cocktail dress dancing to a waltz version of "Eyes on Me"—was iconic among convention goers of the time. It was seen as the very definition of romance. A few of us wanted to recreate that romantic vibe. One such con went as far as to recreate that scene in *Final Fantasy VIII*, enlisting volunteer cosplayers to act like the characters from *Final Fantasy VIII* in that moment as if attendees were immersed in the ballroom scene from the game. I may only have attended three formal dances during my time as a high school student, but if you had told me that anime conventions had a fancy formal ball at their events, I would have immediately gone all-out for it. I didn't have to worry about dancing to random hip-hop or rock that I didn't care for. I could dance to anime and video game music!

I found out that Todd was into ballroom dancing. I just wanted to wear something fancy from anime and dance the night away to anime and video game music. Both of us were hyped for the ballroom dance. The ballroom dance was held at the Sheraton, a few steps away from the main Anaheim Convention Center. Todd and I walked in as Aoki and Karen from *X/1999*. Aoki had a simple matching outfit with Karen: a black suit with a red bow tie. A few anime tunes were played. It was a very bare-bones set-up—a hotel ballroom, some chairs, and a deejay. However, it was the break I needed from the hell that was AX Idol. By the end of the night, Todd and I were officially a couple. We announced our coupledom at Anime Expo 2003.

The return to Anaheim was a bit surreal to me. This was the first time we were using the Anaheim Convention Center halls for the dealers room, panel rooms, and main events. The event was also spread out to the Anaheim Hilton, Anaheim Marriott, and nearby Sheraton. It was definitely more contained and compact than Long Beach, but the numbers were definitely growing at an alarming rate. The advent of Toonami and anime being pushed into the mainstream became evident here with the amount of attendees present. In the hot Anaheim summer, we had plenty of palm trees for shade. Being from the Midwest, Sora was very hyped to see all the palm trees. This also made for amazing cosplay photos.

We even shared the space with the Benny Hinn Ministries. This was not a good mix with the anime crowd. You had your televangelist stans walking past *Hellsing* and *Trigun* cosplayers giving us all the stink eye or a "Y'all need Jesus!" The *Hellsing* Catholic clergy cosplayers and the Wolfwood cosplayers carrying the cross just laughed it up and knew this unsolicited judgment was coming. None of us harassed the Christian con goers; we received dirty looks from both the Benny Hinn crowd and the suburban families on their Disneyland vacations.

Anime Expo 2003 was also the debut of Man Faye to the masses. Man Faye was a cosplay wonder and a legend to those who remembered him back in the 2000s. You either loved him or you hated him. There was no in between. Man Faye is a cosplayer best known for cosplaying as Faye Valentine from *Cowboy Bebop*. This was, however, a hairy dude with a dad bod rockin' Faye's revealing yellow short shorts and crop top. It was meant to be a gag, and it made a lot of people literally gag. After Anime Expo 2003, Man Faye would go on to late night talk shows and Stan Lee's reality TV show as his own personality. For a few years in Anaheim, we did have one cosfamer clad in yellow with hairy legs getting positive and negative attention. Man Faye had said that his skimpy and scandalous take on the sexy femme fatale from *Cowboy Bebop* was satirical; it seemed acceptable for women to wear skimpy clothes and cosplay at anime cons, but when a male did it, he was met with criticism and much more scrutiny. This viewpoint was up for debate considering the amount of slut-shaming that was geared towards femme cosplayers dressed in skimpy outfits worn by anime characters.

Anime Expo 2003 finally ended. However, the summer had a few local events. Anime-related events did not end here. Los Angeles

Aizen cosplayer from *Bleach* at Nisei Week, a celebration of Japanese American culture. Cosplayers were welcome to march in the annual parade in downtown Los Angeles.

had Nisei Week. Nisei Week was always looking for cosplayers to march in their parade celebrating Japanese American culture. Nisei Week is a huge cultural festival in the middle of summer in Los Angeles. Food booths, games, and cultural presentations honoring the Japanese American experience were scattered throughout the Little Tokyo neighborhood. The festivities culminated in the parade. It was an honor for the anime community to be invited to be a part of this time-honored event.

My new boyfriend, Todd, joined me for that event in Little Tokyo. We went as Nadeshiko and Toya from *Cardcaptor Sakura*. In hindsight, it seemed odd that we went as mother and son, but that's what we had in our cosplay lineup. Then we started making future cosplay couple plans together. I told him that I also ran convention reports and would love to have an assistant to make things easier. And thus Traveling Valentine—the cute cosplay couple and convention blog squad—was born.

19

Branding Cosplay Identity

Todd was a huge *Lupin III* fan. I also enjoyed the *Lupin* franchise for what little I had watched.... I had only seen a few episodes on Toonami and maybe three movies. I enjoyed the madcap comedy and how it had been a long beloved anime. The Toonami run encouraged me to check out this retro anime. So, out of the Lupin gang, it made sense for me to go as the femme fatale, Fujiko Mine. I found two Fujiko outfits that I loved and that I could get from a vintage consignment store without any issue. One of them was a pink dress from the 1970s and the other was a short green dress. I was looking forward to wearing retro outfits to anime conventions. I wasn't too crazy about cosplaying as Fujiko; she wasn't really my favorite character. Yet, I had a bigger love for vintage fashion. For a period in the 2000s we were known as the Fujiko and Lupin III cosplayers.

Todd also had a car, a simple Toyota Corolla that could go places. This was important for me as a college student who did not have access to a vehicle all the time. I was looking forward to taking road trips to conventions with him at the wheel. We rebuilt my website to reflect Traveling Valentine branding. Before we knew it, we were seen as the cosplay sweethearts of the West Coast. We became the poster children for everyone's hopes and dreams for finding romance and true love in fandom. I didn't know what to make of it. I was only 19, and while it was nice to have my con reports in the spotlight, I was not sure what to make of our romance being branded and idolized by the masses.

I started my second year at Sonoma State University. Todd and I were thinking about what events and conventions to hit up. Fanime, Cherry Blossom Festival, and Recca Con were on the list. My aunt had given me frequent flyer miles for American Airlines. She only had enough miles for one traveler. I was making plans to fly out to Baltimore and to find friends to room with for my first Otakon. I had friends from Chicagoland who were going. I

161

wanted to see them again. I also wanted to see my convention senpai, Robert Black, again. I was not going to be alone. I was going to be in good company.

"But what about me?" Todd asked. I only had enough miles for one round trip, and I wanted to focus this Otakon visit on hanging out with friends I did not get to see often. I wanted to focus on seeing them again. Todd and I would have so many local Bay Area events together. Todd didn't like the idea of me going to anime conventions solo. To save myself from drama, I opted not to go to Otakon and used "Anime Expo is going to cost a bit" as the excuse to tell my friends outside of California. Inside, I felt I was letting my friends down. I'd known them longer than Todd. I had so many more memories and shared experiences with them. I really did want to go to Otakon and felt let down. I lived vicariously once again through Kevin Lillard's Otakon 2004 coverage posted on Fansview and felt a sense of melancholy that I was missing out on seeing my friends.

This episode was the first indication of Todd's controlling nature. Yet, I swept that under the rug. I wrote it off: Couples have problems all the time, I told myself. It's not going to be 100 percent perfect. Right? In truth, I just wanted to try a brand new con on my own and catch up with the friends I had not seen in a year. I missed them so much.

First cosplay where I presented masculine as Nicholas Daniel Wolfwood from *Trigun* while cruisin' around San Francisco's Japantown.

Todd was a public relations major. He was signing Traveling Valentine up for media credentials for conventions. Great! I didn't have to pay $50 for a three- or four-day weekend badge! I had the website design skills, the storytelling voice, and my trusted digital camera. I still paid for my website space from my student assistant campus job.

However, with us getting media credentials, I had to remove old content from Scarlet Rhapsody. Reports from 2000 to 2003 were taken down because they did not meet a professional appearance or expectations. They were written as a cringey blog written by a high school fangirl in cat ears. But that's who I was at the time—teenager excited about attending anime conventions and giving a firsthand account of experiencing something new and meaningful. They were supposed to read like blogs. I had to delete the reports from 2000 to 2003 on Scarlet Rhapsody to meet with our new standard in getting approval for press. We had to look professional to present as credentialed media.

The joy of the San Francisco Bay Area fandom is that events were plentiful. There was no shortage. Anime was becoming more and more accessible. One of our video stores at the mall called the anime DVD section the "otaku section." I was fond of that acknowledgment. Borders had children parked in the manga section reading books. My friends in university snickered at the children who were checking out manga. "This is not a library!" "Borders is not a babysitter!" They

Browsing San Francisco's Japantown in my Tohru Honda (*Fruits Basket*) cosplay. I had to stop by Japan Video to see what DVDs were in stock!

163

sighed. As someone who only had access to the *Sailor Moon* Japanese manga in middle school, I was happy these kids had access to manga translated into English. I was happy they were reading something that was inaccessible to me when I was their age. I was happy to see kids reading books in general. I had no problem with this. Yet, I didn't want to lose friends. I kept silent. You never wanted to start drama. That was the unwritten rule. If it felt upsetting, you kept your head down and stayed quiet.

As a broke college student, I went to the local Borders and I took whatever was the latest volume of *Fruits Basket* and bought myself a coffee and continued to read about the adventures of Tohru and the crazy Sohma family. Anytime there was a buy-one-get-one-free sale at Borders, I would put that towards *Fruits Basket* so I could have the entire manga series— and it was a long series that expanded outside the anime at the time! I had the thrill of keeping up with the manga while I was at the Borders cafe, and then I could buy these books during a major sale so I could read them any time in my college dorm.

This was also the time we started seeing wearable anime products in stores. Hot Topic at the time was seen as the devil's living room. Scrawled lettering in Hot Topic's logo, the blaring of indie rock music, vinyl records from indie groups, and gothic clothes at an affordable price characterized the store. Emo kids went there for their anime fix. A controversial item then was a red trench jacket that looked a lot like Vash the Stampede's signature red trench coat from *Trigun*. This sparked discussion in the cosplay community about whether cosplay was getting too mainstream because a look-alike jacket was found at Hot Topic. I shrugged it off because I felt that if it was accessible to the masses to make cosplay easier for newbies to get in, so be it. This was also the time that retail stores started selling *Naruto* headbands bearing the leaf village insignia. Folks who had made *Naruto* headbands for cosplay from scratch were furious to see this in stores. While I felt that their anger was valid—after all, it takes hours to perfect and make your craft—I was okay with *Naruto* ninja headbands being sold because of the easy access and affordability for newbies. *Naruto* was becoming more and more popular. It was taking the cosplay world by storm. I couldn't get into *Naruto*. Todd showed me a few episodes and it seemed like something I might have watched when I was six or seven years old if it was airing on television. Yet, I could understand the popularity that it was getting from younger audiences. It was action packed and had tons of likable characters, and so many people who grew up with *Naruto* took his catchphrase to heart: "Believe it!"

A Sakura Kinomoto (the heroine of *Cardcaptor Sakura*) cosplayer enjoying ParaCon 2003 (Santa Clara, CA) at Great America.

In the 2000s the audience skewed much younger. The younger millennials and members of Generation Z were watching anime by whatever means necessary, even if it was watching an episode on YouTube in three parts. Living in the Bay Area at the time, I would occasionally see a *Naruto* fan at the mall wearing the headband. I thought to myself, "Cool!

165

Let them live their best ninja lives!" Other cosplayer friends snickered and judged from afar. "Why would you wear that in public?" they would say.

BitTorrent and downloading anime on a digital platform made anime much more accessible and consumable. When I started torrenting anime it was still a niche thing to do. The target market was adapting to the times. More and more anime was being subtitled into English and uploaded onto torrent servers the very next day. You could immediately download the latest English subtitled episode of a series you were watching within 24 hours of the original Japanese broadcast. Spoiler talk about *Fullmetal Alchemist*, *Death Note*, *Bleach*, etc., became more and more common. More and more newer titles were popping up on the torrent websites. Keeping up with anime did not mean having to wait months for a DVD release or weeks for several episodes on VHS tapes. You could have it in an instant. As a studious college student, it felt difficult to keep up—shonen anime was big in the 2000s. I gravitated towards *Fruits Basket*, *Paradise Kiss*, and *Nana* during my university days. The shonen and seinen anime of the 2000s did not do it for me, but I would not decline to watch an episode if friends wanted to have a watch party. I did enjoy the seinen series Eddie had showed me at Sonoma State University. Maybe there was something different about '90s seinen? And because these anime genres were taking over, for anything magical girl or girl power focused, you really had to dig around for femme-centered titles. *Sailor Moon* and other magical girl shows were fading into the background. Not even the live action tokusatsu *Pretty Guardian Sailor Moon* could spark a Moonie renaissance. We would not see our moon princess make a comeback until *Sailor Moon Crystal* in the 2010s.

The best part about attending San Francisco Bay Area anime events was riding the BART in cosplay. Because the Bay Area still had its "let your freak flag fly" mantra, it was fun cosplaying on public transportation. Yeah, we got stares, but nothing hostile. I wore my Tohru from *Fruits Basket* on the BART on the way to the Cherry Blossom Festival and I was able to spot some *Yu Yu Hakusho* cosplayers on the train. We all huddled together and became instant friends engaging in conversation to kill travel time and then walking together to the parade spot.

And I was finally able to check out the Cherry Blossom Festival! Todd lived close to the BART line. I would come down from university and stay with him overnight. My first Cherry Blossom Festival was wild. This was similar to Nisei Week in Los Angeles, a citywide celebration of Japanese culture and a celebration of the achievements of the Japanese American community in the greater San Francisco Bay Area. I loved seeing

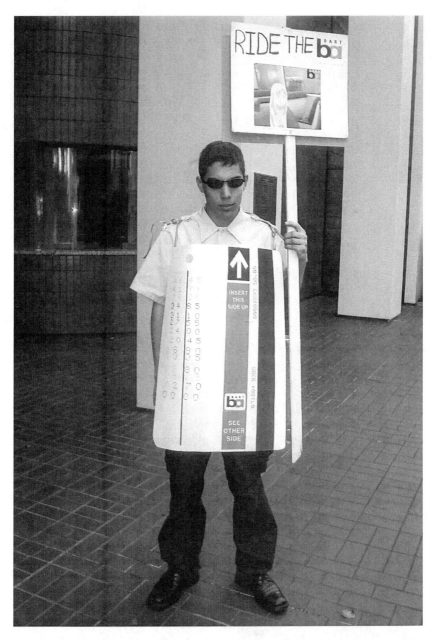

BART Boy, a San Francisco Bay Area personality, pays homage to the Bay Area's rapid transit system by combining his day job and his love of anime and cosplay.

A *Katamari Damacy* cosplayer arrives at the City Hall plaza to get ready to march in the annual Cherry Blossom Festival parade.

all the cultural floats and displays. I loved seeing the taiko circle rehearse at the starting point of the parade. We cosplayers gathered at the San Francisco Civic Center. We were assigned numbers for the cosplay contest. Our costumes were judged based on accuracy to character and craftsmanship. Winners would ride on the Safeway float. The rest of us would march from the San Francisco Civic Center to Japantown. Once we got to Japantown, we could finally check out more cultural displays or sit in one of the restaurants and have some of the best Japanese food on this side of the Pacific! Our tradition was to eat at this place called On the Bridge. This was a Japanese–Italian fusion place that had a lot of unique flavors. It had a soy-based pasta and the best parfaits, and it also served as a manga cafe. Japantown was definitely the central hub for otaku of the San Francisco Bay Area. So much so, even Japantown started hosting events for our nerdy community.

Japantown Anime Faire was a convention on the grounds of San Francisco's Japantown. Todd and I entered the cosplay contest as Lupin III and Fujiko Mine. We noticed that the contest had an interview-style format where a cosplayer went onstage and was interviewed by the emcee. This was not our style. We wanted to show off our dramatic flair and theatrical style. We wanted to give the audience a show. We had a friend be our bumbling buffoon of an Interpol agent, Zenigata, to chase us offstage. We planned a skit because having a performance act for a cosplay contest was the expectation if you really

At the Tokyo Pop booth at Anime Expo 2004 (Anaheim, CA) cosplaying as Fujiko Mine from *Lupin III* collecting and buying as many Lupin manga as I could!

Sochie Heim cosplayer from *Turn A Gundam* at Japantown Anime Faire 2006 (San Francisco, CA).

wanted to show off and win over the audience. Basically, the skit went that Zenigata would see that these international thieves would be onstage and then chase us offstage. We would run back and forth onstage to create confusion for Zenigata. We did not place, but we gladly entertained the hundreds of people gathered in Little Tokyo's public plaza. Japantown Anime Faire lasted for a few years. However, a lot of Bay Area otaku felt they did not need a convention to enjoy Japantown. In Japantown it was pretty common to see people wearing their anime shirts or Lolita fashion or *Naruto* fans in their headbands. Going to Japantown was like a special occasion. It was like going to church. Even if it was mainly for just hanging out with friends. Many of us didn't have cars. We would trek in on the BART or MUNI. Bay Area otaku generally weren't drivers who had reliable vehicles. We were happy when we had friends with cars and forever thankful for it. Yet, if one was going to hang out in Japantown, it would be a full-day affair. This was our favorite space for food, movies, shopping, or just hanging out over crepes.

In downtown San Francisco, there was a building that looked like it came from the future. In the evening, it had a gentle blue glow, beckoning the folks on Market Street to come right in. Once they set foot into this building, they were greeted by chrome and club music. The high-tech vibes and gentle blue glow were inviting. This establishment is known as Sony's Metreon. When I was visiting the San Francisco Bay Area to tour the colleges that accepted

Sugar from *A Little Snow Fairy Sugar* at Japantown Anime Faire 2005 (San Francisco, CA).

171

me, my brother wanted to stop by this high-tech shopping center. The Metreon had movie theaters, a Discovery store, an arcade, a Sony PlayStation store, and an anime store. The anime store had a Gundam sitting right in front of it. You could also pick up anime figures and merchandise. The Metreon also hosted their own one-day event every fall: Metreon Anime Festival. I only went one time for a few hours just to check it out in between studying for midterms because it was always during peak study time. I liked it because it gave cosplayers a chance to pose with the futuristic-looking design of the building or something as peaceful as the outdoor gardens and fountains next door. It was really an excuse for cosplayers to just hang out and take photos. I couldn't justify the $30 cost for one day when I could go there for free and wear cosplay. Yet, the Sony Metreon became one of the hangout spots for us Bay Area otaku. "Meet me at the Metreon! We can get dinner there after the movie!" I recall playing a lot of *Dance Dance Revolution* with friends at the arcade and seeing friends test out new PlayStation 2 games at the Sony store. Other than Japantown, this was our hangout zone.

Theme parks also hosted anime events. The Bay Area had ParaCon at Six Flags Great America. ParaCon was short for "Paramount Con." Imagine cosplayers at the theme park. Todd and I dressed up as Subaru and Seishirou from *X/1999*, a toxic but pretty canonical male pairing, for the theme park convention. We were wearing suits to the theme park. It was our most theme park–friendly cosplay. Imagine cosplayers going on

Attending ParaCon 2003 (Santa Clara, CA), an anime convention at Great America, cosplaying as Seishirou from *X/1999*.

A *Battle Royale* cosplayer at Recca Con 2003 (Pittsburg, CA).

looped roller coasters and merry-go-rounds, taking photos at a theme park! There was a cosplay contest. I don't remember who placed, but I remember that Viz gave us free *Ah! My Goddess!* and *Lupin III* soundtrack CDs. ParaCon did not last very long, but it was a memorable event. None of us came home empty-handed.

It's no surprise that community colleges were still hosting anime events. That's how Fanime had its start. The Bay Area also had Recca Con, a convention that took place at the local community college in the East Bay. This one-day event was the perfect hangout event. There were two Recca Cons per year—one in the spring and one in the fall. The community college's main student union had plenty of space to entertain the hundreds of Bay Area anime fans. It was a simple setup with a game room, swap meet, a few panel rooms, and a main stage. I remember entering the cosplay contest as Yomiko Readman. The last time I ever placed in a contest was Ani-Magic 2000, my first event. I entered as a beginner, but somehow, because the organizers knew me, I got bumped up to the veteran category. I ended up placing as Yomiko Readman for the rather small cosplay contest.

And if you traveled an hour south of San Francisco, you could find even more events. The Bay Area also had Anime Overdose at Santa Clara University. It was a one-and-a-half-day event. I was surprised it even had

A Chun-Li cosplayer posing for a photograph around the vendor hall at Fanime 2005 (San Jose, CA).

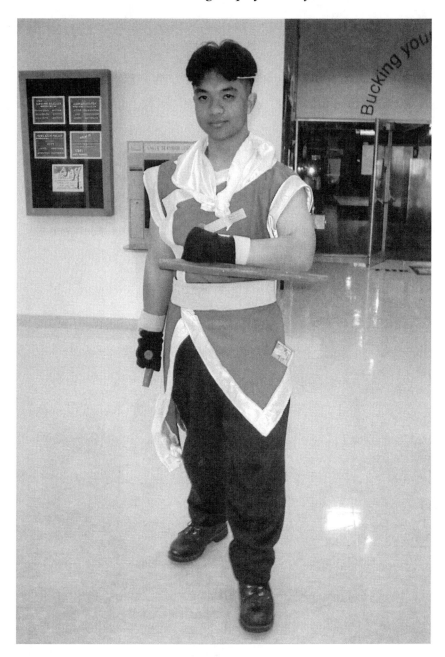

Suikoden cosplay at Anime Overdose 2005 (Santa Clara, CA) at Santa Clara University.

anime's best frenemy, Carl Macek, as a guest of honor. Depending on your version of history, Carl Macek can be seen as either as public enemy number one or a legendary pioneer of bringing anime to the West. He's best known for *Robotech*, having combined three different anime into one anime called *Robotech*. I missed out on his panel on day one, but I would have loved to have heard him. He passed away in 2010.

Anime Overdose, like Recca Con, took place at a student center. As anime was getting more and more accessible via Toonami and torrent sharing, the audience was getting younger and younger. There were a lot of 12- to 13-year-olds being dropped off at the con with their friend groups. I remember seeing a lot of younger cosplayers and otaku hailing from anime such as *Naruto, Fullmetal Alchemist, Fruits Basket,* and *Bleach* during this time period. I remember when I was the youngest person at an anime con and how my parents were strict about me attending one. The anime that I enjoyed in high school was slowly fading. Yet, I did welcome the newer generation. While my friends complained about the *Naruto, Bleach,* and *Fullmetal Alchemist* cosplayers taking over as the top fandoms, I was simply happy to see that these kids could get official *Naruto* headbands at Hot Topic so they could represent their fandom. It reminded me of wearing cat ears with my school uniform.

Anime Overdose would later rebrand

An anime fan patiently awaits a voice actor roundtable panel at Animation on Display 2006 (San Francisco, CA).

itself to Animation on Display. A few concerned parents did not feel comfortable taking their children to an event associated with the word "overdose." They were afraid that the use of "overdose" in the event title meant that this convention had something to do with drugs, alcohol, or addiction. The more family-friendly Animation on Display would then move to San Francisco. During their inaugural year in San Francisco, they characterized themselves as an animation convention. Rob Paulsen and a few voice actors from Hollywood attended in their first year in San Francisco. We also had the creative team behind *Wallace & Gromit: The Curse of the Were-Rabbit* and *Happy Tree Friends*. It was nice to see all types of animation represented at Animation on Display. They really did live up to their broad-based name. However, the biggest draw was the visual kei group, Psycho Le Cému. Psycho Le Cému brought in a huge amount of attendees from all over. Psycho Le Cému was best known for their vivid, anime-inspired outfits. They even had *Lupin III*–inspired outfits for one of their magazine photoshoots. This was one of the rare times you could have seen them live. Luckily, I was there for their concert—our press credentials

Stopping by Mitsuwa Marketplace in San Jose's Japantown to pick up snacks before Fanime Con.

177

gave us the front row. This would be the first of many anime, J-pop, and J-rock concerts I would see in the front row because of my reputation for media coverage.

And of course, Fanime was THE main event to attend in the San Francisco Bay Area. Fanime was growing and found a new home in San Jose in 2004. Fanime was a long-running convention in the San Francisco Bay Area that started in a community college and was now heading to the San Jose Convention Center. It went from being a three-day event to a four-day event. Even when I was attending Anime Expo and Ani-Magic in 2000, I did hear about Fanime and had considered it. I finally attended in 2003 during its last year at the Santa Clara Convention Center. My first Fanime was a positive experience, and it did live up to the "by fans for fans" motto.

Fanime drew in a few thousand Californians each year. They were known at the time to have a robust artist alley, arcade, and one of the best masquerades in the country. While organization and starting on time was not their forte, this was a big party event for Bay Area anime enthusiasts and California fandom more generally. It felt like a true 24-hour convention. People were still gaming in the main convention hall and there were raves going on. Late-night adult programming went into the wee morning hours; you had all night hentai playing with audience lampooning included and you also had the bishōnen auction hosted by Yaoi Con. Friends could just chill, chitchatting at the tables in the convention center enjoying the nightlife. As Anime Expo was becoming larger and larger, many veterans of Anime Expo were canceling plans to make it down to Anaheim in favor of Fanime being their main event for the year. A lot of cosplayers began to bring their A game to Fanime. I enjoyed both Anime Expo and Fanime. Fanime was my party con with my Bay Area friends. Anime Expo was my homecoming con to get excited for main events, guests, and autographs.

Also, as the university years went on, it was trippy to see advertising for Anime Expo in downtown San Francisco. I spotted a poster for Anime Expo right by the mall in South City and another one at the Daly City BART station. Anime Expo continued to thrive in Anaheim. During the time it was in Anaheim, Anime Expo brought in a ton of all-stars from Japan. Most notable was CLAMP, the artist team behind *Cardcaptor Sakura*, *X/1999*, and *Magic Knight Rayearth*. I admired their art and their storytelling. I loved how femme-centric their manga was. Also, I admired their unapologetically queer subplots and subtexts. I had so many questions for them the year they came to Anime Expo. I needed to meet the creators behind my favorites.

Gentleman thief, Lupin III, waltzes right into Fanime 2006 (San Jose, CA).

Yet, questions for the all-star manga team were limited to preselected questions and questions about the new *Tsubasa: Reservoir Chronicle*, the convoluted multiverse connecting all CLAMP franchises and characters together. I wanted to ask about queer representation and presentation, but I was not given the chance. CLAMP only had one panel and one signing, but the signing was limited to specific items bought at the convention.

Many people recall Anime Expo's golden years at the Anaheim Convention Center. I wish I took time to appreciate this era. This was also the time I was brought in on staff to help out with the ballroom dance. Anime Expo staff heard about my suggestions from the 2003 ballroom dance, and they wanted me on board with their cosplay events staff. I would help select music and help out with the dance lessons. It was a commitment, but it was one that I enjoyed. I would continue to staff the ballroom dance until Anime Expo 2008. I always found it nice that anime conventions had ballroom dances—it was like cosplay prom. You could dance to anime and video game tunes instead of a curated list of Top 40 hits. You could be with your friends and perhaps find romance with a fellow otaku. You could wear a formal version of a character you liked—or make one up if there was no canonical formal version. Staffing the ballroom dance was my favorite part of Anime Expo during the Anaheim era. Not only did it earn me a free badge that covered the entire weekend, it was a chance to be a part of the creative team behind my favorite Anime Expo event.

There was no doubt that Anime Expo was growing out of control as anime was becoming much more accessible. The audience kept getting younger. I started seeing more teens attend these events through the likes of *Naruto, Fruits Basket, Bleach, One Piece, Prince of Tennis*, or anything that may have been trending on Toonami or Adult Swim. Cartoon Network had a huge hand in bringing anime to younger audiences, and they kept the convention scene thriving with cosplayers and hotels filling up fast!

20

Fake It Until You Can Make It

Content for Traveling Valentine kept growing and growing. We saw no shortage of anime conventions and events in the Bay Area. I was seeing my leadership potential in running a conventions media website. I was also pursuing leadership positions with my university's Asian Student Union, taking the lead with a few community events. Being seen as local cosplay celebrities and hometown heroes for being cosplay sweethearts that took a lot of convention and cosplay photos empowered me. I had to think about what would be the next best thing to do to grow and expand Traveling Valentine outside of cosplay photos and convention reports.

I had Windows Movie Maker on my laptop. Todd would sometimes record random convention shenanigans on his camera. I did make a few anime music videos, but I never entered them into an anime music video contest. I took some of the recorded video and I put it to music. At last, I had created a convention music video. I was inspired by the "Crash and Burn" video Sora made for Anime Central 2001. I wanted to bring this spirit of the old days into my new life as a college student in San Francisco. I wanted to make a memorable convention music video set to a song I felt resonated with my convention memories.

I would post the convention report and photos. I would then also find a song that would describe the vibe I felt at the event. Austin Powers was a huge thing back in the 2000s. Because Todd and I were known for our Lupin III and Fujiko cosplays, I picked out "Soul Bossa Nova" for Japantown Anime Faire because Lupin III is as close as they come to a Japanese Austin Powers. I liked Billy Joel's "We Didn't Start the Fire," and I used that for a con and highlighted a cosplayer or a moment with each piece of the historical listicle song.

Traveling Valentine was entering a new age of convention music videos. It elevated our success as a cosplay media website.

"I love your music videos!"

"Thank—"

And before I could finish my sentence, it would become apparent that the compliment was not directed at me. Time after time, Todd was given the praise, even though the credits also listed me as the editor for the music videos.

"We would love to use your videos to promote our convention. I would love to talk to Todd about it sometime!"

I was always in the shadows. Video editing was part of my university major. I was a media studies and communications student hoping to get a behind-the-scenes job in the entertainment industry. Todd was a public relations and business economics student.

"And I love your videos!"

A convention chair approached Todd with compliments.

This was when I started seeing the misogyny at conventions. My high school years were full of whimsy and joy. Maybe there was misogyny going on that I was not aware of, but I was not a witness to it because I was in the pure bliss of fandom sensory overload. With Traveling Valentine gaining so much popularity in the San Francisco Bay Area for being the cosplay sweethearts and a cosplay media duo, I wanted to say something, but there was that cardinal rule—don't start drama.

LiveJournal was at times a good place to vent, but you also had to be careful about how often you vented. After all, no one wanted a constant pity party or to read another emo post. "I had to unfriend them because they got too emo," I would hear friends say. I wanted to keep my cosplay friends. I would show happy couple photos of us to balance things out. I didn't know how to talk about it. There was that "no drama" rule. You didn't share your drama. You kept it to yourself.

And if it wasn't sexism, I started to see racism.

I transferred to San Francisco State University after two years of general studies at Sonoma State University. Our communications major was seeing some significant cuts. I had to do what was best for my career down the road. San Francisco State University was an hour south of Sonoma State. I would also be closer to my friends in San Francisco and San Jose. Transferring to San Francisco State was better for my media studies major. After really getting immersed into the subject matter in my Asian American studies course at Sonoma State, I wanted to switch my minor to Asian American studies. The best part was that San Francisco State was the university for ethnic and cultural studies. I knew I had to make this upgrade.

20. Fake It Until You Can Make It

I was an avid member of the Asian American Student Association at Sonoma State. My final push to transfer to San Francisco State was a comment made by one of our leadership team member's regarding *American Idol*'s Jasmine Trias, a Filipino American from Season 3. "Did anyone see that stupid Filipino on *American Idol* last night?" It was the first thing I heard when I stepped into the club during one meeting. It was said by one of the white members of the club who happened to have an officer position. Culture themed student organizations could not discriminate. And why use the word "stupid" to describe someone? I did notice a number of white male members of the Asian American Student Association.

"Look at them! They probably don't speak English!" said a college friend with whom I enjoyed watching Hong Kong movies as we were watching *American Idol* and the camera panned to Jasmine Trias's parents. Sonoma State's casual racism was not for me.

I was happy to finally be living in San Francisco. The Paris of the Pacific. I was ready to exchange my cottagecore life in wine country for the city by the Bay. Living in San Francisco put me in a much more diverse part of the Bay Area. Wine Country felt too homogeneously white, and it would be nice to be close to real Chinese cuisine, not some imitation

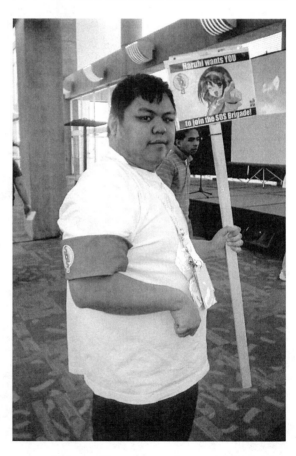

A Fanime 2005 (San Jose, CA) attendee shows his love for *The Melancholy of Haruhi Suzumiya*. Will you join the SOS Brigade?

fast-food version of it. I was looking forward to spending my free time finding dorm decoration and Asian snacks in Chinatown and exploring Japantown. I was not thinking about diversity and culture as a social factor at Sonoma State, but after a few encounters of casual racism, being in a city that had people that came from my culture did not feel as isolating. At least I did not have to worry about people speaking English slowly to me as if I did not understand the language.

The first club I joined at San Francisco State was Anime FX. A lot of the members recognized me from the local convention scene. "You're that Traveling Valentine cosplayer!" I was very humbled. We were seen as hometown celebrities. I made friends at San Francisco State's Anime FX so fast. So it was no surprise that I gained leadership within our niche anime community on campus in no time. I rose through the ranks to vice president, having organized our annual swap meet. I looked forward to every Friday, when we would hang out in one of the science building's lecture halls to watch anime or just talk and catch up. Anime FX was 50 percent "let's watch anime" and 50 percent "let's go into an empty classroom to game, share anime music videos on our laptops, or geek out." I was part of the social crowd, and I was taking the lead.

Living in San Francisco meant access to Japantown all the time. I could take the MUNI bus to Japantown after class or during the weekend to have soba with classmates, pan Japanese–Italian fusion dishes with cosplay friends at

An anime convention goer sporting a beanie from the slice-of-life anime *Azumanga Daioh* at Ani-Magic 2004 (Lancaster, CA).

On the Bridge, or sweet crepes with Anime FX club members. I was living the life.

I returned to Ani-Magic in 2004. This time around, it was not off the dark desert highway in Lancaster. Ani-Magic 2004 took place at the rather fancy and bougie resort area of Valencia. One of the Asian performing guests of honor invited us to lunch. She noticed that I was also a student at San Francisco State University. Since the musical guest was a Bay Area local, I was thinking of maybe discussing giving her a singing gig on our campus. After all, I was happy to take the lead on some of our Asian Student Union events. "Filipinos aren't Orientals," she said. "Filipino skin is too dark." I didn't know how to address this, but it made me feel uncomfortable. I didn't know who had the authority to say where Filipinos are from, but it wasn't going to be some random guest at Ani-Magic.

Around the time *Memoirs of a Geisha* came out in cinemas costume design, Colleen Atwood received heavy criticism for her interpretations of how a maiko should look and dress. She took liberties with the design of traditional maiko dress. I was really uncomfortable with this given how obsessed I was in researching all the fine details I had to do for cosplay. I called this out on my blog, and I was met with so much heavy scrutiny by non–Japanese friends who were superfans of anime. "Who cares?" "They were on a budget!" "It's just a movie." "But it looks pretty!" I honestly thought this community was all about celebrating Japanese culture, but when it came to defending whitewashing and cultural appropriation, I was shocked. I ended up losing friends because of having opinions that defended authentic Japanese culture. Am I allowed to start drama?

San Francisco State's business students told me that my pursuit of an Asian American studies minor was a vapid, futile attempt. "That's a bullshit program!" one of my peers in my marketing class said. I went into it wanting to get to know more about my culture and myself. San Francisco State would be the best place to study the subject because it was where the very idea of ethnic studies originated. These classes gave me the language to stand up for myself, but I then realized that I could not speak too loud. Speaking too loud would get me labeled as a starter of drama. And I didn't want that.

With my Asian American studies minor, I ended up taking classes on art as activism, independent Asian American cinema, and histories of Asian American immigration. I decided that for my senior project I would create a docuseries about the rise of Japanese pop culture in media. *Kill Bill*, *Avatar: The Last Airbender*, anime on Western television, Japanese

An elegant gothic Lolita–inspired outfit at Fanime 2005 (San Jose, CA).

Lolita street fashion appearing on *Project Runway* and being sold at stores like Hot Topic, *Spirited Away* winning Best Animated Feature at the Academy Awards, manga flooding the shelves at bookstores, and conventions sprouting up all over the Bay Area all gave me justification for this thesis. I spent most of my last year at university taking all of the technical things I learned in my media studies major and mixing it with a heavy dose of firsthand research into modern otaku fandom to create a four-part documentary created on Windows Movie Maker. Our anime club, Anime FX, even had a screening and Q&A of my senior project. I was very thrilled to achieve this much. A radio play producer at 15, I had become a documentary filmmaker in my fourth year of university. I pitched this documentary to a few local conventions for screenings and Q&A, and it was picked. I haven't run a panel since my voice acting days at Anime Central. I hosted screenings at a few California conventions including Animation on Display and Anime Los Angeles. I really did boost myself up to be a local hometown celebrity even more. Cosplayer, convention blogger, and documentary filmmaker—I was having it all.

But what else was out there other than anime that I could explore?

21

Outside Anime Fandom

The more involved I was in the anime cosplay community, the more I started looking to other fandoms outside of anime. *Kingdom Hearts* brought in Disney cosplayers to conventions. This was so unheard of when I first started. In fact, there was a ton of anti–Disney sentiment when I first converted to an otaku. It was refreshing seeing people start Disney cosplay gatherings at Fanime.

I also befriended Karisu, resident cosplay mom. This cosplayer had a husband and two kids that all cosplayed. And they also had Welsh corgis! I admired that someone who was of boomer age still enjoyed the hobby. Karisu would talk about the taboo of cosplay from something outside of anime at anime conventions and what a ridiculous community standard that became. At the time, I was shifting from anime. There weren't a lot of new anime that called to me and getting the older stuff meant shelling out my allowance to spend $30+ on a DVD. A broke college student could not do that. Things like *Star Wars*, Disney, Broadway, and even J-fashion like the gothic Lolita trend were calling to me more.

I had attended San Diego Comic-Con in 2002, and the more I opened myself to fandoms outside of anime, the more willing I was to give these conventions another shot. The Bay Area had SiliCon in San Jose at the original site of the first Anime Expo. I wore Yukino's basic school uniform from *His and Her Circumstances* to keep things simple. It was a small con. It was also a very quiet convention. Yet, an older costumer told me, "You're not wearing a real costume. That's normal clothes!"

I also tried my hand at Worldcon in Anaheim. Karisu had recommended this one to me. With a name like Worldcon, I was expecting all things pop culture past and present. I wanted to see *Star Wars*, *Back to the Future*, *Twilight Zone*, retro science fiction, and giant robot anime— whatever! Worldcon had a "taster" badge where you could pay $75 to roam around for three hours. If you liked what you saw, you could pay the difference for a full-day badge. I heard amazing things about this convention's

I'm cosplaying as Yukino from *His and Her Circumstances* in a cosplay made from things from my closet and parts of my middle school uniform at SiliCon 2005 (San Jose, CA).

masquerade. At the very least, I wanted to check out the world's top tier cosplay contest.

The "taster" badge didn't include for masquerade. So, we were wandering around the Anaheim Convention Center looking at exhibits focusing on old-school science fiction and fantasy. L. Ron Hubbard's foundation had a booth. The only anime I saw was hentai figures for sale. The only thing that millennials would recognize was a DeLorean from *Back to the Future*, but it would cost you if you wanted a photo with it. I tried my best to keep an open mind. Yet, I did not feel I was within the target audience for Worldcon. I wished there was some attempt to get millennials in. It seemed that this was simply for boomers who wanted to party. And there's nothing wrong with that! I just understood that I wasn't the target market.

The Bay Area did have WonderCon, but it would usually fall during my spring midterm study time. WonderCon is a younger sibling con to San Diego Comic-Con. San Diego Comic-Con had a smaller, lighter version of their show in the Bay Area that took over the Moscone Center. WonderCon was a big deal in San Francisco fandom. Almost every Western fandom that was mainstream was present. However, the timing of WonderCon would always interfere with my midterms. I could only show up for a Saturday, but even then, my plans would be halted because of an emergency or I needed extra time to study. The times I did attend for a few hours on a Saturday allowed me to explore the dealers hall in the later afternoon and watch the cosplay contest in the evening. We would top off the day at Mel's Drive-in for burgers and shakes.

The target demographic of anime was getting more shonen driven. I was seeing a ton of bright orange ninjas, shinigami in black, pirates in straw hats, tennis teams causing a racket, and short-tempered blondes in red coats complaining about their lack of height. The audience was getting younger. I've heard the complaint, "I don't like shōjo. Anime has too many weak female characters!" I really missed peak '90s shōjo like *Sailor Moon*, *Magic Knight Rayearth*, and *Cardcaptor Sakura*. Yet, I didn't want to be seen as an old otaku waving their cane to the kids. I didn't want to be seen as a jaded curmudgeon.

Todd also wanted us to pair up in cosplay to keep the Traveling Valentine brand relevant. Lupin and Fujiko, Yuki and Tohru, Sousuke and Chidori, Henrietta and Jose, Riza and Roy, Integra and Walter, Faye and Spike. We had the reputation of cosplay sweethearts. I started seeing that I didn't have many opportunities to cosplay solo. It's normal and healthy for couples to have different interests. My formative years were defined by the girl power that was shōjo anime. As '90s anime fandoms were slowly fading from the cosplay scene, and I wanted to go back to cosplay plans I originally wanted to do when I first started. I had a ton of cosplay plans from magical girl anime I wanted to go forward with. When I said I wanted to cosplay Umi from *Magic Knight Rayearth*, Todd replied, "Well, what about me?!" If there was not a character for him, there would be no going forward.

Obtaining cosplay in university was very tricky. Most of my cosplays were clothes and knickknacks found in my closet or at Goodwill or Forever 21. I was a broke university student, but I started feeling the need to learn how to sew. I did save up annually for my special commission from Amethyst Angel. I had Mulan from Disney and Christine Daaé from *Phantom of the Opera* during my university days. At least I had two non-anime cosplays to bring to themed cosplay gatherings or pop culture themed conventions where non-anime cosplay might be appreciated.

22

Cosplay Is Serious Business

Cosplay photography was turning into an art of its own. I never considered myself to be a cosplay photographer. I saw myself more as a convention journalist like Kevin Lillard. I like to capture moments in time, as they're happening. I liked to capture cosplayers in the wild of the convention halls. Cosplay photographers were upping their game. It was no longer a simple digital camera and a quick photo of a cosplayer in the convention hotel or hall. Cosplay.com was offering paid photoshoots. Higher end digital cameras were hitting the shelves. Cosplay photography was a mostly male-dominated part of the cosplay scene. While cosplay photography was a good service to the cosplay community, this also had its issues. Issues such as overweight cosplayers being ignored and photographers mainly focusing on conventionally attractive cosplayers became topics of discussion. And the discussion was never pretty. "But photographers should be able to choose who they work with!" "It's the choice of the photographer!" There were a lot of male photographers defending whom they could and should photograph. I did not fall on the conventionally attractive side, and my cosplays were mostly conservative and covered up. Most of my cosplays were Goodwill finds or a nice dress that I had commissioned. It did not have the San Diego Comic-Con "wow factor." I wanted to be comfortable on my vacation at a con. It was really hard finding a photographer to work with because many photographers were males who were looking for conventionally attractive women to book a photoshoot with. Thankfully, I had the goodness of my friends and my digital camera to document my cosplays in the 2000s.

By this time, Kevin Lillard's health was starting to fade, and he pulled the plug on Fansview. He wasn't attending as many conventions. We were slowly seeing an end of an era. We were sad to see this website remain dormant. Many of us in the community spent time visiting Fansview to combat our fear of missing out when a major convention was happening. We mourned the community's loss.

Beyond discussing and planning for conventions, Cosplay.com opened up Cosworx. There was a need for a wig store that sold wigs for cosplay. While one could go to a Party City or a Halloween store or attempt to dye a wig with a Sharpie, selection was very limited. Alternatively, you could order wigs from Japan. The Japanese cosplay stores had a variety of colors and the fibers were soft enough to make it look like real hair instead of the plastic feel Halloween wigs had. However, ordering from Japanese brands directly from Japan meant you also had to pay high shipping prices or use a go-between. Group orders were very popular, but it could be tricky getting people to join in with you on an order. Cosworx was a game changer.

Cosworx also sold cat ears by Yaya Han. When I saw the black and pink cat ears, I knew I had to own them. "I want these to be a trend!" said an energetic Yaya at Anime Expo 2006 when she debuted the ears. Cosworx was valuable at the time. And even with that, Cosworx also created competition—Arda Wigs and Epic Cosplay would soon follow in the cosplay wig business. More and more, you would see entrepreneurs provide service to the cosplay world. Wigs were the best start. And by this time, I could finally get a Utena wig that would complement my mocha skin tone.

Cosplay.com also collected photos from Western cosplayers for Japanese cosplay magazines. When asked for cosplay submissions for the magazine, I submitted the photo Lionel Lum took of me at Anime Central when I cosplayed Soletta Orihime from *Sakura Taisen*. I was beautiful in the photo. I had a je ne sais quoi expression on my face. I looked away from the camera with the elegant, sophisticated air of an opera prima donna. I thought it would be perfect for publication. And guess what? The photo was selected! I was so happy that I would be featured in a Japanese cosplay magazine! However, Todd was not happy about this.

When he found out I was in an issue of a cosplay magazine, he threw an angry fit at me. I was happy that Lionel Lum's photo of my Soletta Orihime cosplay made it into a Japanese cosplay magazine. Anytime I looked at *Animerica*'s cosplay coverage, I always wanted to see my photo. I dreamed I would flip through the pages of *Animerica* and find that one of Kevin Lillard's snaps of me had made it to publication. When Todd found out, he got furious that I was featured. His raging fit made me cry. What was supposed to be a joyous occasion for me turned into a sour memory. I thought Todd would be happy for me that my photo was published to be

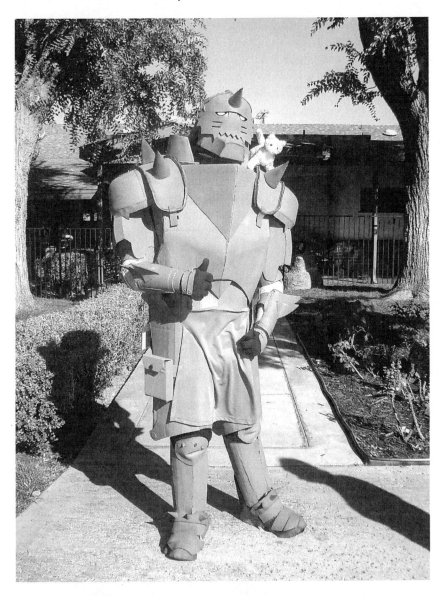

Alphonse cosplayer from *Fullmetal Alchemist* at Ani-Magic 2005 (Lancaster, CA).

seen worldwide. Yet, it became clear to me that if there was any aspect of my life that he was not involved in, I would not hear the end of it. I was being emotionally manipulated.

I knew I wanted to get out, but he did not make it easy. I tried talking to friends, but they would tell me, "But you're a cute couple!" "When's the wedding?" "You better get married before it's too late. You don't want to wait!" Even friends who were organizing conventions were making offers to us, "We have an extra ballroom for rent right before the con starts. You can have your wedding there." I got so drained thinking about these comments. I was about to graduate from university in media studies. I wasn't even sure what I was going to do with it given that I was graduating during the time of the writers' strike and the economic crash. Elder millennials like me who finished college at this time were entering one of the messiest economies in recent memory. I was worried about money and landing a job after university. Marriage was not priority number one.

"But you're not really bisexual. You have me." I ignored my bi identity for years since graduating from high school. It didn't help that the LGBTQ+ organizations at both Sonoma State and San Francisco State showed biphobia and their leadership was predominantly white. People suggested I wander in the yaoi or boys love circles. But boys love was not my thing. I preferred WLW and shōjo-ai manga. I was a fan of *Utena* and *Dear Brother*. I also appreciated the shōjo-ai subtext of *Rose of Versailles*. Yaoi was all over, but being a cis female who loved WLW content, I felt like the odd one out. These shōjo-ai stories resonated with me more. It didn't help that the yaoi community had internalized misogyny: "I hate this female character! She's weak and ruins my ship!" I missed the Queer Kids Table of Anime Expo where we would just gush over whatever. I didn't appreciate seeing my identity being fetishized and my gender identity also being scrutinized. I felt I did not belong with the yaoi crowd. My queer identity was about more than just two pretty boys engaging in buttsex.

I was torn between two routes. I presented too heterosexual to mingle with the millennial otaku queer community of the Bay Area, and I was too much of a kept woman to escape the closet. I hadn't consciously gone back in the closet or grown comfortable there. It just happened when I wasn't thinking about it. I missed the time of Anime Expo 2000 where I could freely talk about my identity. I missed having those spontaneous conversations without having to discuss anal sex between two pretty boys as the meme du jour.

After graduating from university, I was met with the start of the economic depression. Full-time jobs for new graduates were scarce. I wanted to go into the business side of the entertainment industry, but the 2007 recession did not make it easy landing a job. And with a looming actors' and writers' strike on the horizon that would affect all sections of Hollywood, I had to put my dreams of being a documentary filmmaker on hold. However, I was fortunate to land some temporary administrative work to carry me through the worst parts of the recession. I went from temp job to temp job during the start of the 2007 financial crisis. But what to do in this ennui? What did I need to do to keep me busy?

I phoned a friend from Anime FX: "Hey Cici ... do you have a free weekend?"

23

Lesson One
How to Sew Straight

Renderings of 1950s gowns, swatches of cotton sateen, and the busy buzz of sewing machines. I needed one more elective to maintain my full-time status at San Francisco State University. I enrolled in a costuming class in university with a few personal goals in mind—learn how to read a sewing pattern and have the confidence to make a simple garment. I walked into the three-unit theater costuming class. I was excited to learn. I was excited to take on challenges. By the end of the semester, I wanted to make a whimsical ball gown for my final project—something like Yukari's blue butterfly dress from *Paradise Kiss*. However, I was met with disappointment. I came in with high puppy energy hoping to be fed with the knowledge of being a professional-grade seamstress by the end. I had so many questions, but the course professor seemed distant. I was asked to steam and iron costumes for the upcoming production of *West Side Story*. I looked at the 1950s fancy bell shaped dresses. I wanted to make one of those. The semester consisted of ironing, steaming, and the occasional stitch and fix. My personal learning goals were not met.

I picked up a tiny sewing machine at CVS. I was practicing making doll clothes for my Asian ball-jointed dolls. A friend gave me an Asian ball-jointed doll for the Lunar New Year. She needed some simple, country-style Lolita dresses—she needed to look like *Anne of Green Gables* in her calico printed skirts, Victorian blouses, and boater hats with the ribbon.

I subscribed to a doll collector's magazine that had patterns for doll clothes. On a sunny fall afternoon, I invited my friend from the anime club, Cici, to teach me how to sew. Cici was an award-winning cosplayer. She had been going to conventions longer than I had. She had done a *Sailor Moon* masquerade act that had the Sailor Senshi redesigned as 1960s go-go dancers set to "Mr. Wonderful." She also had a masquerade act poking fun at the censorship the *Sailor Moon* series underwent when brought to the United States. Most of all, Cici had the best convention horror stories— some funny, some cautionary. I felt like I was listening to an elder Gen X cosplayer telling stories from the past. Cici became my cosplay senpai.

I had a lot of respect for her love of the craft. I would show her some of the cosplays I bought in the past, and she would break down how she would have done it differently. She definitely knew what she was doing. I could trust her in teaching me how to sew. She was very patient with me. Unlike my college professor, she was just as eager to teach me as I was to learn.

We had the tiny machine from CVS to work with. It wasn't a "real" sewing machine, but it was travel sized sewing machines that you could get for $30 to patch up a tear or two. However, it was enough for Cici to show me the basics. We threaded the thread through the machine and made sure we had the bobbin in order. I had a ton of scrap fabrics from my grandma's collection. I had the doll sized dress pattern pieces cut out.

And with that tiny sewing machine, I was able to make doll clothes out of scrap fabric. I felt accomplished and a sense of pride after creating my first doll dress. The seams were small, but working on a smaller scale would make the human sized projects a walk in the park.

My next lesson was picking and choosing fabric. I had listed two projects I wanted to get started on—Reira from *Nana* and Rei Hino's school uniform from *Sailor Moon*. I was reading *Nana* in university and after graduation. I loved the use of high fashion and josei manga coming together to tell a story about two girls from two different worlds and their unlikely friendship. Reira happened to be the front woman of a band who wore dresses inspired by Vivienne Westwood.

Cici took me on the train to 16th Street and Mission in downtown San Francisco's Mission District. We walked a block or two to Fabric Outlet. This massive store had everything. Cici showed me how to break down what materials I would need for the outfit. We would find a sewing pattern similar to the dress and uniform I wanted to create. The pattern would tell us how much fabric we would need and any additional supplies like zippers or buttons. Cici would show me how to pick out the fabric and what fabric I could use for each of these projects. There wasn't a dedicated cosplay section at fabric or craft stores; we had to navigate supply shopping on our own.

Freya, another cosplay crafter friend of mine, had a brilliant idea of having a sewing sleepover weekend. I would bring a project that I was working on. I also had another project in mind—Galaxy Mage from *Disgaea 2*. This outfit consisted of a simple white dress and a Victorian-style overcoat. I figured this would be an easy project to start off on. The white dress looked like any 1950s housewife dress. I could find a Mrs. Claus pattern for the overcoat.

Freya had told me that the Jo-Ann's in her neck of the woods was massive. I wanted to take the shopping skills I learned from Cici to see if I could pick out the fabric I wanted.

Freya had a professional-level machine and a serger. I knew I was in good hands. We reviewed threading the machine. Yet, before we could really get to work, we had to wash and pre-shrink the fabric we had bought earlier that day. "Always wash your fabric," Freya said. We reviewed the pattern pieces I bought. Freya taught me how to "franken-pattern," or how to adjust the default pattern measurements to your actual measurements. Factory-made patterns aren't always going to be perfect. Freya showed me how to ensure that the pattern piece given will best flatter my measurements. Once the fabric ran through the washer and dryer, it was time to cut the pieces out and then sew them together. By the end of the sleepover weekend, I was able to finish the main dress. After that weekend, I gained more confidence in being able to sew on my own.

After I finished university, I ended up moving back home to the Los Angeles suburbs. My aunt had an extra Brother machine she had been meaning to give me. Anime Los Angeles was coming up, and I wanted to enter masquerade with my first sewing project. I went forward with Reira from *Nana*. She too had a simple white dress with a few accessories added on. I was able to create the simple white dress in about a week's time. For her gloves and neck piece, I was able to find feathered trim to complete the look. I used Cosworx to get a simple wavy brown wig.

I didn't place at the Anime Los Angeles masquerade that year, but I was proud that I was able to enter with the first cosplay I ever created from scratch. I still take pride in utilizing closet cosplay in my earlier days and hiring commissioners. After putting in time with my first projects—Reira and Galaxy Mage—I understood why commissioners charged as much as they did, especially if I was hiring an award-winning cosplayer to take on the labor.

However, I did have new friends in Los Angeles that I made through the years I attended Anime Expo while spending my summers in between university. After my first Anime Los Angeles, we went on a field trip to Los Angeles's massive fabric district. This is where Hollywood costume designers and Fashion Institute of Design and Merchandising students would shop, where other sewing enthusiasts based in Greater Los Angeles would get their supplies. And everything was a low, low price. Some stores even advertised themselves selling fabric for $1 per yard. It was sensory overload. I was not prepared for this. Fabric, lace, trims, zippers, supplies, etc., of all kinds were out there in the open. I found bridal satin for less than $3 a yard. I found imitation Louis Vuitton fabric for $5 a yard. I could even find cheap pairs of shoes to modify!

Simon, one of the new cosplay friends I made in Los Angeles, showed me where his go-to shops were. He had a favorite trim shop that had so many different trims. I came to the fabric district with a few projects to shop for, but looking at all the different variations of trim, I wanted to do something with some of the fancier and floral trims I came across. But no, I could only carry so much fabric with me back to the car. I had to focus on Dawn from *Pokémon: Diamond and Pearl*, Chane Laforet from *Baccano!*, and Grandis from *Nadia: Secret of the Blue Water*.

And after we went fabric shopping in Los Angeles, our tradition was to stop by Little Tokyo. It was a stone's throw away from the wonderland of cosplay supplies. We would leave the parking structure from the fabric district and then proceed to park in Little Tokyo. We would have lunch at Curry House. Over our delicious spicy curry and tropical iced tea, we would discuss upcoming cosplay plans and where and when we would wear them, share ideas on cosplay construction, and plan travel for upcoming conventions. After lunch at Curry House, we would look at a few stores, and every now and then, we would find cosplayers having fan-run meetups in Little Tokyo.

Little Tokyo was a haven for anime fans. Around this time, the term "weeb" started taking shape. "Weeb" became the term that millennials were using to describe their anime enthusiast selves. "Otaku" was fading from ubiquity. "Weeb" was self-depreciating and an honorific at the same time. The origins of the term "weeb" remain nebulous at best. I never liked the term because it was used more as an insult towards younger, socially awkward anime fans who wore *Naruto* headbands in public, as a put-down rather than a way of characterizing oneself or the people in one's tribe. "Look at that weeb! They must have bought their cosplay from Hot Topic!" I was not comfortable with putting down younger anime fans. I wanted to be welcoming, and if they wanted to wear a *Naruto* headband, as long as they were not harming anyone, I said let them be. I remembered what it was like to be an awkward teen into anime, and back then I had wished that major stores carried anime goods!

These younger millennial cosplayers donned *Naruto*, *Bleach*, or *One Piece* cosplays and gallivanted around Little Tokyo. There were meetups going on, organized on Facebook, for these hangouts to happen. You could find these younger fans at the main Anime Jungle store or at the Little Tokyo mall just hanging out in Naruto or Bleach cosplay. No formal photoshoots; it was just cosplayers hanging out as if it were the last day of Anime Expo. There were differing opinions on this. It gave young people a sense of community and a safe place to find peers. Older fans felt secondhand embarrassment. My friends had mixed feelings about seeing cosplayers casually hanging out in Little Tokyo. However, inside, I was happy that high school–aged kids could have a community.

I felt the cosplay community shifting. There was a real fear of being trolled online if your cosplay was not good enough or if you did not look like an idealized version of a character. I knew a lot of friends who became sticklers for accuracy, and it made it hard for them to get things done and ultimately led to their burnout. I knew I was still a beginner seamstress. My cosplay sewing mentors had applauded how much I had learned and improved within a few months. Yet, I learned that sometimes it's not the lack of skill that gets you anonymously trolled. Some bullies will project their

Brain Age Guy wandering around Fanime 2006 (San Jose, CA).

anger against you by posting one of your cosplays on these anonymous websites just because. They did not need any particular reason to project their insecurities. I was posted once on one of these anonymous troll forums and was called a "Fail Lolita" when in fact I was posting privately on my Live-Journal to show off my new haircut. I just happened to be wearing a lacy business casual blouse with a headband that had a huge bow. Lolita was not the intention, but it seemed that someone had beef with me and decided to post my new haircut photo meant for the eyes of close friends on one of these public anonymous troll sites. It was not the trolling from the anonymous folks that got to me, but that a private photo meant for friends was shared for the sake of getting trolls to say nasty things about my new-hair-cut selfie.

I never liked bullies, and I didn't like participating in conversations about them. After all, I survived bullying from high school and middle school. I did not want to be part of that in a community where, ideally, I could truly be me. I stayed focused on my cosplay creation and leveling up my sewing skills. I kept friends who were more into the craft rather than those who were easily distracted by drama and gossip. I avoided any form of social forum whenever I sewed. The only media I had with me in my sewing space was maybe my laptop playing anime or a movie while I sewed. I couldn't be bothered with community gossip. I grew out of that in high school. The more I focused on creating, the happier I was and the more productive I could be.

24

Cosplay ...
in This Economy?

Graduating university in 2007 meant graduating into a failing economy. I began work towards my master's degree in school counseling. I did like helping my brother and his friends navigate and complete their state college applications. Also, I just simply like giving advice and helping confused people. I was never a gatekeeper. Also, in between my temporary office work during the economic downturn, I began taking cosplay commissions. I became a seamstress for hire during the start of the 2007 recession. I started a small business taking in simple commission requests. Once I started sewing, I felt confident enough to take orders for simple projects, whether it was a dress or modifying an existing piece of clothing.

I met one of my best friends during this time period. Dia and I were huge into *Pokémon Diamond and Pearl*. We had seen each other at conventions and events but never took the time to really get to know each other until we started playing *Pokémon Diamond and Pearl*. We bonded through this gaming hobby. We talked about building teams for battle and teams for aesthetics. After all, *Diamond and Pearl* also had those Pokémon beauty contests in the game. I wanted to build an all-kitty team both for battle and for contests. We would discuss strategy and also play along together on our Nintendo DS. From there, we would then talk about our strict Asian upbringing. Dia is Korean American and had rigid expectations culturally and religiously. We ended up sharing this connection. "LOL Asian Parents!" we would say anytime our parents were giving us grief for not being the perfect child. The two of us had a found family thing going on. I considered Dia the younger sibling I never had. While I did have a younger brother by blood, this bond was much stronger.

Dia was also a cosplayer and they needed a new Kagura from *Fruits Basket* cosplay done. I had materials ready. Kagura's flared mint-green sundress was simple enough to make. Because of our obsession with *Pokémon*

Hanging out at Fanime 2007 (San Jose, CA) right before the festivities began!

Diamond and Pearl, we wanted to go as Dawn and Ash. Dia had always liked Ash and could do a spot-on Pikachu impersonation. I really liked playing as Dawn in *Diamond and Pearl*, and her friendship with Ash is just so wholesome. In the anime, Dawn was more focused with beauty contests, and in the post-game for *Diamond and Pearl*, I was more into Pokémon beauty contests than battles. I proceeded to make Dia an Ash cosplay. It was a simple vest with a yellow stripe. It was one of my first projects. I would also make Dawn's outfit, which consisted of a pink skirt from one of the stores in the LA Fashion District and a black vest. Dia and I each carried our character's Pokémon. Dia had a Pikachu, and I had a Piplup. For the first time in a while, I was excited to team up and collaborate on cosplay. Simon would also join us as one of Ash's gym leader rivals, Volkner, the electric gym leader. Todd would join us as Brock. Because we had a full team, it made sense for us to enter in a cosplay contest. And why not?

Mikomi Con was one of those small university cons hosted by an anime club. California State University–Northridge is no stranger to geek connections. The original *Star Trek* series was filmed there. However, the night before Mikomi Con, I broke up with Todd. My life was heading in a new direction. I knew I was not the same person as I was in 2003. Todd wanted marriage and a baby. I wanted to focus on getting my master's degree. I wanted to focus on my career and where it might take me. I was still in my early twenties, and I felt marriage was not something I wanted when I was still figuring myself out. I couldn't even fathom the idea of having kids so young. I could not handle the pressure. We broke up the night before the cosplay contest.

Yet, the show had to go on. Our group did not know that we had called it quits.

It was Saturday night at Mikomi Con. All of us were in the *Pokémon Diamond and Pearl* cosplays waiting in the wings ready for our turn. We did not have prerecorded audio. We were going on live. We had a very simple skit. Ash and Brock would go up against the electric gym leader, Volkner. Brock would make a few quips, such as the line inspired from the play *Jersey Boys*, "Ash, there's two types of women: Nurse Jenny and Officer Joy. Both will break your balls." Ash would find a new friend, Dawn. My part was short, and I just had to look cute onstage. The point was, we all had fun going up there.

I never stay for awards. My anxiety gets the best of me. The tension backstage can be very daunting. Did I win something? And if I didn't win anything, what went wrong? I know cosplay contests are supposed to be fun, but even for the smallest competitions, I can't shake off the anxiety. To catch a breather, I went out to grab dinner at the Red Robin near the university. Dia and Simon stayed behind. When I got back from dinner, Dia and Simon were there in the parking lot. "WE WON!" screamed Dia. Wait.... I haven't really placed in a cosplay contest in years. This was my first time back onstage in a while. I remembered my first time as Gary Oak's cheerleader eight years prior in Lancaster. A silly *Pokémon* skit that we had made up on the fly won Best of Show. This was a grand victory for our friend group.

But I was still breaking up with Todd. And it was for the best. I could finally be my own person again. I could run Scarlet Rhapsody, not Traveling Valentine, on my own. It was back to basics. I knew how to pitch Scarlet Rhapsody as a convention media website. I notified my convention contacts that I was running Scarlet Rhapsody now. I brought Dia and Simon on this project to help me out with having a podcast branch of reporting on conventions. Podcasting was becoming a brand new thing. I needed to evolve with the times. Also, I would later bring on a copy editor and a secondary writer to assist me with keeping up the website. I brought on Jay, another Southern California cosplay native who was a graduate student in media studies. Jay attended anime cons that I had not checked out—Sakura-Con and Anime Vegas. I felt we could expand our coverage to conventions outside of California. Jay had that itch to travel. I appreciated that this new team brought in a different perspective and another voice to Scarlet Rhapsody's growing website.

I knew I had the confidence to lead this again. I'd been running this endeavor for eight years, and I did not see any reason to stop anytime soon. I was a graduate student still figuring her life out, but I knew I was an important voice in the convention community. I'd seen friends and colleagues come and go, but like Sailor Pluto, the guardian of time, someone had to stick around to see how this would all play out.

Epilogue
In My Ancestor Era

October 2023. The Torrance suburbs. Del Amo Mall. The mall of my childhood. The Aladdin's Arcade where I played *ParaParaParadise* and *Dance Dance Revolution* after school in my uniform is no longer there. The Mitsuwa Marketplace where I bought *Sailor Moon* manga and rented *Sailor Moon* VHS tapes in Japanese found their new home at this mall. On a rainy Saturday, I went to grab groceries for the weekend. I was housesitting and I felt like making yakisoba for dinner that evening. As I made my way to the Japanese supermarket, I came across a few teenage otaku carrying bags from a new anime store that had just opened. They looked like they were waiting for their parents to pick them up from the Mitsuwa Marketplace. Animate, a Japanese anime superstore, had just launched their store at Del Amo Mall.

Groceries could wait just a bit. I wanted to see what this was all about. I went up two sets of escalators. Animate was right next to my favorite upscale dumpling place. I took a look inside. This store touted itself as Tokyo's one-stop shop for anime merchandise.

At the age of 39, I was still an anime fan. And I still represent hard for my fandom. I had *Sailor Moon* Funko Pops gifted from coworkers, Hello Kitty model kit Gundams, a few giant plushes of idols from *Love Live*, and a plush of the cuddly Bond from *Spy X Family* sitting at my office desktop at the University of California, Irvine. Animate was going to be the death of my wallet, but I had to decorate my university office space. After all, pieces of anime merchandise on my desk were great conversation starters with students and staff.

I picked up a few *My Hero Academia* clear files and folders. I could use a Nejire folder to organize documents in my office space. After all, you don't see much merchandise of her. *Demon Slayer* merchandise was fairly common, but there was not enough Shinobu-themed merchandise.

207

Epilogue

Shinobu is best girl after all. Endless rows of *Hololive* or whatever VTuber thing was trending dominated the store. There was a tiny section of *Love Live* keychains. "Wow! I haven't been into this since high school!" a 20-something customer said as she browsed through the *Love Live* charms. I'd been a *Love Live* fan since I got my first "big girl" job in Boston; Nico may have been my first favorite, but Nozomi is still best girl. *Evangelion* merch never goes out of style, yet still no Misato-themed figures and acrylic stands. Oh, the *Genshin Impact* section ... and still they do not have any of my waifus. Sadly, Beidou and Ningguang merchandise doesn't track as well as Yae Miko or the Raiden Shogun.

I browsed the book section of Animate. Oh hey ... two *Sailor Moon* art books featuring scenes and interviews from the latest movies, *Sailor Moon Cosmos* and *Sailor Moon Eternal* ... and an Anna Sui *Sailor Moon* collaboration purse?! Shut up and take my money! It's a wonderful feeling seeing the kids—the Gen Z and Gen Alpha crowd—get excited about the amount of new anime merchandise available to them. I must have spent about $250 on *Genshin*, *Sailor Moon*, *My Hero Academia*, and *Spy X Family* merchandise at Animate's grand opening weekend. I was a office lady otaku with money to spend, and these were gonna have a good home either on my bookshelf or at my office desk. I wasn't a starving college student anymore. I was not relying on an allowance or a part-time job. I had mad money to spend.

There's no doubt that anime is being enjoyed across all ages and generations. I attend San Diego Comic-Con as a guest speaker, and I see families dressed up from *Demon Slayer* and *Chainsaw Man*. Families dress up in costumes they may have gotten from an online storefront or pieced together from department store purchases. I see baby Tanjiros and Denjis.

When I am not at a convention, you might see me taking part in cosplay charity. Cosplayers help at back-to-school events, attend 5K walk-for-the-cure fundraisers to cheer families on, visit children's hospitals, and read to kids at libraries. When I joined, I listed that I had more anime characters than Western characters. It took some convincing to have the organizers understand that children these days truly identify just as much with anime characters as comic book characters. Anime characters showing up at children's charity events make just as much of an impact as Spiderman or Darth Vader. I continue to dress up as Sailor Moon, Yor Forger, and Shinobu Kocho at children's charity events. My best memory is dressing up as Sailor Moon and teaching kindergarteners how to say "Moon Prism Power, Make Up!"

Epilogue

I continue to run Scarlet Rhapsody. It took me almost two decades to be proud of this archive of fandom history, cosplay, and convention lore. When I first started it, I was just another kid with a website. To this day, I'm the only queer female person of color to run such an active archive that has been documenting conventions since the early 2000s. And this ain't a one-gal show! Our team continues to grow. We have Alice, our East Coast representative who covers all the biggest fandom events in the Northeast and mid–Atlantic. We have Ramses, our community moderator and co-panelist for any guest speaking opportunity we get. We also have Azure, one of my buddies from my San Francisco State days cohosting "Convention Tea," a live stream dedicated to convention reviews.

It's so much easier to buy cosplay these days. You no longer have to scour forums or ask for cosplay creator recommendations. Buying quality *Genshin Impact, Demon Slayer, My Hero Academia, Twisted Wonderland*, etc., costumes online has never been better or more affordable. We're also seeing folks sell pre-styled wigs, and wigs now come in varieties of color. In other words, I don't have to get a bright hot neon pink Utena wig that's gonna clash with my mocha skin; I can get that airy and dreamy milkshake pink that works perfectly with my skin tone. Cosplayers these days have it much easier and have much more access in dressing up as their favorite character. I wish I had this access when I was in high school, but I do admit, there was a certain joy in making something homemade or finally tracking down the legendary Setsuna Kou in hopes she would finish your cosplay just when you needed it.

At least in Southern California, there's a major event going on almost twice or thrice a month. Even after the 2020 pandemic when conventions slowed down and had to be put on hold for a year or two, conventions started to spring back up again. Yet, they were different. Many anime conventions in SoCal would highlight American voice actors as their headlining guests. It would have been an otaku's dream come true to meet so many American voice actors all at once. You could have 10, 20, 30 ... or a full cast reunion at these events. Yet, these events were not the same as the all-night weekend parties at some hotel or resort. Most of these conventions would close doors at 6 p.m. Sure, there would be an afterparty that consisted of a dance and 18+ programming, but if I recall, convention dances and late-night programming used to be part of general admission.

I still attend a few anime events for the guests and the concerts. I have a soft spot for idols. But I decided to take a new role in my community. Tik-Tok was calling me a Cosplay Ancestor. I decided to take leadership roles in my community—Cosplay Wrestling Federation, California Cosplay Gala, ZotCon, and various opportunities where I get to judge cosplay contests. Judging cosplay contests for kids is always my favorite because you're encouraging and enabling the next generation of cosplayers and potential leaders in the community.

Some of my friends have chosen the route of retirement and moved on to new fandoms or live the lives of normal human beings. Some have chosen to have families and raise their children in the geeksphere. Some have sought cosplay fame and fortune but returned disappointed because cosplay fame is but a myth. I have done panels on cosplay creation and construction, and every time I conclude these panels to a room full of impressionable youth, I always end with the same advice: "Do it for the love, not the likes."

Social media is just as much a part of cosplay as the costumes themselves. For better or for worse, this is the reality. Instagram and TikTok have replaced the traditional DIY websites and cosplay directories to post photos. Though I have been around for about 20 years, I have a small, humble following, and I wouldn't want to change that. I am happy with the friends I have made and the communities I have stepped up to lead. I live in Southern California where fame is always being chased and that's not why I cosplay. Cosplay to me has always been about creatively expressing myself in fandom; it's walking fan art. It's an art. It's showing your love of a series or character and bringing it to life. Also, Halloween should come more than once a year.

When *The Avengers* came out in theaters, the comic con scene exploded to a degree none of us saw coming. The all-heroes-team-up movie made audiences want more and also to be a part of that world. Southern California not only saw the growth of San Diego Comic-Con, but also had more comic cons sprouting up to meet the demand for pop culture gathering spaces—Long Beach Comic-Con, Los Angeles Comic-Con, Comic-Con Revolution in Ontario, California, among others that have come and gone. Even more pop culture–focused cons popped up across the country and the world. So many people were busting out Avengers- and Marvel-inspired cosplay at these events. San Diego Comic-Con was seen as THE main event for all geeks. It became the dream and bucket list item for all self-proclaimed geeks.

Yeah, I liked *The Avengers*. But getting tickets to San Diego Comic-Con as a regular attendee was next to impossible. I expanded my coverage for Scarlet Rhapsody, the little anime convention blog site that could, to these pop culture weekend parties. However, even with the popularity of Marvel and DC coming in at an unprecedented rate, I still felt that anime was my home. Anime Expo, Fanime, and Anime Central were still home to me. I tried to dip into the Marvel scene, but I realized it was not for me. I was happier in my anime spaces—maybe because there was all-night karaoke? Maybe because anime cons lasted beyond 6 p.m.? Maybe because anime outfits had more variety? Whatever the reason, I always found myself gravitating to where I started.

The past 20 years of fandom conventions have been a whirlwind. Sometimes a blur. Sometimes joy. Sometimes drama. Sometimes spending it with the best friends I could ever ask for. I don't see myself retiring from covering and documenting fandom events anytime soon. I know I will always be an anime fan. *Sailor Moon*, *Magic Knight Rayearth*, and *Cardcaptor Sakura* have taught me that it's okay to be feminine, girly, and have the will to help others, even if it means saving the world. These still resonate with me today and are why I have chosen a career in helping others in education. You can thank Naoko Takeuchi and CLAMP for motivating me to earn my master's degree in counseling!

And so, I have the Sailor Moon cosplay I made during the 2020 pandemic lockdown hanging in my closet next to the Princess Mars cosplay I wore to my senior year homecoming dance. Why yes, I still fit my high school measurements. I have a framed photo of Mari Iijima and me from Ani-Magic 2000 next to the photo of me cosplaying as Nero Claudius from *Fate* prepping for Cosplay Wrestling Federation on my home office desk. Sometimes, I'll visit the Disneyland Hotel, not for the Dole Whip, but just to walk around the hotel, take a selfie where I met Jimmy, and send him a message asking, "Hey! Remember when we met here 20 years ago?" Twenty years ago may have been my cringe era, but it is an era that I would relive over and over again if I could. There was no better feeling than being a teenager at the turn of the millennium during the rise of anime fandom culture in the West. I may have been cringe, but I was cringe with the best friends I could ever ask for. The memories we made—unwavering desire for pocky, late nights on iParty, slumber parties at anime cons, sharing our favorite anisong MP3s via less-than-legal means, being unhinged anime characters on the masquerade stage—this was my life as a teenage fangirl, and it was the best.

Index

Index